THE LIFE AND WORKS OF W. G. COLLINGWOOD

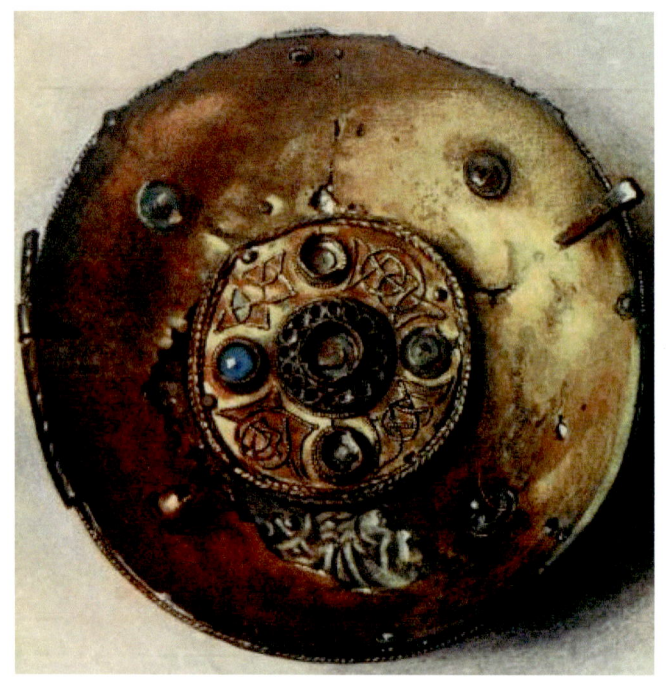

The Ormside Cup
TCWAAS XV, 1899 facing page 385

# The Life and Works of W. G. Collingwood

A wayward compass in Lakeland

## Malcolm Craig

Archaeopress Publishing Ltd
Summertown Pavilion
18-24 Middle Way
Summertown
Oxford OX2 7LG

# Archaeological Lives

ISBN 978 1 78491 871 2
ISBN 978 1 78491 872 9 (e-Pdf)

© Archaeopress and Malcolm Craig 2018

Front Cover: W.G. Collingwood at age 43: Self portrait as Sea Captain.
Back Cover: W.G. Collingwood aged 52. Collingwood (R.G.) Archive Cardiff University.

All rights reserved. No part of this book may be reproduced, or transmitted, in any form or by any means, electronic, mechanical, photocopying or otherwise, without the prior written permission of the copyright owners.

This book is available direct from Archaeopress or from our website www.archaeopress.com

Dedicated to Margaret Craig

# Contents

Chronology ..................................................................................................v
Figures ....................................................................................................ix
Abbreviations ...........................................................................................x
Conversion note .....................................................................................xi
Preface ....................................................................................................1

## Chapter I Collingwood Family (1761-1854) ........................................14
Family Influence ....................................................................................14
William Collingwood ..............................................................................15
Hastings .................................................................................................18
Liverpool ................................................................................................19
Plymouth Brethren .................................................................................21
Parents William and Marie .....................................................................21

## Chapter II Boyhood (1854-1872) ..........................................................27
Liverpool Family ....................................................................................27
Schooling ...............................................................................................28
Northern Influences ...............................................................................30
Icelandic Connections ............................................................................30
Lakeland ................................................................................................31

## Chapter III Student Days (1872-1876) ..................................................34
University College Oxford ......................................................................34
Philosopher Bosanquet ..........................................................................34
John Ruskin ...........................................................................................36
Translation Work ....................................................................................40

## Chapter IV Becoming an Artist (1876-1882) .........................................43
Slade School of Art ................................................................................43
Alphonse Legros ....................................................................................44
Living in London ....................................................................................45
Artist or Academic .................................................................................46
Joining Ruskin .......................................................................................49
Painting Ruskin at work .........................................................................49
On Tour with Ruskin ..............................................................................51

## Chapter V Edith Isaac (Dorrie) and Marriage (1877-1884) ....................60
Young Edith ...........................................................................................60
Courting Edith .......................................................................................65
Early-Married Life ..................................................................................68

## Chapter VI Life at Gillhead Windermere (1883-1891) ..........................71
Home at Gillhead ..................................................................................69

    Earning a Living ................................................................................ 70
    Hill Walker ......................................................................................... 73
    Move to Lanehead ............................................................................ 75

## Chapter VII Working with Ruskin (1881-1900) ............................. 77
    John Ruskin ........................................................................................ 77
    Relationship with Ruskin ................................................................. 78
    Brantwood .......................................................................................... 79
    Daily Routine ..................................................................................... 82
    Severn Family .................................................................................... 84
    Lawrence Jermyn Hilliard (1855-1887) ........................................ 86
    Sara Anderson (1854-1942) ............................................................ 86
    Guild of St. George ........................................................................... 87
    Ruskin Biography ............................................................................. 90
    Brantwood after Ruskin .................................................................. 92

## Chapter VIII Life in Lakeland (1891-1932) ................................... 94
    Family Home ..................................................................................... 94
    Home Schooling ............................................................................... 97
    Religious Education ....................................................................... 100
    Lanehead Magazine ....................................................................... 104
    Collingwood Childrens' Development ....................................... 106
    Arthur Ransome at Lanehead ..................................................... 108
    Lake Artists Society ....................................................................... 113

## Chapter IX Researching the Past (1884-1932) ........................... 115
    Northernness .................................................................................. 115
    Pre-Norman Interest ..................................................................... 116
    Gifted Amateur ............................................................................... 119
    Roman Lakeland ............................................................................ 124
    Anglo-Saxons, Background .......................................................... 125
    Researching Anglo-Saxon ............................................................. 126
    Artifacts ........................................................................................... 127
    Early Industrial Archaeology ....................................................... 133
    Study of Carved Stonework ......................................................... 134
    Gosforth Stone Cross .................................................................... 141
    Giant's Thumb ................................................................................ 143
    Hogbacks ......................................................................................... 144
    Angles and Norse ........................................................................... 146
    Norse Anglo-Saxon Dilemma ...................................................... 149
    Beyond Pre-Norman ..................................................................... 151
    Collingwood's Inventories ........................................................... 152

## Chapter X Scandinavian Studies (1895-1928) .................................................. 155
- Early Interest ........................................................................................... 155
- Viking Club ............................................................................................. 156
- Norse in Lakeland .................................................................................. 158
- Place-name Research ............................................................................ 159
- Mapping Norse Settlements .................................................................. 165
- Writing the Lakeland-based Sagas ........................................................ 165
- Icelandic Sagas ...................................................................................... 168
- Lakeland Sagas ...................................................................................... 170
- Iceland Early History ............................................................................. 173
- Land of Volcanoes ................................................................................. 174
- William Morris and Iceland ................................................................... 174
- Iceland Expedition ................................................................................. 180
- After Iceland .......................................................................................... 185
- Reflecting upon Iceland ......................................................................... 186
- Scandinavian Settlements in Lakeland ................................................. 187

## Chapter XI Academia and Lanehead (1905-1917) ........................................... 190
- Reading University College ................................................................... 190
- Denmark Lecturing Visits ...................................................................... 191
- Viking Club President ........................................................................... 194
- German Miners ...................................................................................... 195
- Surprise Visitor ...................................................................................... 197
- Bewcastle Cross ..................................................................................... 197

## Chapter XII Naval Intelligence (1917-1919) .................................................... 200
- London Base ........................................................................................... 200
- Maps and Manuals ................................................................................. 203
- After the War ......................................................................................... 204

## Chapter XIII Later Research (1920-1930) ....................................................... 206
- Roman Sites ........................................................................................... 206
- Ambleside Roman Camp ....................................................................... 206
- The Tenth Iter ........................................................................................ 207
- Hardknot Castle ..................................................................................... 213
- Wild Northumberland ............................................................................ 215
- Towards a Corpus .................................................................................. 215
- Gosforth Cross Reconsidered ................................................................ 216
- Dykes ...................................................................................................... 217

## Chapter XIV Future of Lakeland (1932-) ......................................................... 220
- Difference of Opinion ............................................................................ 220
- Reflections ............................................................................................. 223

**Chapter XV Father and Son (1889-1932) .................................................. 226**
    Father's Influence ....................................................................... 226
    Summary ...................................................................................... 229
**Chapter XVI Last Years (1928-1932) ........................................................ 233**
    Coming to a Close ....................................................................... 233
    Final Works .................................................................................. 234
**Appendix ........................................................................................................ 237**
**Acknowledgements ..................................................................................... 248**
**Books by the Author ................................................................................... 249**
**Index ............................................................................................................... 250**

# Chronology

| | |
|---|---|
| 1854 | Born at 87 Chatham Street Liverpool to William and Marie Elizabeth née Imhoff. |
| 1856 | Birth of only brother David in Liverpool. |
| 1858 | Birth of only sister Ruth in Liverpool. |
| 1859 | Attended Liverpool Collegiate. |
| 1872 | Student University College Oxford, tutor Bernard Bosanquet. |
| 1873 | Death of Mother, Marie. |
| 1873 | Visited John Ruskin, with father, at Brantwood. |
| 1874 | Worked on John Ruskin's road building project at Ferry Hinksey. |
| 1875 | Began translation work for Ruskin in April, 'The Economist of Xenophon'. |
| 1876 | Translation work with Alexander Wedderburn completed in July. |
| 1876 | First in Greats at Oxford University in September. |
| 1876 | Joined Slade School of Arts in October, tutor Alphonse Legros. |
| 1876 | Met and corresponded with Edith Isaac. |
| 1876 | Made applications for University Fellowships. |
| 1877 | Alpine Tour. |
| 1878 | Made summer visit to John Ruskin at Brantwood. |
| 1879 | Made summer visit to Ruskin at Brantwood. |
| 1880 | Exhibited at The Royal Academy with portrait of his father. |
| 1880 | Met artist Edward Burne-Jones and tutored his son Philip. |
| 1881 | Began working with John Ruskin as Geological Surveyor and Draughtsman or 'General Assistant' initially from September to early January 1882. |
| 1882 | Painted picture of John Ruskin, in January, at work in his study at Brantwood, Lawrence Hillier as model. |
| 1882 | Toured France, Switzerland and Italy (including Alps) with John Ruskin, early August to early December. |
| 1883 | The 'Philosophy of ornament published. |
| 1883 | 'Limestone Alps of Savoy' published, based upon geological data collected during the tour of 1882. |

| | | |
|---|---|---|
| 1883 | Married Edith (Dorrie) Isaac in December at Kensington Registry Office London. |
| 1883 | Moved with Dorrie to a cottage at Gillhead Windermere. |
| 1883 | Visit to Brantwood (Ruskin) with bride, December 29 to January 6. |
| 1885 | 'Book of Verse' published. |
| 1886 | Birth of first child Dorothy (Dora) Susie at Gillhead. |
| 1886 | 'Astrology in the Apocalypse' published. |
| 1887 | Birth of second child Barbara Crystal at Gillhead. |
| 1887 | Joined Cumberland and Westmorland Antiquarian and Archaeological Society. |
| 1887 | Lawrence Hilliard (Ruskin's Secretary) died. |
| 1889 | Birth of only son Robin at Gillhead. |
| 1889 | Visit to Seascale with Ruskin, Arthur and Joan Severn. |
| 1889 | 'Biographical Outline of John Ruskin' published. |
| 1889 | Two Sonnets in Igdrasil (Journal of Ruskin Reading Guild). |
| 1890 | Six Papers published in Igdrasil. |
| 1891 | Birth of fourth child Ursula Mavis at Gillhead. |
| 1891 | 'The Art Teaching of John Ruskin. |
| 1891 | Edited 'Poems of John Ruskin' in two volumes. |
| 1891 | Moved family from Gillhead to Lanehead, house on the east side of Coniston Water. |
| 1892 | Excavation work on Peel Island, Coniston Water, with Dorrie. |
| 1893 | 'The Life and Work of John Ruskin', published. |
| 1893 | Edited three volumes: 'Writings of John Ruskin'. |
| 1894 | Joined the Viking Club. |
| 1895 | 'Thorstein of the Mere' published. |
| 1896 | 'The Bondwoman' published. |
| 1896 | Arranged exhibition in Coniston of Ruskin memorabilia. |
| 1897 | 'Book of Coniston' published. |
| 1897 | Visit to Iceland with Jón Stefánsson. |
| 1897 | Excavation at Springs Bloomery, Coniston. |
| 1899 | Became a member of the Alpine Club. |
| 1899 | Edited work of W.S. Calverley published. |

| 1899 | Coniston Tales published. |
| 1899 | 'A Pilgrimage to the Saga-steads of Iceland' published |
| 1900 | Death of John Ruskin, buried at Coniston. |
| 1900 | Forward to the John Ruskin Exhibition published. |
| 1900 | Editor of Transaction (TCWAAS). |
| 1901 | Designed the Ruskin Cross for his grave at Coniston. |
| 1901 | 'Life and Death of Cormac the Skald': translated with Jón Stefánsson. |
| 1902 | 'The Lake Counties' published. |
| 1902 | Ten papers published in various journals (see Appendix A). |
| 1903 | Death of his Father, William. |
| 1903 | 'Ruskin Relics' published. |
| 1905 | Lecturer at University College Reading. |
| 1905 | Became President of the Viking Club (served two years). |
| 1905 | Lecturing visit to Denmark. |
| 1906 | Second lecturing visit to Denmark. |
| 1906 | Nine papers published in various journals (see Appendix A). |
| 1908 | 'Scandinavian Britain' published. |
| 1908 | Celebrated, at Reading, 25 years of marriage. |
| 1908 | Appointed professor of Fine Art at University College Reading. |
| 1909 | 'Thorstein of the Mere (Revised Edition). |
| 1910 | 'Dutch Agnes her Valentine' published. |
| 1911 | Wrote Forward to 'John Ruskin' by Andreas Mollerup. |
| 1911 | Provided costume sketches for 'Danish Scene' at Festival of Empire. |
| 1911 | Resigned from post at University College Reading. |
| 1912 | 'Elizabethan Keswick' published. |
| 1913 | Became member of the Fell and Rock Climbing Club of the English Lake District. |
| 1913 | Elected to the Society of antiquaries of Newcastle-upon-Tyne. |
| 1917 | 'The Likeness of King Elfwald' published. |
| 1920 | Nominated President of the CWAAS. |

| 1924 | With daughter Barbara designed the 1914- 1918 War Memorial to be placed on the summit of Great Gable. |
| 1925 | 'Lake District History' published. |
| 1926 | C.A. Parker's 'The Gosforth District' revised by W.G. Collingwood. |
| 1927 | 'Northumbrian Crosses of the Pre-Norman Age' published. |
| 1929 | Ten papers published in various journals (see Appendix A). |
| 1932 | 'The Lake Counties' revised. |
| 1932 | 'A Pedigree of Anglian Crosses, Antiquary Journal (last paper). |

# Figures

Figures from author's collection unless stated otherwise in parentheses

Frontispiece The Ormside Cup
Figure 1 Interior by William Collingwood..................................................................20
Figure 2 Approach to Ambleside by William Collingwood 1841................................22
Figure 3 Gershom's School Report ............................................................................29
Figure 4 Dressler's Bust of Ruskin .............................................................................36
Figure 5 Ruskin's road building at Ferry Hinksey ......................................................39
Figure 6 Ruskin's Boat. By W.G.C..............................................................................42
Figure 7 Ruskin in his library by W.G.C. 1882 (Ruskin Museum Coniston) ...............51
Figure 8 Lady of Lucca by W.G.C...............................................................................54
Figure 9 Ruskin in Troyes by W.G.C...........................................................................55
Figure 10 Ruskin, centre, with Collingwood (left) and Randal ...................................57
Figure 11 Edith (Dorrie) Collingwood ........................................................................61
Figure 12 Envelope addressed to Edith by W.G.C. ....................................................62
Figure 13 Postcard to W.G.C. from Dorrie.................................................................64
Figure 14 Reverse Runic side of Postcard. Collingwood (R.G.) Archive Cardiff University ...64
Figure 15 Nursing baby Dora at Gillhead Cottages by W.G.C....................................67
Figure 16 Mist on Mickledore Scafells by W.G.C. .....................................................72
Figure 17 Dorrie's Drawing of Baby Ursula ...............................................................73
Figure 18 Lanehead, based on photograph by H.J. Taphouse ....................................74
Figure 19 Brantwood showing the Turret Room. Photograph by John McClelland ..78
Figure 20 Susannah (Susie) Beever by W.G.C. ..........................................................81
Figure 21 Dorrie with the four children ....................................................................97
Figure 22 Puff and Fluffs (1) from 'Nothing Much'(AH)...........................................101
Figure 23 Puff and Fluffs (2) from 'Nothing Much'(AH)...........................................101
Figure 24 Ormside Cup by W.G.C............................................................................129
Figure 25 Gosforth Cross by W.G.C.........................................................................136
Figure 26 Giant's Thumb by W.G.C. ........................................................................138
Figure 27 Kist Wood Panel by W.G.C. .....................................................................157
Figure 28 Distribution Map of Norse Danish Settlements ......................................160
Figure 29 Thingbrekka Iceland By W.G.C. (AH).......................................................177
Figure 30 Thingvellir Icelandic Parliament by W.G.C. (British Museum).................178
Figure 31 Altarpiece at Borg Iceland by W.G.C. ......................................................180
Figure 32 Wedding Anniversary Scroll. Collingwood (R.G.) Archive Cardiff University.......193
Figure 33 Gershom feeding cat with L-R Robin, Ursula and Dorrie. (ULC). ............196
Figure 34 Figured Samian Ware Ambleside by R.G.C..............................................201
Figure 35 Thirlmere before the Dam. Thomas Allom c. 1832.................................218
Figure 36 Acca Cross Upper ....................................................................................234
Figure 37 Acca Cross Lower ....................................................................................234
Figure 38 Gravestone for Gershom and Dorrie.......................................................236

# Abbreviations

| | |
|---|---|
| (AH) | Abbot Hall, Kendal. |
| (CACU) | Collingwood (R.G.) Archive, Cardiff University. |
| (CW1) | First Series of Transactions of the Cumberland and Westmorland Antiquarian and Archaeological Society. |
| (CW2) | Second Series of Transactions of the Cumberland and Westmorland Antiquarian and Archaeological Society. |
| (CW3) | Third Series of the Transactions; does not apply to Gershom's period. |
| (CWAAS) | Cumberland and Westmorland Antiquarian and Archaeological Society. |
| (EI) | 'Dorrie' Edith Issac |
| (E.M.D.C.) | Edith Mary Dorothy Collingwood. |
| (Igdrasil) | Journal of the Ruskin Reading Guild: quarterly magazine and review of art, literature and social philosophy. |
| (JDANHS) | Journal of the Derbyshire Archaeological and Natural History Society. |
| (JFRCELD) | Journal of the Fell and Rock Club of the English Lake District. |
| (NCM) | Northern Counties Magazine. |
| (PPHFAS) | Papers and Proceedings of the Hampshire Field Club and Archaeological Society. |
| (PSAN) | Proceedings of the Society of antiquaries of Newcastle-upon-Tyne. |
| (R.G.C.) | Robin George Collingwood. |
| (RPI) | Retail Price Index. |
| (RWS) | Royal Water Colour Society. |
| (TCWAALS) | Transactions of the Cumberland and Westmorland Association for the Advancement of Literature and Science. |
| (TCWAAS) | Transactions of the Cumberland and Westmorland Antiquarian and Archaeological Society. |

| | |
|---|---|
| (T D & G NHAS) | Transactions of the Dumfriesshire and Galloway Natural History and Antiquarian Society. |
| (TNNAS) | Transactions of the Norfolk and Norwich Archaeological Society. |
| (THSLC) | Transactions of the Historic Society of Lancashire and Cheshire. |
| (ULC) | University Library Cambridge. |
| (W.C.) | William Collingwood. |
| (W.G.C.) | William Gershom Collingwood. |
| (YAJ) | Yorkshire Archaeological Journal |

# Conversion note

### Length
Miles, Feet and Inches are shown together with Kilometres, Metres and Centimetres, decimal values in parenthesis.

### Pounds, Shillings and Pence
Money values vary over the years so only Pounds, Shillings and Pence are used. To help the reader unfamiliar with this currency: 20 shillings to the pound sterling and 12 pence to the shilling (240 pence to the pound). The currency was in use during Gershom's time and in the UK until 1971. When seen as appropriate, a comparison is made between these money values compared with equivalent value, 2010-2015, using the retail price index (RPI).

# Preface

Preface, something readers skip in a book? Please do not skip this one especially if you are not familiar with the works of W.G. Collingwood, he does not come readily to mind when thinking of notable lives such as Darwin, Freud or Churchill. W.G.C had a varied complex life and a more detailed background is needed to 'set the scene' which is to be found in this preface.

To close friends William Gershom Collingwood was known simply as 'Gershom'. I have been presumptuous in using Gershom too where a more friendly tone is felt appropriate otherwise 'W.G.C.' or 'Collingwood' has been adopted when a formal tone seemed appropriate, also to be in keeping with the sensible practice of his generation, addressing people only by their surname to avoid over-familiarity. Only to John Ruskin, who liked inventing nicknames, was Collingwood known as 'Collie' or 'Colliewallie'. Long before writing this biography, I became confused between W.G. Collingwood and R.G. Collingwood, thinking there may have been a small printing error and they were not different people, especially when both were at times writing about the same subject set in the same area (archaeology in the English Lake District). Son Robin introduced the 'G' (George) later in life leading to possible confusion between W.G. and R.G. Collingwood.

R.G. Collingwood moved during his life between: philosophy, history, archaeology and music; in a way similar to his father (W.G.) who moved between: art, antiquity, archaeology, history, writing fiction and non-fiction.

John Ruskin quickly summed up his young friend when he and Gershom met in Oxford, describing him as like a compass needle *'that would find some attraction one way or another'.* From this insight I thought of a title 'Wayward Compass in Lakeland' because in my view Gershom never did have one attraction or career settled in one direction or another and spent most of his life in Lakeland, becoming an authority on the history of the place and its people.

Gershom was born in Liverpool in 1854 and died in Lakeland in 1932. His father William Collingwood was a well-known Artist and Mother Marie Elizabeth née Imhoff was Swiss. The name 'Gershom' pronounced Gur-shahm has a Hebrew meaning of 'a stranger here' or 'exile' leading to speculation that the Collingwood family could be Jewish, especially when he married Edith *Isaac* but there is no evidence of a Jewish connection in either family (being Jewish comes through the mother's bloodline). When daughter Dora Collingwood was older, she remarked that, 'we have a great deal of Hebrew blood in our veins though I am thankful to say our ancestors changed their religion a hundred and fifty years ago'. I have not been able to find evidence to justify this statement. Though when writing about evidence I am reminded that archaeologists regularly point out that absence of evidence is not evidence of absence.

One of a number of titles given to W.G.C was 'antiquary' normally used for someone who studies ancient artefacts but for Gershom this also included imagining how people lived, what people made and what, possibly, they could have felt and thought, even to imagining the existence of ghosts based upon folklore tales told to him as a boy. Grevel Lindop in his 'Literary Guide to the Lake District' (1993) wrote that Gershom *almost single-handedly transformed the historical and archaeological understanding of the Lake District.* This influence alone should establish him, in Britain at least, as a well-known figure of the latter nineteenth and early twentieth centuries, but adequate recognition did not come. The Dictionary of Literary Biography, late nineteenth century and early twentieth century ought to have acknowledged his fiction and non-fiction writing but listed only his work as a writer of biography, although the review by Phillip Mallet did include most published fiction and non-fiction, briefly, in vol.149, 1995.

Lack of recognition is difficult to understand, though he readily admitted to shunning publicity of any kind; an important question is to ask is why recognition was not thrust upon him? Gershom was a writer of well-received books both non-fiction and fiction, wrote numerous learned papers (Appendix A) and as an artist exhibited paintings at the Royal Academy, he also helped establish the Lake Artists Society; served as Editor then President of the Cumberland and Westmorland Antiquarian and Archaeological Society (CWAAS) and worked closely with John Ruskin for 19 years. A friend of Gershom, writer and Oxford University lecturer Edward Thompson, wrote in the early 1930s that *'versatility has been one thing that has kept him* [Gershom] *from recognition'* Edward John Thompson was around 30 years younger than Gershom and correspondence passed frequently between them, mainly Gershom giving encouragement to the younger man. Thompson was a Methodist minister and later became Lecturer in Bengali at Oxford University. Various possible reasons for a lack of prominence in W.G.C's own right are explored in this book but in the use of one word 'versatility' Thompson possibly comes closest to explaining the lack of adequate recognition.

Despite his many achievements, anyone referring to a biography of W.G. Collingwood would have to explain, in most cases, what he did. One possible reason for lack of full recognition could be a difficulty in pigeonholing him. He had a wide range of interests and expertise, described as: Author, Editor, Poet, Lecturer, Artist, Antiquary, Iceland Explorer, Comparative Philologist, Amateur Geologist, Amateur Cartographer and Amateur Archaeologist. A list of this kind attributed to one person almost inevitably leads readers to think he must be a professional in one and an amateur in all others. Where the word 'amateur' is omitted it can be assumed that Gershom was professional in that he was paid either directly or through royalties, and where amateur is stated he received no financial reward. The terms 'amateur' and 'professional' are not used here to indicate proficiency, as is now common, but is used in the traditional sense, unpaid or paid respectively.

Another possible reason for lack of full recognition was that Gershom spent most of his life in, at that time, an infrequently visited part of Lakeland; Ruskin who lived nearby had made a name for himself when he moved, aged 52, to Lakeland in 1871. Taqui (Barbara) Altounyan, writing about her maternal grandfather (W.G.C.) in her book 'Chimes from a Wooden Bell' expressed surprise that her mother Dora in a letter to her sister Barbara wrote that: *'the Collingwoods were lacking in something, some vitamin necessary for complete success in life, causing inability to take opportunities. Perhaps lack of perspicacity in choosing what horse to back is part of it'*. While the comment could possibly be applied to Dora's father (W.G.C.) it did not apply to her brother, Robin George Collingwood or to her paternal grandfather William Collingwood, so the broader reference to 'Collingwoods' in Dora's statement is difficult to justify. Inspection of published obituaries in the National Press and Journals invariably show specialisation as a dominant theme in the lives of men and women recognised with obituary notices; in this respect, Gershom went against the trend because despite his life as a polymath, obituarists served him well. Obituaries of William Gershom Collingwood appeared in newspapers and journals, which offered additional insights. The most detailed obituary appeared in The Times newspaper of October 3, 1932 written by his son Robin George. There were suggestions that this obituary partly compensated for Robin saying little about his father in his own writing (and even less about his family); he was very close to his father, which made this neglect, if that is what it was, difficult to understand. In fairness to Robin George, he did say in the preface to his autobiography (1939), *'the autobiography of a man whose business is thinking should be the story of his thought. I have written this book to tell what I think worth telling about the story of mine. An autobiography has no right to exist unless it is 'livre de bonne foi'* (a book in good faith).

This would be a reasonable explanation for Robin's lack of recognition of his father in earlier works, which were mainly about philosophy or history; they were primarily about his thoughts.

Peter Johnson (Intention and Meaning in R.G. Collingwood's autobiography 1995) makes the point that R.G.C's autobiography was: *'written in the light of his present concerns and aspirations, and these govern his principles of selection and inclusion. What is to count as omission therefore, must be seen in this light.'*
Both the Alpine Club and the Fell and Rock Climbing Club of the English Lake District paid generous tribute to W.G.C. in their journals. Contributors from both clubs, mountaineers W.P. Hasket Smith and R.B. Graham respectively, highlighted a part of Gershom's life largely overlooked by other writers. He had an enduring

love of mountains, especially in the Alps and Lakeland, a love he shared with John Ruskin: whether Mont Blanc, Jungfrau, Coniston Old Man or Langdale Pikes, to be in the presence of mountains brought him great joy to the end of his life.

Another obituary for W.G.C. printed in 'The Vasculum' for November 1932 (vol. 18, No. 4) was in recognition of his valuable contribution to that journal of papers relevant to the Northern Counties.

In the Transactions of the Cumberland and Westmorland Antiquarian and Archaeological Society (TCWAAS), there was recognition of the massive contribution made by him with his papers based upon rigorous research and for his editing of the transactions over many years, but author of this obituary is not clear. This obituary in particular pointed to Gershom's lack of prominence: '*From a young man of brilliant promise, with striking gifts in art and literature, a witty talker and cultivated musician, he had become a scholar and something of a recluse. He had sacrificed all hope of a career to the duty, as he thought it, of tending Ruskin's declining years; painted merely for a livelihood, wrote merely for his own amusement, and turned increasingly towards the past to find an object for his thoughts*'.

While the overall thrust of the statement could be correct, there are certain 'persuader' words, typical of a journalist's writing, particularly the words 'merely' and 'amusement'. Painting for a livelihood is what professional artists do, it is far beyond being 'merely' and to complete his vast literary output demanded a strong interest in the subjects and rigorous scholarship from him, far more than 'amusement'. Possibly this is why Douglas, H. Johnson in 'R.G. Collingwood Studies', thought the hand of a journalist wrote this obituary. One possible name comes to mind: Arthur Ransome, a journalist, may be discernible in this obituary. To accuse an antiquary of turning increasingly towards the past (last line); is rather silly? The highly respected science journal 'Nature' October 15, 1932 also contained a tribute to his life, pointing in particular to his book on stone crosses in 1927 as his most significant work.

Gershom contributed six papers to the Yorkshire Archaeological Journal between 1906 and 1926 and the printed obituary recognised his wide interests and characteristic generosity. Typically when during the 1914-1918 war to raise money for the Red Cross Society he sold presents given to him by John Ruskin, the only way he could offer support because he was too old for active service and was never a wealthy man. Finally, an In Memoriam, published in the Transactions (TCWAAS) of 1953, noting how '*the New Series* (CW2, from 1900) *of the Transactions owes to him its inception, and the standard which subsequent Editors have been glad to keep before them as an exemplar*'. There was no branch of the society's activities which did not owe much to his influence, whether by personal research and writing or by the encouragement and support of other members.

The many obituaries did not enhance his reputation, though any enhancement at this time would be rather late. It was recognition during his lifetime that was lacking; his only son Robin George received his due recognition both before and after his death, but not his father. An interesting comment on this lack of recognition came from the 'In Memoriam' of 1953 that: *'though the outer world thought more highly of his brilliant son, Robin George Collingwood (1889-1943), posterity will perhaps reverse the judgement of their contemporaries.'*

W.G.C, through his research and writing, had great influence upon our understanding of pre-Norman history in Northern England (first to eleventh centuries) sometimes referred to as 'Early Christian Period', a more appropriate term than 'The Dark Ages' often used to describe the period sixth to eleventh centuries. Thinking about this period and arrival of the Normans W.G.C. wrote, *'the Normans arrived late here in the north-west. The date 1066 means to us Stamford Bridge; Hastings is foreign history. East Cumberland and Westmorland hardly began to feel the influence of the invaders before the twelfth century; the sea coast not until much later; the mountains, never, until after the Normans had given place to the new English of the thirteenth century.*' The Battle of Stamford Bridge, referred to by Gershom, was fought between the armies of English led by King Harold Godwinson and Norwegian led by King Harald Hardrada. After most of the Norwegian leaders died and with the battle won, King Harold travelled south to fight the Battle of Hastings only three weeks later. Officially, the Battle of Stamford Bridge marked the close of the Viking Age in England. For W.G.C. it was the close of his main period of study too. Understandably, for him and his study of the north, the battle of Stamford Bridge was far more significant than the battle of Hastings.

An important part of Pre-Norman study was an understanding of Anglo-Saxon carved stone crosses and their further development by Scandinavian settlers. W.G.C. became an authority on this subject after editing the work of William Slater Calverley, publishing in 1899. In this book, W.G.C. pointed out that the Norman Conquest was at first a political fact rather than a social overturn, at least in the North-West of England. *'To the masses it meant new lords, but not new habits of life and thought'.*

Gershom's main interest was in the lives of people in Anglo-Saxon and Scandinavian settlements, although he could not altogether ignore the earlier Roman period of almost 400 years in the north-west of England.

Archaeological work led him to Roman sites and their remains where he developed his own ideas about the extent of Roman influence in Lakeland. Robin George (R.G.C.) accompanied his father on archaeological digs from a very early age and developed a stronger interest in this period to become an authority on Roman settlements in the north and north-west, particularly along Hadrian's Wall. Few scholars had a better understanding of Romano-British life.

When writing his book 'Lake District History', Gershom described the Roman occupation of the area as just *'an episode but the Britons lasted'*.

> 'Indeed, it is more likely than not that most of us have a drop of the old British blood in our veins [possibly a comment that could be read as valid in 1925]. The idea that the Anglo-Saxons and Scandinavians made a clean sweep of the ancient race, especially here in the North-west not only neglects the evidence of place-names but also leaves the whole evolution of our nation unexplained. If they had done so, we should be Danes or North Germans. The rapid and brilliant flowering of the Northumbrian people in the times of Bede and the Bewcastle cross can only be understood only when we regard the Angles of Deira as a mixed race, combining the sturdiness of the Sassenach with the artistic temperament of the Cymru'.

These ideas, followed through by W.G.C. until the end of his scholarship in this field of research, were brought to fruition in his book 'Northumbrian Crosses of the Pre- Norman Age' (1927). Richard Bailey in the Preface to his book 'Viking Age Sculpture' (1980) wrote about Gershom's Northumbrian Crosses. 'That this classic study is a book which remains both an impressive memorial to a pioneering scholar and a constant point of reference for following generations of students; no one will ever match his artist's instinctive understanding of the mind of the medieval sculptor'.

To mark the golden jubilee of the book, a Collingwood (W.G.) Symposium was held (1977) on insular sculpture from 800 to 1066. Typically, when writing about Scandinavian influence, Gershom would make incisive statements based upon rigorous research as in his book 'Scandinavian Britain' writing: *'The Norse settlers did not come as conquerors, entrenching themselves against the natives, but as immigrants seeking a livelihood'*. The settlers were heimafolk, not aggressive heimsfolk.

Not surprisingly, some of W.G.C's conclusions have not stood the test of time but in his later years, in true scholarly style, he was always ready to revise earlier ideas in the light of new evidence. One of the most significant examples was to change his ideas about early settlers or visitors to Peel Island on Coniston Water; the name 'Peel' (Peel Island) is suggestive of fortification similar to towers built in the sixteenth century. After some excavating on the island with his wife Edith (Dorrie), he thought the remains were of Norse origin, tenth or eleventh century, but later revised this idea to the remains being from a fourteenth century fort. A significant part of Gershom's life was spent researching the past: through carved stonework (Chapter IX) and Scandinavian influence (Chapter X) in both cases, he struggled with considerable uncertainty emerging from results of past studies and from results of his own research; inevitably a number of conditional tenses have to be used in describing these periods of his life. He had to accept uncertainty; the idea: because there is no such thing as certainty, there cannot be uncertainty was only of interest to his son and other philosophers.

The first men to arouse interest and stimulate further research about pre-Norman life in Northern England were Dr Charles Parker and Rev. William Slater Calverley; Gershom befriended both pioneers after settling in Lakeland and collaborated with them when beginning his antiquarian and archaeological research. After they died, Gershom became recognised among scholars as an authority on the Early Christian Period in his part of the world; recognised not only in Britain but internationally too.

Letters provide the richest source of details about his life: family, friends and Gershom himself were prolific letter writers and much of this correspondence has survived, held in various archives, though one difficulty has been in reading Gershom's almost impenetrable writing, likened to a spider crawling first through spilled ink then over his notepaper. Fortunately, a number of his letters are transcribed for the Archives at Abbot Hall (AH), Kendal, which inevitably leads to questioning of the transcriber's interpretation of certain words. Although Gershom kept a diary at times, he was not a diarist or as he said 'no Boswell', he learned a great deal from John Ruskin but did not follow his example by writing an account of each day. Ruskin was assiduous in recording thoughts to diaries and journals.

When writing about Great Gable in the English Lake District (2010-11) I felt greatly in debt to W.G. Collingwood for the detailed research he had carried out in the area, and naturally wished to know more about the man. No autobiography or biography could be found. After further searching, I discovered that five writers described something about his life and work but none in a purely biographical way. Mathew Townend in his outstanding book 'The Vikings and Victoria Lakeland' (2009) wrote in the Introduction *'that it is by no means a narrow biography of Collingwood alone'*. A biography of W.G. Collingwood could not be described as *narrow*. The point made by Townend, as I understand it, was that the aim of the book was to contribute to the scholarship of regional medievalism in which Gershom played a central part, but not forgetting a number of key antiquaries who also played their part in our understanding of this subject. The book comes closest to providing a biography of W.G.C.

Jeremy Collingwood's book 'A Lakeland Saga' (2012) provided good coverage of Gershom and family life, including a family tree, but here Gershom shares stage with journalist and childrens' author Arthur Ransome. Taqui (Barbara Harriet) Altounyan, a granddaughter, in her books 'In Aleppo Once' (1969) and 'Chimes from a Wooden Bell' (1990) provide useful information about her grandfather.

In addition to these books, are papers by Douglas H Johnson and another granddaughter of W.G.C. Teresa Smith in 'Collingwood (R.G.) Studies' (1994-99); all write about Gershom from a particular perspective at a particular time but none of the man during his whole lifetime, to embrace his many interests. Janet Gnosspelius planned to write a biography of her grandfather W.G.C. and collected material over a period of fifteen years but died in 2010 before completing her research. On the evidence of what Miss Gnosspelius did write, in note-form, now held in the R.G. Collingwood Archive at Cardiff University (CACU) her finished work would have satisfied my curiosity about her grandfather, making this biography unnecessary. I was pleased to read the notes and letters related to the research done by Miss Gnosspelius; her approval I would most like to have, but sadly not possible.

A number of comments about W.G.C. during his life and afterwards point to lost opportunities, but the main opportunity he supposedly lost would most likely have been something in academia as a senior academic. In hindsight he sacrificed very little; a wonderfully varied life replaced what could have been one of rigid conformity in a monastic-like brotherhood, typical of universities at that time (1870s – 1910), or in the words of a fellow student of Gershom at Oxford Oscar Wilde, when asked what he will do with his life, '*God knows. I won't be a dried-up Oxford Don, anyhow*'.

Today, the Collingwood name (apart from admiral in Nelson's fleet) is known mainly through the work of Gershom's son Robin George well known as philosopher and historian, a scholar studied closely by members of the R.G. Collingwood Society and by others with an interest in philosophy or history, or both. I am not an historian or philosopher and, apart from a few comments in the conclusion, do not attempt to assess any influence W.G.C. could have had upon his son R.G.C. towards becoming known, internationally, in both disciplines. I trust that sufficient detail exists here that any reader knowledgeable about the work of R.G.C. may find help in assessing any influence from his father.

The Lives of other notable people sometimes reveal Gershom by association, the strongest being John Ruskin his 'employer', for some years it could be said that Gershom's view of Ruskin from their first meeting at Oxford University until the professor's death almost thirty years later verged on idolatry. Gershom said, '*I don't ask anybody to like Ruskin; I did, because I found him interesting; not because I found him always right. He was extraordinarily nice to me for 30 years, and more of an all-round man than anybody I came across*'.

Through an association with Ruskin, Gershom was fortunate to meet some influential people of the time, especially in the arts; helpful when Gershom was hoping to become a recognised artist himself. Edward Burne-Jones associated with the Pre-Raphaelite Brotherhood helped Gershom during his early years when attempting to become an artist. William Morris, a close friend of Jones, who with his co-authored work on Scandinavian history inspired and helped Gershom with his Scandinavian studies. Another artist, friend of his father, William Hunt (RWS) wrote a letter to John Ruskin introducing Gershom, a student about to enter Oxford University. Beyond the art world, and any influence of Ruskin, there was journalist and foreign correspondent Arthur Ransome, best known for his children's books. He looked upon Gershom and Mrs. Collingwood (Dorrie) as second parents and was somewhat in awe of them, yet one way some general readers know of W.G. Collingwood is through the early life of Ransome, but Ransome turned to the two senior Collingwoods for guidance and advice during most of his life. Gershom or Dorrie proofread most of Ransome's published writing. Gershom, who knew Oscar Wilde at Oxford, advised Ransome against writing a book about Wilde but he went ahead, leading to a worrying period in Ransome's life.

Son Robin wrote that his father had sacrificed a good part of his career in devoting time to Ruskin's work, this statement is debatable. During the years working for Ruskin and subsequently helping to care for him until his death (1881-1900) W.G.C. wrote and had published eight books: 'The Philosophy of Ornament', 'A Book of Verses', 'Astrology in the Apocalypse' 'Thorstein of the Mere', 'The Bondwoman', 'The Book of Coniston', 'A Pilgrimage to the Saga Steads of Iceland' (with J. Stefánsson) and 'Coniston Tales'. None of these books was for, or about, John Ruskin and in addition, he wrote 12 Journal papers not related to work done for the Professor. In the same period, W.G.C. edited five works by Ruskin and wrote his biography in addition to a biographical outline; also 'The Art Teaching of John Ruskin.

There were many advantages attached to working with Ruskin: access to a fine library with rare books, meeting many interesting visitors, access to a stimulating environment at Ruskin's home Brantwood. Not least access to Ruskin himself, a man with one of the finest minds of the nineteenth century; a century not matched (nor probably will be) for the existence of fine minds. More correctly, W.G.C. worked *with* John Ruskin rather than *for* him from autumn 1881 until around 1895; during the last five years of Ruskin's life (1895-1900) his role was that of carer and to a lesser extent had been caring since 1890 helping Mrs. Joan Severn, Ruskin's cousin, at Brantwood.

W.G.C. in addition to carrying out projects for Ruskin, and extensive independent research, produced works of art to help support his young family, a fee of around £100 per year from Ruskin paid only the rent. When working with Ruskin he was not an employee in the conventional sense of the word; no fixed hours of work and no regular tasks as part of a job description. His working relationship with Ruskin could be loosely defined as one of assistant, sounding board and friend. There were moments between the two men when they would indulge in what we now call small talk. On one occasion Ruskin was reminiscing about how he attended the

Queen's coronation (Victoria) in 1838 (sixteen years before Gershom was born), dressed like a dandy. Gershom showed him a photograph of a young man dressed in this way and asked '*did you ever wear a coat like that?*' Ruskin replied '*I'm not so sure that I didn't.* Ruskin normally dressed in homespun woollen clothing and not silk finery, unless for special occasions: Queen Victoria's coronation or presented at Court. Ruskin's clothing is discussed extensively in J.S. Dearden's book 'John Ruskin's Life in Pictures.'

In addition to a retainer-fee paid by Ruskin, the Collingwood family subsisted on earnings from the art of Gershom and Dorrie his wife, together with generous support from a neighbour Susannah (Susie) Beever, and Emma Holt a wealthy visitor from Liverpool. In 1887, after being settled for a while with a young family at Gillhead near Windermere (not lake, Bassenthwaite is the only lake in the Lake District others are either waters or meres). Dorrie wrote in a letter to Ruth her sister-in-law (CACU) of their concern about paying bills, in her words '*Gershom came back and pulled from his pocket two crackling bank notes of £10 each; Miss Beever had got an unexpected £40 and thought I ought to have half. I need hardly tell you she knows nothing whatsoever of our money circumstances.*' Dorrie may well have been right in saying Susie Beever knew nothing of their money circumstances, but Miss Beever may have suspected that Gershom, Dorrie and their young family could be in need of some extra support. In addition to the gift of £20, Susie Beever gave Dorrie three beautiful gold rings that she was going to leave to Dorrie in her will but decided she ought to have them sooner. One ring had six diamonds, one had three moonstones and the third a sapphire; described as blue as our lake when the northeast wind blows. Susie Beever was friend and support for Gershom's family soon after their arrival at Gillhead in 1883. Two years later, he dedicated his book of verse to Susie Beever.

Gershom by force of circumstances had to appreciate the need to make a living but in a letter 1887, (AH) his reference to money as 'filthy lucre', after buying a Palaeolithic chert for a friend, says much about his attitude to finance. Dorrie benefitted from wills left by some of her own family members: in 1915 from the will of Thomas Dains of Ipswich and in 1916 half the estate of Thomas P. Isaac, her brother, amounting to around £800. Money coming to Dorrie in this way, and from her painting, simply helped the family to survive; she left very little money at the time of her death. In her will, it was stated that all her estate pass to her husband then to son Robin absolutely.

For many lovers of Lakeland's past (not now) the thought of living 40 years beside Coniston Water or in any other part of Lakeland would be bliss, idyllic. I now realise that for the Collingwoods their life was fraught with difficulties; few days passed without worries about income and paying bills, they never had much money.

William Gershom Collingwood, in stature a short well- built man with piercing blue eyes and blond hair turned snow-white with age. In character he was generous to a fault, today he would probably be described as naïve; Dorrie kept an eye on him to prevent his generosity being taken too far such as giving his best suit to any passing traveler or a gold sovereign to a beggar. Granddaughter Taqui herself described Gershom as *'sweet, kind and perhaps rather ineffectual person, with many interests but no real brilliance'* this suggests that he could be thought of as dreamy and unworldly with few attributes, not until she read his obituary in The Times did Taqui discover the extent of his achievements; very sad. 'Sweet and kind' were appropriate descriptions but ineffectual can be described as easy-going. Words to a baby granddaughter Barbara Harriet (changed to Taqui) Altounyan from Gershom in a letter, May 17, 1917 (AH) serve well to reflect his nature: *'Darling Little Barbara, I hope you'll like this world, for a visit, a good long one, as much as I do. It is a mixed sort of place, my dear, but there is a lot of good in it, especially mountains and blossoms on trees, and little girls, and nice mothers and aunties <u>and</u> old grandparents'.* [Barbara (Taqui) died aged 84 in 2001].

He was equally generous with his time and knowledge being ready to help anyone without question of payment. Numerous letters exist in archives from W.G.C. to people wanting information: students writing dissertations, amateur geologists, archivists or followers of Ruskin, he replied conscientiously to everyone. John Ruskin defined poverty as 'not having what you need', Gershom would shrug off the idea of being poor by saying the family had all it needed, which was true but nevertheless maintaining even a basic level of income could be a worry from day to day. Gershom worked with almost a complete disregard for monetary reward. To quote from an obituary (TCWAAS): 'In his life he was no less simple and abstemious than if he had been vowed to poverty'.

Strong and energetic he climbed and walked on the mountains and hills of Lakeland throughout his adult life until shortly before his death aged 78. He disliked the idea of growing old and at the age of 40, he shed tears at the thought of his climbing days being over and for a while behaved as though his active life was over too, but soon after the next climb, he realised there could be many more ascents. He continued to paint Lakeland landscapes, often high among mountains, in all weather and in loving detail. Creative artistic activity was a strong theme in the lives of Collingwood families; art in the household meant only one thing, *taking part*, and features strongly throughout this book. A grandfather of Gershom an architect, father prominent as an artist in watercolours, Gershom himself artist and creative writer through to his wife and children with their impressive output in painting, sculpture and writing. Published work from three generations of the Collingwoods helps reinforce the idea that art played a major part in the life of the families. Gershom's father William Collingwood wrote and had published 'The

Value and Influence of Art as a Branch of General Education' (1862); his son wrote and had published a well-received book 'The Art Teaching of John Ruskin'(1891). Gershom's son Robin wrote and had published 'Principles of Art' (1938) and devoted the first chapter of his book 'Speculum Mentis' to the subject.

Gershom had a wonderfully varied life where experiences were valued over recognition, financial gain or the acquiring of possessions, but he was not too well suited to an age of acquisitiveness and increasing specialisation.

Education today drives students towards being monomaths; in contrast, polymaths are often seen as dabblers or worse dilettantes. In the nineteenth century especially at the time of Empire building and before the rigid division between disciplines, the polymath was highly respected. There were individuals helping to establish the Empire who within one career would organise the building of a railway and design a sewerage system in some far-off land, also give advice on forestry, paint watercolours and write poetry. Working in remote parts of the world called for strong individuals who, not able to call upon specialists, showed how initiative and wide-ranging interests and abilities were essential. Gershom was very much of this generation but unfortunately, people like him were becoming a dying breed. Bill Rollinson, a much respected writer of Lakeland life, described W.G. Collingwood as the person he would most like to have met; a sentiment that can be shared by many serious followers of life in England's north-west.

As a researcher and writer, Gershom's output of scholarly work was prodigious especially in the Transactions of the Cumberland and Westmorland Antiquarian and Archaeological Society (TCWAAS) where he contributed 66 papers (Appendix A). In addition, six papers in the Yorkshire Archaeological Journal covering mainly Anglian and Anglo-Danish sculpture across the East and West Ridings of Yorkshire. Most papers were the result of travelling to sites, some remote, spending time doing extensive fieldwork. Research done for the Transactions and other journals greatly helped in the later writing of 'Northumbrian Crosses of the pre-Norman Age' (1927), which is still highly regarded. In addition to learned papers, Gershom wrote and had published 19 books between 1883 and 1927 in addition eight edited works and one of translation between 1876 and 1926. The books he wrote included biography, poetry, geology, art, guides, history, travel and fiction. Edited works included poetry, writings of John Ruskin, politics and local history.

His book 'Lake Counties' (1902) continues to be widely read; revised by Gershom in 1932, reprinted in 1938 and 1939, a new edition in 1949 and published with revisions by Dr William Rollinson in 1988. Added to scholarly work he made observations as an amateur geologist resulting in a book 'The Limestone Alps of Savoy'. As a writer of fiction, he used his knowledge of 10 and 11- Century Lakeland to write two outstanding novels: 'Thorstein of the Mere', a story of Norse settlement in and around Coniston, and 'Bondwoman', re-published later as 'Bondwomen';

son Robin described the outburst from the Press about Bondwoman as 'obloquy for its immoral tendencies'. A similar fate had befallen 'Jude the Obscure' Thomas Hardy's book reviewed by scandalized critics a year earlier, one called it 'Jude the Obscene'.

The work of writing this biography in narrative form uses varied sources, but to allow the diverse nature of this life to flow as a story references appear in the text wherever possible rather than as footnotes. Further references appear under Notes. The reader wishing to know more about a particular source of information should find sufficient leads either within the text or from the Notes.

The many different activities and interests in Gershom's life occurred often in parallel and unlike many recorded lives; it is difficult to put any one activity or interest into a convenient time-slot of one year or even a period of years. I have listed main events in his life chronologically, but when writing the text, details inevitably overlap.

When Gershom was writing about Rev. William Slater Calverley, a friend and close collaborator, he remarked that, 'he [Calverley] would have been the last to wish his biography written'. There must be a suspicion that Gershom would feel the same about any written record of his life; though his modesty would prevent him suggesting that a biography could be written. I offer this account purely out of respect and gratitude, feeling that W.G.C.'s life and works ought to be better known.

Malcolm Craig
Histon, Cambridge, 2018

# Chapter I
# Collingwood Family
# (1761-1854)

## Family Influence

There is little doubt that the greatest influence upon Gershom came from his father, which continued well into adult life. There were times when William could not influence his son as much as he would have wished, despite vigorous attempts. Most resistance came from Gershom when he opposed his father's wish that his son should follow him as a leading figure, or indeed with an ambition to become *the* leading figure in the Plymouth Brethren. Throughout Gershom's time at Oxford and afterwards in London he was active with the Brethren, it seems mainly to please his father; when at Oxford in 1872 he wrote apologetically to his father about going to chapel, saying it was 'a quiet pleasant way to begin the day'.

According to W.B. Neatby (A History of Plymouth Brethren), early leaders of the Brethren came mainly from theology graduates but over the years, there were fewer learned candidates. William Collingwood was well aware that the Brethren needed people of higher education and saw his scholarly son an ideal candidate for a high position. Not long after Gershom left Oxford, it became obvious that he wished to become a professional artist, even though he did respond to prompting from his father to apply for University Fellowships, making several attempts. Eventually it became obvious to his father that whether his son was a Fellow of a university or a recognised professional artist he was not going to devote some of his time to the Brethren. The strongest indication of this change in attitude came from a letter to his father from Gillhead[1] in which he expressed grave doubts about the Brethren and suitability of some members. This led inevitably to some tension between father and son.

Going back a generation, William's father Samuel Collingwood (1786-1852), Gershom's paternal Grandfather, was a contractor and architect, he lived all his life at Greenwich in Kent. Samuel married a cousin in 1813, Frances Collingwood. Frances was Gershom's paternal Grandmother, who was born, and grew up in Oxford. Her Father, also a Samuel Collingwood (1761- 1841) was for most of his working life a printer to the university in Oxford a city that, like Liverpool, featured strongly in lives of the Collingwood family. For many years, printers were recognised as aristocrats of skilled tradesmen, demanding the longest of apprenticeships.

---

[1] Letter, 1885. W.G. Collingwood to William Collingwood. Abbot Hall, Kendal.

Samuel came originally from Rochester in Kent where he trained to be a compositor in the printing business and in 1792 became an Overseer at the Clarendon Press in Oxford where, at his retirement in 1838 he was Procurator of the University Press. Samuel, the Printer, had four wives and eighteen children, only the fourth wife and four children survived him; he died aged 79. Frances Collingwood, William's mother, was the second daughter of Samuel the Printer.

Frances and Samuel the Architect had six sons all born in Greenwich: Samuel 1815, William (Gershom's father) 1819, John 1821, Edward 1824, Cuthbert 1826 and Alfred 1831. Essential details of William Collingwood's life come from the writing of his son Gershom, typed in 1968 by a granddaughter Janet Gnosspelius[2] now held in the Collingwood (R.G) Archive at Cardiff University. William left six diaries recording important family events but he wrote in the first diary that he would not record personal anecdotes; most of what we know of Gershom's father is in the form of bald facts.

## William Collingwood

William Collingwood, a second son and father of Gershom plays no small part in this story, he became an established artist, a member of the Royal Watercolour Society (RWS) and close friend of much underrated artist Samuel Prout a painter known and respected by art-critic John Ruskin. Ruskin published notes about Samuel Prout after an exhibition at the Fine Art Society Galleries in Bond Street between 1879 and 1880. Ruskin, for his notes, chose around 70 illustrations by Prout, drawn during one of the artist's typical working tours travelling between Calais and Rome. Over the years Prout was often in Ruskin's thoughts, he kept up a correspondence with one of the Prout's daughters and he continued to admire her father's artwork. William Collingwood's paintings, which still appear on sale at various galleries, were exhibited at the Victoria and Albert Museum, London; at the Whitworth Gallery, Manchester; the Walker Art gallery, Liverpool and Ruskin Museum, Coniston. Many of his works are in private hands. Most of his better-known watercolours feature Alpine mountains: Jungfrau at evening, Matterhorn from the Zermatt Valley, Dent du Midi, Weisshorn and many other mountains. For most of his life, he followed the example of Prout's work.

As a boy, William attended two famous old schools in Oxford. James Hinton founded the first in the eighteenth century where William attended as a boarder at the age of seven. The second school William attended at the age of twelve was the Cathedral School founded in the sixteenth century. William's development was

---

[2] W.G. Collingwood, written by him and typed from MS. by Janet Gnosspelius in 1968. Collingwood Archive, Cardiff University.

advanced for his years, something of a child prodigy especially in the study of Greek and Latin though weak in mathematics; an academic career beckoned but was unfulfilled.

There had been suggestions that Admiral Collingwood was a member of the family. Although records of Gershom's ancestry have been traced to the seventeenth century there is no connection with Admiral Cuthbert, First Baron Collingwood (1749-1810) who served under Lord Nelson at the Battle of Trafalgar. A connection has been claimed in published writing by Wawn, 'The Vikings and Victorians' (2000) by quoting Jón Stefánsson from his memoirs, written late in life, Úti i heimi (1949), Stefánsson associated Gershom's family with the Collingwood of Trafalgar fame by stating that a relative of Gershom took over from the fallen Lord Nelson at Trafalgar. A draft family tree[3] created by Charles Harold Collingwood (1867-1961) traced the family back to John Collingwood of Lambourne in Essex (1660-1734), who came from Northumberland; seven generation before the birth of Gershom but no link was found to Admiral Cuthbert Collingwood. There are many Collingwoods in Northumberland, the Admiral's home county: records from a Mormon Index for baptism and marriage from before 1700 show there were approximately 360 Collingwoods in Northumberland, and in nearby Durham 430 persons with that name. Apart from Lincoln with 560 Collingwoods, the majority of other counties numbered less that ten with that name; Scotland was not recorded.

Gershom once referred to Northumberland Collingwoods as 'Cavaliers of the North', suggesting that branches of his family were from that county and while this is true, there is no evidence of any being in line with the famous Admiral. Janet Gnosspelius (1926-2010) updated the family tree in 1969. There is evidence of Northumbrian connections in the Collingwood family. The family tree names members in a number of places in Northumberland and Scottish Border Country: Wooler in 1346 to Haggerston in 1512, including Etal, Capheaton, Norham and Berwick. Taqui Altounyan a granddaughter of Gershom wrote in her book 'Chimes from a Wooden Bell' (published in 1990) that throughout his life William Collingwood (her Great-Grandfather) was a deeply religious man. When aged fifteen and offered a place at Christ Church, Oxford, he declined because of doubts he felt towards parts of the thirty-nine articles, which state the doctrinal position of the Church of England. To accept the place offered he had to follow the teaching of the established church and although rules of this kind were soon afterwards relaxed, he could never feel comfortable being associated with that church. William's father Samuel, known in religious terms as a dissenter better known as nonconformist, Congregationalist, or Independent, and may have been sympathetic

---

[3] A Pedigree of the Collingwood Family, from John Collingwood, Lambourne (Family Tree). Collingwood Archive, Abbot Hall Kendal.

towards his son's decision. He arranged for William to work as a live-in apprentice for Ackermann, a supplier of artist material in the Strand, London, and he was able to return home to Greenwich at weekends. During this time, William became self-taught in the skill of drawing with some assistance from a friend of his father James Duffield Harding who helped and encouraged a number of artists between the 1820s and 1840s. As a young man of 22 John Ruskin took lessons from Harding during autumn of 1841and, Ruskin referred to the artist when writing 'Modern Painters'. An artist rebuffed Harding as a boy and the event made him promise that should he become an artist he would teach anybody who asked for help; he did become a landscape painter and lithographer and, keeping his word, was a great help to young artists. In addition, he was well known to Ruskin. At the age of 18, William won two prizes at the Society of Arts for painting of landscapes and at the age of 19 exhibited a drawing showing Greenwich Church; he was among older artists belonging to the Royal Society of Artists, a group of around 30 members, based in Suffolk Street London. Harding recognised William's ability to become a gifted artist and persuaded the management of Ackermans to release him from his apprenticeship agreement. After release from his apprenticeship, William began to spend weeks in Hastings, living in a lodging house and working as a freelance artist, which brought him into contact with Samuel Prout an established artist some years older. Prout had moved to the town in 1837 from Brixton for health reasons. He was a topographical water colourist who travelled widely in Europe painting and drawing landscapes and buildings. When not working in watercolours he made fine drawings on white paper with black Cumberland lead. There can be little doubt that he influenced William to follow a similar path in developing his own career primarily as an artist in watercolours, in particular that when looking for suitable subjects, especially mountains as background, an artist must be prepared to travel beyond England's shores.

Prout found pupils for William to bring in fees, adding to the sale of his pictures in shillings rather than pounds; they were close friends until Prout's death in 1844. Shortly before his death, Prout moved back to London to live at number five De Crespigny Terrace Denmark Hill near the home of John Ruskin and his parents. Inevitably, with young Ruskin's interest in the work of various artists, it was not long before he and Prout met. William too met Ruskin (later, William arranged through an artist friend an introduction to Ruskin for his eldest son Gershom). During his time in Hastings William Collingwood also made friends with William Henry Hunt, a well-known artist working mainly in still life. Hunt spent winters in the town, away from his home, 62 Stanhope Street, Hampstead. Like Prout, Hunt was of interest to Ruskin. William was steadily drawn into close contact with both artists, Prout and Hunt by this time were both well known to John Ruskin who was becoming a respected commentator on the work of artists.

## Hastings

The coastal town of Hastings was popular with aspiring artists who were attracted to the fine beach, fishing boats, pier and the crags of West Hill with its picturesque ruin of a Norman castle built in the eleventh century. Soon after William Collingwood arrived in the town, he recorded in his diary that first visit (1838); during the three weeks spent there, a chance meeting occurred while sketching on Pier Rocks, which led to a friendship with the Maw family lasting most of his life, and one son Arthur Maw became a close friend of Gershom. The meeting was with John Hornby Maw (1800-1885), retired and wealthy from a business making surgical instrument, he was also a gifted amateur painter. The work being done by William, then only nineteen, must have impressed him because he asked the young artist to West Hill House, his home in the town, where artists Turner, Prout and Hunt had been visitors.

In the house, William could see Maw's collection of drawings and paintings by J.M.W. Turner. John Maw and his wife Mary Anne (née Johnson) had a young family at home the eldest Anne Mary who was eight, George six and Arthur four. Over the years, William became close to this family, especially Arthur and his sister Anne and stayed regularly with Arthur. The Maw family moved around the country: Guildford, Worcester and Bideford, and finally in 1850 to Broseley in Shropshire. In later years, Gershom and his family also came to enjoy the friendship of the Maw family.

After a number of visits lasting weeks in Hastings William had two respected professional painters (Prout and Hunt) and a wealthy patron of artists (Maw) as firm friends. Unfortunately, these regular visits to Hastings lasted less than two years despite encouragement from Prout and Hunt, and led to a productive period for William. Both artists helped him to sketch and paint scenes around the coastal town and suggested opportunities for him to gain commissions for portrait painting.

A chance meeting at Christmas 1838 led to William having the opportunity to teach art in Liverpool and importantly help secure a regular income. With this appointment as 'Professor of Drawing' also went the title, teacher of drawing and dancing but he would have laughed at a title 'Teacher of Dancing', William did *not* teach dancing. William valued his skill of drawing: '*He who can draw can tell his thoughts to the whole world, and not fear that his language shall ever be a dead one, so long as his canvas or paper exists*'. '*A pencil will last a month, costs less than a cigar that is gone in an hour, the poorest can learn to draw*'. This love of drawing he passed to his eldest son.

## Liverpool

The city of Liverpool in the nineteenth century was a vibrant international port; ships lined the many docks loading and unloading cargo for trade throughout the world. 'Engine of the Empire' described docks of the city. Trade was most commonly with Far-Eastern countries, but from around 1850, Cunard liners crossed the Atlantic to a set timetable.

Though in places the city was grimy and rather sordid William settled there for 45 years; the Collingwood family home at 87 Chatham Street is now part of the University campus. Gershom grew up in a city of two halves; there were prosperous Georgian town houses where professional men and their families lived, yet nearby were streets of slums where families lived in extreme poverty, despite the increasing affluence of the city as a centre of business. Liverpool is fittingly referred to as a city of laughter and tears. Augustine Birrell M.P. (1850-1933) wrote 'Some Early Recollections of Liverpool' published in 1924, which covered the period that Gershom was at school in the city.

Moving to Liverpool did not end William's contact with Hastings and the Maw family, a week was spent there in 1840, and between 1842 and 1845 he made one visit to the town each year. In 1842, Maw commissioned William to paint a picture of a room in his house, his first interior painting. This was followed by a more ambitious commission in 1843 when William spent four weeks painting a picture of a drawing room (Figure 1) There was a suggestion that the Maws contributed to The Brethren by William's reference to breaking bread (a weekly event for Brethren) in 1848 at the Maw's home in Guildford.

During William's early years in Liverpool, he earned a living by teaching art, and selling his artwork, which thrived. Working in both oils and watercolours William produced impressive images, mainly buildings of historical interest, interior as well as exterior, and landscapes. Still a single man, William taught techniques of the artist and whenever possible travelled to capture scenes for painting and sketching.

Beginning in 1839, he walked through Yorkshire to the Lake District and in the following year walked in Scotland; among his most notable work at this time were impressive street scenes in Edinburgh. No doubt while in the more rugged areas of Yorkshire and the Lakes, he was thinking of his artist-friend Prout and his journeys to the Alps looking for suitable mountain landscapes. William returned to the Lakes in 1841 and made illustrations that prove to be of value as a record of places in Ambleside that had changed little since Wordsworth's day (Figure 2) Drawn to the mountains, William visited North Wales and was so impressed, particularly by Snowdon, he returned the next year. Being not far from Liverpool the English Lake District offered him ample opportunities for landscape painting, and eventually he

Figure 1 Interior by William Collingwood

was able to introduce his eldest son (Gershom) to the delights of that area, similar opportunities for landscape sketching and painting were to be found in North Wales and further afield in Scotland. The craft of the landscape painter consists of so many elements, that it can only be fully appreciated by someone who has devoted most of his or her life to that form of art. Some years later, he was to take Gershom, then eleven years old, to Wales where they sketched and climbed Snowdon. Another painting in the Lakes that year showed Grange-in-Borrowdale; a rare attempt to paint in oils with Maiden Moor as background shrouded in mist. After becoming a member of the Liverpool Academy, he visited the Alps in 1844, a time when Alpine valleys were unspoiled and many peaks were still unclimbed. He could record Alpine-valley scenes that had remained unchanged for centuries.

## Plymouth Brethren

The religious life of William, which had made him spurn the opportunity of study and possibly an academic career at Oxford, took a dramatic turn when, in 1844, he left the Congregationalist church to become closely involved with 'The Brethren'. The Christian movement, founded around 1827 and in the 1840s was relatively new to England after coming from Ireland in 1831. A fundamental belief held by The Brethren was that the bible is the supreme authority and following the doctrine of Brethren led William to resign from the Royal Watercolour Society (Royal Charter was not granted until 1881 but had generally been known as the Royal Watercolour Society). The main reason for resigning was the Society's insistence upon members having life insurance. Brethren believed in divine providence or God being able to protect and care for humankind, insurance seemed to him in conflict with providence; a question that appeared to be logically sound to any religious believer was, 'why have insurance when we are under God's care?' Here there seemed to be a recognition of Calvinism and doctrines of predestination; God foreordaining. After formation in Ireland, the Brethren emerged first in Plymouth and went by the name 'Brethren of Plymouth' before changing to the now familiar name, 'Plymouth Brethren'. Another strong belief held by the sect was in Millenarianism; that there would be a second coming of Christ and God's Kingdom would last a thousand years, or more. There was no organised ministry, each gathering of Brethren in a meetinghouse or hall (not chapel) was autonomous and William helped finance a permanent place for them to meet in Liverpool. He was concerned that The Brethren needed a place of their own after moving around the city; first in an old schoolroom in Canning Street, a former church in Oldham Street and a room in the Mechanics Institution. By 1858, the Brethren established a meeting place in Crown Street, and remained there until 1886. In addition, he planned to save sufficient money from the sale of his art, produced from scenes in England and Switzerland, to allow a missionary journey to China. Lord Congleton, living nearby in Cheshire, back from being a Brethren missionary in Baghdad, was an influence in William joining the sect and in pointing the way towards missionary work. The aim to be a missionary in far-off China would be feasible only if William remained single, or found a wife with missionary ambitions or sympathies; he did neither.

## Parents William and Marie

An account of William Collingwood, while alone in Switzerland during an artistic tour, meeting a Swiss girl and bringing her home as his wife as stated by Henry Currie Marrillier in his book 'Liverpool School of Painters' is appealing but not

Figure 2 Approach to Ambleside
by William Collingwood 1841

correct. William travelled extensively in Switzerland but only after marrying a girl from that country. The girl Marie Elizabeth Imhoff beautiful, confident and self-willed, with long auburn hair, he saw possibly for the first time in England. She travelled in September 1846 from Paris to London in the company of William's eldest brother Samuel and his wife Frances (née Swallow). Marie was then 20 years old. Marie stayed with the Collingwood family for at least one year before returning to Switzerland.

Later, Marie Imhoff travelled to London in 1851 to visit the Great Exhibition held at the Crystal Palace in Hyde Park, a short distance from the Serpentine Lake. While staying with friends of the Collingwoods Marie met William (again?) and on Boxing Day of that year married him. The months immediately leading up to the wedding day are of interest but the sketchy records leave more questions than answers. Early in November of that year (1851) Marie was staying at Oxford in a household of William's relatives, William travelled from Liverpool to visit the family and there met Marie on the fifth and three days later William accompanied Marie back to London. Soon afterwards, William returned to Liverpool, but on December 18 he went back to Oxford to spend Christmas, and among the family gathering was Marie.

They married at a nearby village of Woodstock on December 26. They spent their honeymoon in Hastings where they arrived next day, staying at number 11 Caroline Place. Both Marie and William had travelled many miles before finally coming together. What appears to be a series of chance meetings between Marie and William at a Collingwood home may have been planned by William after their first meeting.

Family background and early life of Marie is vague and difficult to record with any confidence, Janet Gnosspelius in researching for a possible biography of W.G.C could find only fragments of family history about his mother. Marie had two sisters, one married into a German family Werl, the other married into a family of Hamburger. Marie's only brother Edward became a banker in Milan and an Elder of the Waldensian Evangelican Church in Turin. A cousin of Marie put together a rough family tree together with notes and from this, we learn that Marie's paternal grandfather was a house builder and moved to Arbon from Altnau four years before Marie was born.

Marie was one of four children of a public official and Protestant Pastor in Arbon, a town in the Canton of Thurgau in the northeast of Switzerland. Marie lived in Arbon on the west shore of beautiful Lake Constance (Bodensee); the town lies across the Lake almost opposite the main town of Lindau. After marrying William, she was to spend the remainder of her life in Liverpool, apart from occasional visits to Switzerland or the Home Counties. Her main escape route for short periods away from Liverpool with William and their young family was north to the Lake District, a cottage at Gillhead on the eastern shore of Windermere where rolling hills come close to the water, a landscape similar to her childhood home beside Lake Constance, otherwise known as Bodensee.

Marie began to make a home in Liverpool from January 1852 in what were lodgings at 10 Moss Street in the city, there is no evidence that she adopted William's beliefs but was baptised that year by John Price of the Brethren. She and William went to Switzerland in July. From William's diary, we learn a little more about Marie because during that tour the young married couple was on a steamer from Geneva to Vevay on Lake Geneva when Marie pointed to the shore at Ouchy where she passed two years at Dr Mellet's school. Before having children, Marie took the opportunity to pay a long visit to her own country. At the beginning of July

1853 Francis Collingwood and Marie arrived in Ostend to begin a tour. Frances kept a journal where at least the outline of their journey could be followed. When they took the route to Mannheim and Schaffhausen, it was clear that Marie was heading back home, to stay at Lindau on Lake Constance. Marie visited the Imhoff family after the death of her father in March of that year. From Lindau they travelled west to Brunnen on Lake Lucerne. In Lucerne, a meeting of the ways in Switzerland, they joined up with William Collingwood and his brother Samuel. The party then went on to Andermatt and crossed the Grimsell pass to reach Meyringen and eventually Rosenlaui. They spent time visiting the summit of the Faulhorn 8,792 feet (2,680 metres) which features in one of William's paintings; there are many easy ways to the top and even in the mid nineteenth century, a hostelry-type building stood at the summit. The four travelers could enjoy one of the finest views in the Alps, looking across to the mountains Eiger, Monch and Jungfrau, giants of the Bernese Oberland.

Other tours followed but on their return to England, home for William and Marie was always Liverpool.

After marriage to Marie, and settling in Liverpool, William was closer in distance to the Maw family now living in Broseley, Shropshire. John Hornby Maw helped his two sons George and Arthur buy a struggling tile manufacturer and established Maw & Co making ceramic floor tiles normally used to form geometric patterns. The tiles featured in the construction of some prestigious buildings throughout the world. The manufacture of these tiles appealed to Maw senior, because he could combine business and art; his ideas about art he shared with William Collingwood. John Maw continued to provide commissions until 1854 when his daughter Anne advised William about the subjects to paint when in Speke Hall, Liverpool. In April of that year Gershom was born, William and Marie stayed one week with the Maw family in Broseley. William was abroad painting in the summer of the following year and Marie with baby Gershom spent one month with the Maws in Broseley. On his return that year, William was again at Broseley in November while producing a painting of a room in the home of Richard Groom, timber merchant of Arleston. For many years, leading up to Marie's death in 1873 the Collingwood's young family visited the Maws. In 1870, the Maws stayed over a weekend in Liverpool at the Collingwood home and the following year William, Marie and the three children stayed at Severn House in Broseley. In 1872 after Gershom had gone to Oxford the family was in Broseley for a few weeks from November 17 to December 9, mainly to help Marie recover from illness.

This was the pattern of William's work for the next twenty years: committed to his religious work with The Brethren, teaching art and fulfilling commissions for painting interiors and landscapes. A painting William did of the alpine mountain

Jungfrau came to the notice of John Ruskin when it was at the Watercolour Society in 1856 and gave his judgment about the work:

> 'Striking in effect, and an attractive picture, but sadly wanting in accuracy of detail. If the artist would show the mountain carefully, and then work out the same effect, with rock substance beneath it, he might produce a valuable drawing. And the effect itself, simple as it is, would have been twice as good if the artist had not indulged himself with a bright yellow light on his cow, and spots of pure white and yellow about the roots of his pines, while the first rays of dawn are still a mile or two above them, and cannot get down to them for an hour and a half yet, at the very best. The picture as it is , cannot be a study from Nature; and it forms a connecting link between the works above noticed, in which the artists' <u>intention</u>, at least, is to be true, and those forming the larger portions of the exhibition , in which the intention is to be pretty or clever.'

To William the criticism ought to be seen as just; with these words in mind he went to Zermatt that summer and drew the Matterhorn. When Ruskin saw the result he did not put thoughts to words but both men became friends, Ruskin saw a man in William who loved mountains as he did. This friendship led eventually to Gershom's close association with Ruskin. John Ruskin read religious pamphlets written by William Collingwood and valued them even though not agreeing with much of the content, similarly, William found fault with some of John Ruskin's writing.

After some years of poor health, Gershom's mother died of consumption in Liverpool and lies buried in Toxteth Park Cemetery. Gershom was at Oxford, younger brother David followed his medical training in London and only sister Ruth remained at home with her father.

The Collingwoods finally severed their ties with Liverpool in 1884 when health reasons for both widower William and his daughter Ruth made them seek 'better air' and to do this they left the city and went across the Channel to live mainly in Italy. After almost one year, they returned to England to settle in Hastings, an old haunt for William but as at Liverpool, he had differences of opinion with the Brethren. Next stop, the final one, was at Clifton near Bristol, there he found a warm reception from the Brethren and had happy associations with them until his death on June 25 1903.

William died at his home in Abbotsford Road, at the age of 84 and left most of his wealth to his daughter Ruth, she cared for him during the final years of his life and this arrangement was with the agreement of Gershom (David had died 5 years earlier). William had put his wishes in writing, dated May 3, 1900. Both sons had each received almost £1000 to help them with their professional studies, which had not applied to their sister. William had been successful as an artist but also inherited a share with his five brothers of an estate in Buckinghamshire called Lower Glory Mills. Within the National Archive of the Centre for Buckinghamshire Studies, records show that Samuel Collingwood printer of Oxford (William's maternal grandfather) bought parts of the estate in 1828. Samuel added to the estate by buying cottages and two parcels of land between 1838 and 1839; he then had on the estate: cottages, a papermill and 28 acres of land.

When Samuel died in 1841the estate came to his fourth wife, Jemima; only Jemima and four of eighteen children, by previous marriages, survived him. In his will it stated that when his wife died the estate be auctioned, this happened in 1848 and the highest bidder was William's father Samuel Collingwood the architect of Greenwich; money from the sale went to the four surviving children of Samuel and Jemima, one being William's mother.

When Samuel the architect died in 1852, his six sons shared the estate: Samuel, William (W.G.C's father), John, Edward, Cuthbert and Alfred. William's eldest brother was brought up by his grandfather, Samuel, in Oxford despite having a large family of his own. When they leased the estate in 1865, it had been in the Collingwood family since 1828. William was a beneficiary of his uncle's investment, which helped fund his travelling including a year abroad with daughter Ruth. Gershom benefitted during his father's lifetime with sums of money, especially when a student at the Slade and time spent trying to become an established artist while living in London.

This is the background to the early life of William Gershom Collingwood, with a Swiss mother and artist father settled in the city of Liverpool. They were not a prosperous family but comfortable, very comfortable in comparison with many working families of that city. Gershom was to spend the first 18 years of his life in the city with his close family.

# Chapter II
# Boyhood
# (1854-1872)

**Liverpool Family**

William and Marie had three children: William Gershom in 1854, Sophia Ruth in 1856 and David in 1858, all born in Liverpool. With a Swiss mother, brought up in the east of that country, her children grew up fluent in German.

William travelled a good deal to fulfil his art commissions and when in Liverpool was an active member of the Brethren; early upbringing of the children was almost entirely the responsibility of Marie.

David unlike his father or elder brother was either not artistic or preferred a more stable occupation than being an artist, and chose to study medicine; in 1883 he became a fellow of The Royal College of Surgeons at the minimum age for admission. After working as House Surgeon at University College Hospital and Victoria Hospital for sick children in London, he went to Australia in 1884. David was the second Collingwood to make this long journey by sea, an uncle, younger brother of his father, went to Adelaide in 1849, unlike David without any established profession. Edward Collingwood, sailed with his wife and arrived in Australia a widower, Ann Collingwood née Day died during the voyage on a small cramped barque named 'Elizabeth' and was buried at sea. Edward's second wife Helen née MacGowen, he married in Adelaide, she came from Liverpool and five years later Edward was back in England, working as a clerk in London with a family of eight children, four sons and four daughters; it remained a puzzle to the Collingwood family why Edward went to Australia. The journey was long and arduous at that time and the prospects highly uncertain unless like David Collingwood the immigrant belonged to an established profession.

David Collingwood served as a Physician after arrival in Australia and later worked in partnership with Edward Thomas Thring from England; a gynaecologist. The partnership developed to become one of the largest general practices in Sydney. David spent 5 years as a GP but after returning to England with his family his health suffered and a haemorrhage led to his death aged only 40 leaving a widow and two children. In a British Medical Journal obituary[4] David was described as having a vigorous personality, tenacity of purpose, a kindly disposition and a

---

[4] Stanley, D.1889. David Collingwood, Obituary. British Medical Journal, September 30.

gifted teacher beloved by friends and held in fondest affection by family; words that could equally apply to his elder brother Gershom.

Ruth, or 'Ruthie' to the family, was at home most of the time without a career, quite common for middle-class young women at that time. Ruth spent some years looking after her ailing father who lived for 30 years as a widower. Ruth did not marry and after her father died, she moved to Somerset and died in Weston-Super-Mare aged 81.

## Schooling

Schooling for Gershom before going to university was at an establishment founded in 1843, primarily for children of merchants and professional men in Liverpool called Liverpool Collegiate in Shaw Street (later known as Liverpool College). David Wainwright in 1960 wrote of 'Liverpool Gentlemen': A History of Liverpool College (A Vice President of the establishment when Gershom attended was William Gladstone a Liberal member of parliament who was to serve four terms as Prime Minister during the second half of the nineteenth century).

The Headmaster was Rev. George Butler and it may have been his pioneering methods of teaching geography by illustrating lessons with relief maps made of papier- mache that prompted Gershom many years later to make similar maps in the Lake District. Another possible influence in directing Gershom towards the arts was his attendance at classes conducted by Artist W.J. Bishop who was an associate of Liverpool Academy (established 1810) his main subject was ornamental art. Aged only thirteen Gershom illustrated a letter from Switzerland to Ruth his sister showing the workings of a pole lathe.

While at the school, Gershom, together with another student H.V. Pigot, edited the Liverpool College Magazine, achieving a high standard; it existed between 1871 and 1873. Gershom showed early drawing ability when he contributed illustrations, among them one of a master caning a boy Master Yellwell because he refused to do classics; the reason given by the boy was that he planned to be a merchant, not a parson. Gershom did do classics with enthusiasm and achieved good results (Figure 3).

The three Collingwood children will have been conscious of their unconventional family background. Pupils around them at school, and friends, would have fathers working mainly in offices: accountants, solicitors, in senior clerical roles, or as professional engineers, dock managers, master mariners or officers, deck and engineering, at sea. Other schoolchildren in Liverpool would have wage-earning parents, working mainly in the docks, in the many supporting workshops as craftsmen on ships as seamen or in the city as shop assistants. Typical features of working life shared by salaried professionals and weekly wage-earners in a family

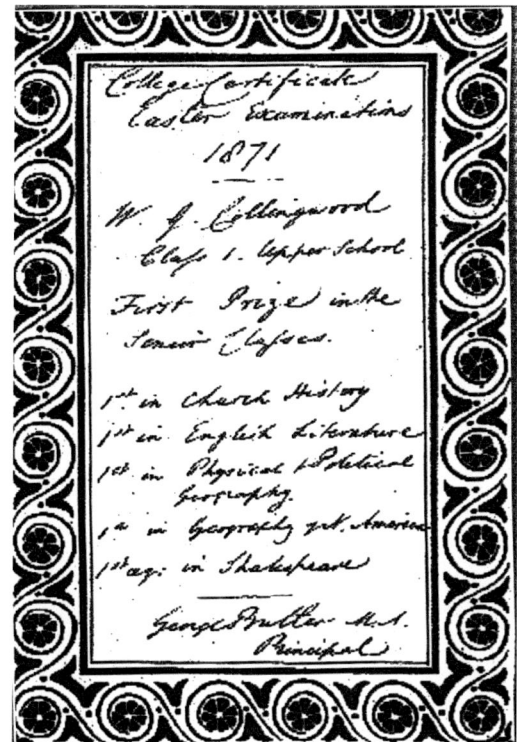

Figure 3 Gershom's School Report

was that they all worked regular hours, normally at the same job for life, with a predictable income. None of these features applied to Gershom's household; his father's ability to provide for the family relied totally upon his production of paintings that clients wished to buy. In addition, he had one Swiss parent and the other English but not from Liverpool, not a Liverpudian; Gershom could be called an outsider and was destined to spend his life looking for somewhere to belong.

Teaching at the college followed closely Church of England principles; Gershom's father must have felt that the good reputation of the college outweighed any misgivings he felt towards the Church of England. Mother Marie brought up in a religious and protestant family did not raise objections, she was probably aware that very few boys left the college without making successful careers for themselves.

When schooling was ending, Gershom was not yet ready to follow his father's example as an artist and given that a place at Oxford University was on offer, an alternative prospect of becoming a member of the professional class of Liverpool would not be considered. Since the age of sixteen Gershom had been entrusted with the task of taking a Sunday school class and his father would naturally hope that his well-educated son could eventually play a leading role in the Brethren.

The faith was not strong in Oxford and Gershom's father had arranged a meeting between his son and Dr Henry Fry a non-conformist clergyman in the city. No relationship developed and Fry died soon after Gershom settled at the University; he made no serious contact with the Brethren until leaving Oxford.

**Northern Influences**

Rivalry existed between the two major cities of the North West, Manchester and Liverpool, a common saying was '*Manchester men and Liverpool Gentlemen*' reflecting a perceived difference between manufacturing of Manchester and the commerce of Liverpool. Another common saying, only believed in Manchester, was that 'one man is worth ten gentlemen of the Liverpool kind'. There was a certain amount of stereotypical-thinking of Manchester folk as hard working and those in Liverpool living at a leisurely pace (pen-pushers, or what now would be key-pressers). Strangely, leisure features in the City's motto from the Roman poet Virgil: 'God has given to us this leisure, or ease' (Deus nobis haec otia fecit).

Gershom as a young man could witness hard work taking place in the numerous docks of his city, contrary to the perceived image of Liverpool just as someone could witness life of a leisured class in Manchester, again contrary to the perceived image of that city. Overall, working life for most people in the north was extremely hard, whether living in Liverpool, Manchester, Sheffield, Sunderland or Newcastle. Working life in the north was likely to have a strong influence upon him. When living at home in Liverpool everyday life in the city could also have a profound affect upon Gershom without him necessarily being aware at the time; in letters whenever away from Liverpool he expressed a dislike of the city, a possible reason for his regular escapes north to the Lake District. Some years later, when writing home from Oxford (CACU) as a student, Gershom remarked how he was much more relaxed when walking the streets of that city compared with his boyhood in Liverpool. When in Liverpool he would dress in a shabby coat so not to draw attention to himself. 'Nice' well-dressed young men alone in the city had to be very circumspect because they may be robbed, attacked or jeered at by locals. The result was delight from Gershom whenever his parents suggested a visit to Windermere.

**Icelandic Connections**

When the young Gershom lived in Liverpool, the city was affluent from its early days mainly as a fishing port. As industrialisation advanced, trade and commerce had, increasingly, a focus on the north of England and in particular, on the west coast at the port of Liverpool, transfer of trade to the south and east of the country had not then taken place. Amongst the worldwide trade was a thriving business in goods from Iceland: eider down, fish oil, swanskins, dried cod and woolen items of clothing. Often boxes of these imports lay on the waterfront near Pier Head making trade with Iceland plain to see by all passers-by. Contact between the city and Iceland was strong (a major retail outlet in Reykjavik, Iceland had the name of Liverpool). A reader in Icelandic worked at the University College of Liverpool, John Sephton a scholar who had written about Iceland and carried out translation from Icelandic. Two famous explorers of Iceland Henry Holland and John Thomas Stanley were from the city, and members of The Viking Club (later, Viking Society for Northern Research) recognised Liverpool as an important centre for study of the Norse-Viking age. People in and around Liverpool with an interest in Iceland were known as 'Cestrian Icelandophiles'. Later in life, Gershom, Liverpool born and bred, was to visit Iceland and became a leading authority on Scandinavian settlements in Northern England during pre-Norman time; we can only guess to what extent this part of trade in the city influenced Gershom to direct him towards a more serious study of Iceland and its people.

**Lakeland**

Whenever possible, William, Marie and the children spent time at Gillhead close to the east shore of Windermere; these idyllic days in Lakeland helped Gershom recognise that this area was where he should belong and was possibly the most formative period of his life. The Windermere of Gershom's boyhood was a magical place where numerous delights could be found along its shoreline, whether east or west; rocky coves, known locally as neuks and nabs, then fringed with natural woodland long before many of the coves became filled by efforts to landscape them to satisfy private dwellings. As a boy with parents, his sister Ruth and brother David they lived in a cottage, home of professional fisherman William Alexander who later married the Collingwood children's nurse Harriet, née Gill in 1868 when the youngest Collingwood child David was ten years old. Harriet died 30 years later, buried at Cartmel Fell close to the cottage.

Gershom met fishermen and local people who told him tales from the past, helping to develop in him a sense of history. Fisherman-William Alexander told tales of old Lakeland, passed down by word-of-mouth. Stories about Monks at Furness Abbey before the reformation, tales about border fights with the Scots and closer to home accounts of strange figures seen over the years, and ghosts, storytelling of this kind helped kindle in Gershom a lifelong interest in the history of Lakeland and in folklore. In the Epilogue to Coniston Tales[5] published in 1899, Gershom wrote in dialect of this time, 'there was Hugh, t'giant o'Troutbeck, and Adam o'Rattlegill, rows wi Scotch Rebels, he co'd em, and Forness monks long sen...

William the fisherman had little formal education, lived a simple life but had an enormous influence upon Gershom before he went to Oxford University. Alexander belonged to a group of full-time fishermen with rights to fish Windermere. The earliest record of organised fishing on the mere comes from Furness Abbey where in, the mid-twelfth century, the monks had permission to use one boat and twenty nets. Fishermen divided the mere into three sections called 'cubbles': high (north) middle and low (south) cubble. William Alexander carried out net fishing in the low cubble from the shore near to his cottage, a method practised to catch char, trout, pike, eel and perch the most profitable being char (Mrs. Beaton in 1888 referred to char as the most delicious of fish), and potted char became a delicacy. The value of char taken from Windermere in any one year at the time Alexander fished was around £1,000 (£88,600 in 2011 using the retail price index). Net fishing on the mere was suspended in 1921 and a final decision made to stop the practice in 1924.[6]

William spent some of his time at the fisherman's cottage taking his eldest son on painting tours among valleys and hills of the district. During the 1860s, Gershom went with his father to Borrowdale, further north in the Lake District, and heard artist-friends of his father compare the valley unfavourably with parts of Wales and Scotland, which he thought invidious. Gershom felt there was ample history to be found in the valley. Borrowdale needed only its own Walter Scott (It is open to debate whether W.G. Collingwood or H.S. Walpole satisfied this need).

As a boy in Borrowdale Gershom heard the story of a cuckoo, how locals built a wall to keep the bird in so it would always be summer in the valley, it hopped over the wall and flew away, alas only one more layer of stone would have kept it in the valley.

Especially in autumn, and before the invasion of motor vehicles, there were few valleys in the world more beautiful than tranquil Borrowdale, or one with a more colourful history.

These tours with his father and later contact with John Ruskin, proved to be major influences upon the young William Gershom Collingwood that helped shape his life: landscape art among fells and mountains together with 27 years under the guidance of Ruskin that were to follow, helped develop in him many other interests.

---

[5] Collingwood, W.G. 1899. 'Coniston Tales.' Ulverston: William Holmes.
[6] Kipling, C. 1972. The commercial fisheries of Windermere. Transaction of the Cumberland and Westmorland Antiquarian and Archaeological Society, vol. 72. pp. 156-204.

In a letter to his father dated April 13 1871,[7] he recalled an ascent of a mountain called Coniston Old Man, alone, at the age of 16 during one of his visits to Lakeland. Gershom went from Gillhead to Coniston; he began by crossing Windermere then walked around Esthwaite Water to reach the villages of Hawkshead and Coniston before climbing the Old Man of Coniston and back to Gillhead, all in one day:

> 'After a breakfast of syrup vulgarly called treacle. Rowed across the lake (Windermere) Icy. Then across Esthwaite Water to Hawkshead. Then I saw the Old Gentleman who was wearing a white hat and asserted his gentlemanly origin by pulling it off to me. I went past the Copper Mines and was soon out of reach of houses and suchlike abominations. There was a blue haze, which spoilt the view from the top, but the near peaks were glorious. I refreshed myself with snow and by 12 of Greenwich Time precisely I got up on the cairn and yelled 'hip, hip hurrah' as I had promised. But the Gillhead people neither heard nor saw me'.

Later, when more familiar with the district, Gershom would remind people that 'The Old Man' refers not to the mountain but to the pile of rocks at the summit commonly known as a cairn; there used to be three cairns descending in size but now only one ('Man' was a term used in the past for a summit cairn.)

This was a major expedition for a sixteen-year-old boy alone and could only have been attempted by building up confidence after spending some hours on the hills with his father.

Gershom had spent long enough in the city to join a group of Liverpool gentlemen, but the last few years had prepared him for a place at university; the next city would be Oxford.

---

[7] Letter, 1871, W.G.Collingwood to William Collingwood. Collingwood Archive, Abbot Hall Kendal.

# Chapter III
# Student Days
# (1872-1876)

## University College Oxford

At the end of Gershom's schooling at Liverpool College in 1872, he prepared for a move to Oxford. Gershom chose to study classics at University College, founded in the mid-thirteenth century (probably the most famous person to study there was Percy Bysshe Shelley). At the time Gershom entered Oxford University there were a number of influential men teaching there, among them Thomas Hill Green (1836-1882) College tutor and philosopher of the idealist movement; Benjamin Jowett (1817-1893) influential theologian and Master of Balliol College and Richard Lewis Nettleship College tutor who as a mountaineer was of interest to Gershom, he died on Mont Blanc.

    Gershom was one of the few students coming from the north, or at least what staff and students at Oxford considered 'north'; coming from Liverpool, he was thought of as a 'northerner'. Gershom belonged to a relatively poor family without inherited wealth, where yearly income could be described as insecure. He found himself in a minority; did not attend school at Eton, Harrow or Winchester. Yet he appears to have settled very quickly as a minority student to lead a largely uneventful life for four years. He was short of money throughout his student days. Gershom was not a bon vivant, and could not be one had he wished; he was not an aesthete, a swell, an athlete, a Mason or belonging to any group of students. In a letter to his father (1872),[8] he described going to a lecture given by John Ruskin on Sandrio Botticelli, and how in his rooms lived on bread and butter with water morning and noon. Work was his main activity and between terms, he had an escape route to the cottages beside Windermere where he could walk and climb on his beloved hills and mountains.

## Philosopher Bosanquet

Bernard Bosanquet was a fellow of University College from 1870 until leaving the University in 1881. He taught Greek history and philosophy.[9] Gershom was

---

[8] Letter, 1872. W.G.Collingwood to William Collingwood. Collingwood Archive, Abbot Hall, Kendal.

[9] McBriar, A.M. 2004. Bernard Bosanquet. Oxford Dictionary of National Biography. Oxford: Oxford University Press.

encouraged by Bosanquet to become a strong follower of the philosophy promoted by Thomas Hill Green. Green died young at only 45; his ideas, not fully appreciated until some years after his death, in particular with respect to levels of Government intervention and individual rights, which are still relevant and his attempts to present a theory of common good in society at a time when dominant ideas were of utilitarianism. We can argue that continued interest in Green's teaching led eventually to Gershom influencing his son Robin and parts of his writing on philosophy many years later, but this is a contentious point. Initially, the main influence at Oxford came from Bernard Bosanquet, his tutor, especially in becoming more idealistic in his approach to the study of philosophy.

Among his many and varied interests, Gershom would not list philosophy but he did have a philosophy; he said 'born an idealist' and remained so throughout his life. Idealism fully emerged in Britain during the 1870s when Gershom was at Oxford and continued to gain strength into the beginning of the next century. Unfortunately, Idealism is too easily misunderstood and difficult to understand clearly. Two Professors David Boucher and Andrew Vincent have written a book about British Idealism with the purpose of presenting a full range of British Idealists' philosophy; anyone with an interest in idealism would do well to study this book;[10] the writers begin by pointing out that: *'idealism is a much-maligned word. In ordinary language it is pejoratively labelled unrealistic, or unduly optimistic.'* It is important to recognise that idealism is about ideas and particularly consciousness rather than ideals, or utopias. *'The mind is not seen as a passive receptor of external stimuli, but active in constituting that very reality of which it is conscious.'* Gershom, feeling a 'born idealist' before meeting Bosanquet had his views strengthened under his guidance. In writing his father's obituary for The Times newspaper, Robin George Collingwood recognised that his father gained insight into history, which his philosophical training alone could give.

Gershom enjoyed success gaining a first in 'Greats' mainly study of Literature, ancient history and Philosophy; he had a viva voce on June 17, and received results in September, 1876. Gershom was following some impressive scholars at Oxford: Green, Nettleship, Bradley and Bosanquet. He also won the Lothian Prize with one of his essays about 'The Institution and purpose of knighthood'. From this point onwards, life as an Oxford academic would seem to be a predictable career path, but one thing Gershom would never be was predictable. Having a strong independent character and being rather unconventional seemed inherent traits in the Collingwood family.

---

[10] Boucher, D. and A.Vincent 2011. British Idealism: a guide for the perplexed. London: Continuum.

Figure 4 Dressler's Bust of Ruskin

Apart from Gershom's tutor Bernard Bosanquet, another important influence upon him as a student and for many years of his life was John Ruskin, a Professor at the University.

## John Ruskin

Many people readily recognise the face of John Ruskin, even now more than 100 years after his death. Paintings, drawings, sculpture and photographs provide a visual record of the man, mainly in old age heavily bearded as in the famous sculpture by Conrad Dressler in 1884 (Figure 4). As a younger man Ruskin drew a self- portrait in 1874 for a close friend Charles Norton, a Professor at Harvard, social critic and reformer who Ruskin inspired during the American's tour of Europe.

Gershom gives a vivid word-picture of the man: *'Ruskin, tall and slim 5ft 10 inches reduced by age with a stoop. A plain old-English gentleman neither fashionable dandy nor artistic mountebank, blue eyes that riveted you, magnetised you, seemed to look through you and read your soul; and indeed when they lighted upon you, you felt you had a soul of sorts. What they really saw is a mystery'.*

Gershom pointed out that Ruskin was fundamentally a Scot, not English, *'like Scots around the world they change their homes but not their hearts.'*

Opinions differ whether Gershom's prospects were either hindered or prospered because of his association with Ruskin; on balance, it seems that he was very fortunate to spend so many years working with the great man. Gershom first met Ruskin in Oxford at the end of October 1872 soon after joining the university. In a letter to his father from Oxford (AH) he described his first meeting with Ruskin. The Professor said he had received a letter from Henry Hunt about him and ought to know his name [Collingwood]; Ruskin ought to know his name, he was well aware of William Collingwood having bought some of his pictures, and admired his work ever since 1856, after seeing his painting of the Matterhorn. Gershom told Ruskin that he wished to be an artist and Ruskin replied that he did not know how he could help him, apart from a few hints. When Gershom asked about the drawing school, Ruskin said that he could come in when it was wet or when he was tired of reading and draw there. Gershom went to the drawing school and with other students went to breakfast with Ruskin at Corpus Christi College. When Gershom went to Oxford he would know of Ruskin primarily as an art critic but soon came to recognise his role as social reformer. He recalled Ruskin sitting in his room at the university saying, '*here I am trying to reform the world and I suppose I ought to begin with myself, I am trying to do St. Benedict's work, and I ought to be a saint. And yet I am living between a Turkey carpet and a Titian, and drinking as much tea* (taking his second cup) *as I can swig*'. Ruskin had a successful period at Oxford as a student, winning the Sir Roger Newdigate Prize in 1839 after two earlier attempts in 1837 and 1838.

(When Ruskin visited Oxford with his father to collect the prize in 1839, they met William Wordsworth who was there to collect an honorary degree.)

Ruskin steered students towards practical tasks rather than spend most of their working time theorising, or taking part in organised sports in their leisure time. During one of his lectures in 1874, Ruskin proposed to students that instead of developing their bodies in pointless games, in *'fruitless slashing of the river'*, in learning '*to leap and row, to hit a ball with a bat'* they should join him in improving the countryside. Ruskin felt the same amount of effort should be expended in producing something useful. One of the Professor's planned activities was to build a road locally. Ruskin never appreciated sport, or any kind of physical activity for its own sake, after watching a game of tennis he was reported to have said that the net seems to get in the way. To Ruskin, activity must have a purpose, an outcome, something tangible, ideal physical recreation for him was to chop wood for the fire. The need for a road near Oxford offered an ideal opportunity to put his ideas into practice. Ruskin warned against the dangers of separating intellectual activity from manual activity, that the traditional definitions of work for gentlemen and work for artisans exacerbated class divisions. In this respect poet, businessman, socialist and designer William Morris shared Ruskin's view; he too argued that all children should be taught practical skills and related knowledge in addition to intellectual knowledge alone.

Gershom was described as not too enthusiastic about the road-building project and apparently this showed during the digging itself; he had the advantage of being physically fit from his frequent fell walking and climbing, though when writing later in 'Ruskin Relics' he admitted to being 'slack' as a digger. He did have the advantage of spending his boyhood in an area where the majority of people toiled at hard physical work, so unlike many Oxford students and staff, including Ruskin, hard physical work was not a novelty to Gershom. One student in particular who disliked sport of any kind, Oscar Fingal O'Flaherty Wills Wilde, needed little persuading to join the 'gang' of student-workmen. Wilde is reported to have said,

'*I play no outdoor games at all, except dominoes, I have sometime played dominoes outside French cafés*'.

For Wilde, getting out of bed at dawn was a new experience; like his mother, he rarely appeared before mid-day but he did rise early for Ruskin's project. A large strong young man Wilde made a valuable contribution to the road building, the big pay-off for him was getting to know Ruskin. Wilde wrote later in a letter to the Professor that the dearest memories of his time at Oxford were of walks and talks with him; '*from you I learned nothing but what was good*'.[11]

What Wilde learned included being taught by Ruskin how to use a wheelbarrow (if the reader doubts the difficulty of this task, try it fully laden, up or down a slope), which he recorded in January 1882 when writing an article for the Nation magazine in America. The group of Oxford students working on the road with Gershom included a student close to him, Alexander Wedderburn. Another 'road builder' that Gershom was to have a good deal of contact with later in Lakeland was Hardwick Rawnsley, a founder of The National Trust. After road building, members of the group gathered together for breakfast with Ruskin in his rooms at Corpus so had the opportunity of getting to know the Professor more informally; this was a great privilege because people flocked to hear Ruskin give his lectures, often in a room full of students and interested people until there was standing room only.

Ruskin's 'road building' has been much maligned over the years but local farmers appreciated their efforts, especially in winter when their carts would be bogged down when travelling between fields. Ruskin felt that students could build a road with a firm surface. The place chosen was Ferry Hinksey a small hamlet near Oxford.

Before road building began there existed only a swampy lane. Not surprisingly, Ruskin was unfamiliar with the skills of road building and underestimated the difficulties involved, without professional help and regular maintenance over the years their labours did not produce a permanent way. The intentions were sound and for Gershom it was possibly the first real lesson in the value of combining practical and theoretical work on a task typically thought of as pure labouring, a lesson he came to appreciate and followed for the remainder of his life and whenever appropriate he passed on to his children Dora, Barbara, Robin and Ursula.

Gershom said that in building the road,[12] Ruskin's intention was not to make them into navies but to give them respect for the skilled use of pick and trowel; just as his drawing school was not to make them artists, but to show them how hard

---

[11] Ellmann, R. 1987. Oscar Wilde. London: Hamish Hamilton.
[12] Letter 1874, W.G. Collingwood to William Collingwood. Collingwood Archive Abbot Hall, Kendal.

Figure 5 Ruskin's road building at Ferry Hinksey

it was. Most student-volunteers for road building were ill equipped physically for the task, which may help explain why at the end the project it could not be called a success:

> 'My disciples alack, are not strong in the back, And their arms than their biceps are bigger.
>
> Yet they ply picks and spade, and glorify the Slade: So to Hinksey go down as a digger.'

Local people around the village became familiar with this road-building project and at times, it became something of a spectator sport; in a photograph, groups of local men and women can be seen to the left of students working on the road (Figure 5).

John Ruskin was the first Slade Professor of Fine Art at Oxford University where he established a drawing school in 1871 (known as the Ruskin School of Drawing). For some reason, Gershom's tutor Bernard Bosanquet appeared to disapprove of him attending meetings with Ruskin, saying *'he would do him no good'*. There may have been some falling-out between the two academics because earlier as a classics scholar Bosanquet followed the writing of the older man and Ruskin shared with him idealism and need for social reform. After retirement from Oxford Bosanquet moved to London wishing to do social work; although a supporter of radical liberalism he had serious reservations about the 'new' socialists, especially with regard to economic policy, so possibly he had moved away from Ruskin's position while still at Oxford.

**Translation Work**

The first intellectual project Gershom carried out for Ruskin was a translation from Greek, done with fellow-student Alexander Wedderburn. One outcome from student gatherings with the famous Professor was that he asked two students Wedderburn and Montefiore, in 1875, to translate the Economist of Xenophon (Oeconomicus).

The translation work contributed towards John Ruskin's 'Bibliotheca Pastorum' published in 1876.[13] Leonard Montefiore of Balliol College became seriously ill, so the Professor agreed to Gershom taking his place (Montefiore died in 1879 aged only 26). Ruskin commented that their share of royalties from this work would keep the two translators in raspberry jam. Gershom recalled in his book 'Ruskin Relics' that he had a postal order for his share, 'regularly these past thirty years'.[14] Ruskin used ideas from this translated work to help develop his writing on political economics. The Xenophon work, based upon debates between Greeks: Socrates, Critobulus and Ischomachus. Ruskin wrote, *'two of my youthful scholars at Oxford, one English* [Gershom] *the other Scottish* [Wedderburn] *in good love and obedience to my wish, have translated, with painful addition to their own proper work at the University'*. It was proper that Ruskin should recognise that this painstaking work took place while they prepared for their finals. A year before they left Oxford, from March to August 1875, Gershom and Wedderburn spent weeks in a cottage at Gillhead beside Windermere working on the translation and making the difficult journey across to Ruskin's home Brantwood only when they needed their work checked by Ruskin. They would sit in his study and read aloud their translated text while Ruskin read the equivalent sections in Greek. The professor had planned a tour on the Continent that summer but remained at Brantwood to oversee the translation work. When staying at Brantwood their working day roughly followed that of Ruskin, apart from rising before dawn; deskwork in the morning and physical work after lunch.

Alexander Wedderburn visited Brantwood regularly after the translation of Xenophon and worked on editing various publications of Ruskin's work. The Stones of Venice (Traveller's Edition, 1879-1881), Arrows of the Chase (1880), On the Old Road (1885), Lectures on Art (1888), Venice Academy Guide (1891) and served as one of Ruskin's literary executors. This work, done by Wedderburn, was in addition to that undertaken by Gershom in helping Ruskin during this period.

---

[13] Ruskin, J. (ed.) 1876. Economist of Zenophon, translated by A.D.O. Wedderburn and W.G.Collingwood. London: Ellis and White.

[14] Collingwood, W.G. 1903.'Ruskin Relics.' London: Isbister & Co.

The main practical work at that time, in addition to the daily wood chopping, was in making a harbour and jetty for Ruskin's boat. With Wedderburn and Collingwood in the house, Ruskin wasted no time in getting the two fit young men to help him build a small harbour for his boat on Coniston Water; the harbour was to be immediately below the house. Both students worked hard in preparing the area but a local stonemason came to finish the task.

Gershom noted that three stone steps built by himself and Wedderburn were preserved at Ruskin's request as a 'monument' to their work that summer. Collingwood and Wedderburn in extending the harbour at Brantwood faced similar hard labouring work they had done as students at Oxford. The harbour was primarily for a small boat belonging to Ruskin named 'Jumping Jenny' named after the boat captained by Nanty Ewart in the book 'Redgauntlet' by Sir Walter Scott. Scott's work said to be John Ruskin's favourite book. He took great delight in reading from it in evenings and discussed it in 'Praeterita' (Ruskin had Scott's manuscripts for the Waverley Novels, bound in crimson Morocco).[15]

The boat Jumping Jenny was designed by Ruskin's Secretary Laurence Hilliard and built in a boat yard immediately across Coniston Water from Brantwood. Two men were responsible for the building, both master craftsmen, Will Bell and Mont-Barrow. Jumping Jenny was Ruskin's own boat, a kind of flagship. Gershom commented about the boat that 'she looked strong enough to outlast us all'; which she has, at the time of writing Jumping Jenny can be seen at Brantwood. He painted a scene showing the boat lying near the jetty with Brantwood behind[16] (Figure 6).

At the end of his time at Oxford, Gershom was swayed in a choice of career, first by Ruskin praising his drawing. Both his tutor at Oxford and his father preferred that he remained in academia. He chose to be an artist and became enthusiastic about joining the Slade School of Art in London. Other opportunities beckoned: civil service, teaching, publishing and more, but art was his choice. Little did he know that a new world of experience would open up beyond Slade, more to do with serendipity than a planned career in some profession.

---

[15] Moore, H.K. 1930. 'Reminiscences and Reflections.' p.19. London: Longmans.
[16] Dearden, J.S. 1999. 'John Ruskin a Life in Pictures.' Sheffield: Sheffield Academic Press.

Figure 6 Ruskin's Boat. By W.G.C.

# Chapter IV
# Becoming an Artist
# (1876-1882)

**Slade School of Art**

Unike his father, Gershom spent four years at University but like him he avoided, or circumstances dictated, that he would not follow an academic career. A further period of study followed his years at Oxford when he went to the Slade School of Art in London from October 1876 to end of June, 1877; a good choice for the young Gershom because the school had built a tradition for fine draughtsmanship. The Athenaeum Journal, registered as a newspaper and published weekly, printed a notice that year about the Slade courses in drawing, painting and sculpture that would begin on October 4 at 9.30am; places were limited due to lack of space. However, Gershom with his results from Oxford University and support of John Ruskin had little difficulty in gaining a place.

William Gershom Collingwood did become a gifted draughtsman and artist in oils and watercolours; his name is not readily associated with great artists but his work is exhibited and sold in fine art galleries 80 years after his death, and his drawings for illustrated books on archaeology are still of immense help to students of the subject. Careful drawing of maps, showing the layout of Roman sites was of great value too. A particularly fine example is of the archaeologically important site near the mountain of Skidaw in the Lake District, Camp Hill Caermot. Francis Haverfield organized exploration of the site and reported the work done in 1902. G.B. Grundy of Oxford University did some surveying and W.G. Collingwood produced a fine map, printed in CW2 vol.3.

In the summer before going to the Slade Gershom had some energetic walks in Lakeland: walked 50 miles in one day over the Stake Pass to Keswick then back to Gillhead past Thirlmere. Another walk was through Little Langdale to the Roman castle at Hardknot (Ordnance Survey spelling) where he made a bivouac among the ruins and made a fire at 4am. had breakfast then climbed up Bowfell on a very hot day then down to the Old Dungeon Gill and home through Langdale, another very long tiring journey.

Gershom in wanting to be an artist had foremost in his mind the painting of wild landscapes. Gershom grew up at a time when many artists practised pictorial art. The aim was to bring to a public faithful representation of the beauties found in the nation's countryside, the sublime in art. The introduction of steel-plate engraving helped make this work worthwhile. Most artists' original work was skillfully engraved, which allowed prints to be made and sold to a wider public. The Lake District offered wild mountain scenery attracting well-known artists: Allom, Turner, Constable and Heaton Cooper (Alfred). He was also following earlier members of his family in producing what we chose to call 'Art', whether working with clay, watercolours, oils or designs in bricks and mortar; mastering of techniques rather than the product of art alone became their main interest. Ernest Gombrich, in his well-respected book 'The Story of Art'[17] wrote *'there is no such thing as Art, there are only artists; 'Art' with a capital A has no existence'*. With a little thought, we can come to realise that the subject of art varies too much to be captured by one simple word [Art]. When someone remarks about a piece of artistic work, especially 'modern', that 'it is not art' he or she is implying that we can define art clearly, when this is not possible. What we chose to call art is ultimately, what an artist produces.

Gershom grew up with strong feeling for art as produced by his father, importantly not simply the finished product but the planning and processes involved in producing a work of art. Travelling with his father, searching for landscapes while at the same time developing appropriate techniques to capture a scene, inspired him to follow a similar path. At the time William Collingwood was most prolific as an artist he specialised in painting watercolours, which did not carry the same gravitas as work in oil; the Queen's (Victoria) enthusiasm for pictures in watercolours probably did much to change attitudes towards that form of art; during her reign, the Royal Water Colour Society was established.

**Alphonse Legros**

While at the Slade Gershom came under the direction of Professor Alphonse Legros. The professor was born in Dijon, France and later became naturalised British.[18] Legros was a larger-than-life character who lived in England for around 50 years and during that time pretended not to speak English, or rather understood only what he chose to understand. Early results at school in France were poor, he had an aversion to writing and study generally, he left school when aged only eleven years old and after moving to England, he learned only Basic English. At the Slade School of Fine Art, Legros came to rely upon more able senior students to interpret for him otherwise he worked using an acute visual sense and probably did most of his teaching through demonstration and gestures. He was a skilled lithographer and portrait painter, and exhibited at the Royal Academy in 1864.

---

[17] Gombrich, E.H. 1978. 'The Story of Art.' Oxford: Phaidon Press.
[18] Wilcox, T. 2004. Alphonse Legros. Oxford Dictionary of National Biography. Oxford: Oxford University Press.

## Living in London

Gershom had first-hand experience of the poor in Liverpool but he could not help be shocked by the level of poverty in parts of the city when settled in London. A few years earlier, the writer Fedor Dostoevsky, when on visits to London, had described conditions of the poor in the city, he too was shocked despite witnessing dreadful conditions in his own country. Like so many people with a living to make,

Gershom had to put troubled thoughts of the poor behind him; he was there to develop further his aptitude for painting and especially drawing; clearly seeing his future at that time as a professional artist. In contrast, when his father encouraged him to follow a career in academia, he spoke to his son as someone who enjoyed success as an artist, but someone also acutely aware of the inevitable uncertainties, especially if one day Gershom married and had a family. Without financial support from his father, Gershom could so easily have joined the ranks of the poor at this time.

During the year that Gershom spent at the Slade School, he lived at a lodging house, 67 Albany Street near Regents Park; while there he visited his Uncle Samuel in Notting Hill at Lancaster Road. In the house was Samuel's daughter Selma and an artist-friend Miss Mary Isaac; it is believed that this was the first time (1876) he met the young lady he was to marry.

After studying at the Slade, life proved difficult for Gershom. He shared with a number of would-be artists the struggle to earn a living in London, an unforgiving place for anyone at that time without independent means of support; increasingly he came to rely upon his father. In letters, (Collingwood Archive AH) he thanks him for the £20 or £10 sent previously. In one letter (1877), Gershom confessed to difficulty in finding direction, *'there is no direction in which I want to work to the exclusion of all others, as people do who have ambition'*. Though wanting to be a painter he did appreciate that much single-minded work was essential, something he may not be able to sustain. At the time, he was also busy with what he called 'fellowship hunting', which proved to be expensive. In addition, being so near to central London inevitably brought visitors, so entertaining added to his costs. According to Taqui Altounyan in her book 'Chimes from a Wooden Bell', John Ruskin kept an eye on W.G. Collingwood and visited him for tea in his flat in London at 67 Albany Street, when a Miss Isaac was also there for tea. Gershom in a letter (AH), Ruskin had with him a bundle of his latest drawings from Venice, which made Gershom promise to read Ruskin's book 'Stones of Venice'. Gershom came to rely totally upon occasional help from his father, and any commissions to paint, especially portraits; if asked to paint a head portrait he could expect a fee of around £10 and if a full-size portrait as much as £40 (value in 2014: £890 and £3,500 respectively by the retail price index). Inflation assumed to average around 3% per year. Commissions were difficult to find; Gershom worked as an impecunious artist, eventually relying mainly upon tutorial work and father's generosity to pay the rent and buy food. When renting rooms at 7 Grafton Street, Fitzroy Square he wrote of cooking for himself and sent father a menu. With tongue in cheek he listed courses in French to make the fare look more impressive but it amounted to little more than bread, soup and water and the total cost was under eight pence (around three new pence) value in 2015 using retail price index, £2.80.

**Artist or Academic**

Despite thoughts of becoming an artist, Gershom decided to follow his father's advice to think instead of an academic career. While a student at the Slade, Gershom made at least four applications for fellowships at Universities, which were all unsuccessful despite leaving Oxford with First Class in Literae Humaniores and winning a coveted prize. Gershom spent most of 1876 looking for fellowships or applying for them. In January of 1877, he applied to New College, Oxford one of the oldest in the University. In a letter dated January 10[19] to his father (Papa) he describes failing the fellowship papers; when he proceeded to an exposition of certain doctrines of Hegel he wrote, 'I couldn't recall what I wanted to say'. After half an hour of deliberation, he gave up and went out, taking the papers with him. The next letter to father, stated that in one application his essay was thought to be the best but he added that 'it is not likely that my specialty will get me a fellowship'. Even then, he was thinking about art, because he visited the drawing school to see a large drawing by Rossetti 'The Passover in the Holy Family', it was half-finished so Gershom made a written analysis of the artist's way of working. Briefly, 'that he [Rossetti] and Burne-Jones work down from very bright colours and not up to that effect'. In letters to Gershom, his father would draw attention to possible fellowships, prompting him whenever possible towards an academic career. In 1877[20] (AH) he was replying to his father's suggestion that he try for a fellowship at Magdalen, Oxford and he pointed out that '*Magdalen is a classical place where they want good composition in Latin and Greek, which you know is not my strong point*' nevertheless he promised to make enquiries. On another fellowship attempt he got the comment that they were impressed by the literary style of his work but thought he probably did not know much about the subject matter, with which

---

[19] Letter, W.G. Collingwood to William Collingwood, 1877. Collingwood Archive, Abbot Hall, Kendal.
[20] Letter, W.G. Collingwood to William Collingwood, 1877. Collingwood Archive, Abbot Hall, Kendal.

Gershom agreed, confessing that he needed to do more reading. The applications took up a good deal of time that ought to be devoted instead to studying artistic methods, if he was to be successful in that direction. One letter in 1877 (AH) addressed to Miss Isaac, he sent her a prospectus of the Suffolk Street Exhibition, giving her advice about hanging of pictures. For Miss Isaac, not yet known as Dorrie, this was one of the earliest contacts by letter, six years before they married.

After a number of attempts to secure a university position, the one failure to make Gershom seek an alternative livelihood was his application to Liverpool University for the Roscoe Chair of Art, endowed in 1881 commemorating William Roscoe of Liverpool, a lawyer who actively campaigned for the abolition of slave trade, and who was a keen collector of art. Gershom again was unsuccessful, despite a strong recommendation from the Master of his Oxford College, G.G. Bradley then Dean of Westminster; he wrote that *'Collingwood was one of the ablest and thoughtful young men I have known at the University, his character was as remarkable as his abilities'*. Artists Sir Edward Burne-Jones and Alfred W. Hunt supported his application, and W.S. Caine M.P. wrote in support from the House of Commons Library. An event that should have given Gershom hope of success at last was in November 1882; the Roscoe Chair sub-committee recommended W.G. Collingwood to deliver a course of lectures in 1883. In January of that year Gershom gave the Council a syllabus of lectures, which was accepted, he was to be paid £75.00 for his day and evening course of lectures upon art. In the following month, before the course of lectures began, Gershom was informed that the Council do not propose to proceed at present to the election of a Professor to the Roscoe Chair of Art.[21] Some weeks after the lectures had been delivered successfully, in April 1883, Gershom was notified 'that the Senate does not think it desirable that Mr W.G. Collingwood should be appointed to the Roscoe Chair of Art; reasons were not recorded.

His granddaughter Taqui (Barbara Harriet) Altounyan in her book 'Chimes from a Wooden Bell'[22] suggested that *'perhaps he did not have the right church-going habits or was too outspoken to the wrong people'*.

His granddaughter may well have been correct by speculating that his attitude towards religion could be a bar to an academic career; at this stage in his life he still veered towards non-conformist religion, more in respect for his father and may have been less than convincing when discussing Church of England beliefs. While religious beliefs could have been a factor in Gershom's failure to gain a fellowship, his comments in letters to his father about being ill-prepared when actually applying for fellowships must also be taken into account and how much

---

[21] Cook, M. 1987. Letter from Archivist of The University of Liverpool to Dr William Rollinson concerning W.G. Collingwood. Cardiff: Collingwood Archive, Cardiff University.
[22] Altounyan, T. 1990. 'Chimes from a Wooden Bell.' London: Tauris.

this lack of preparedness was due to him wanting to be an artist must be open to debate. If an application for fellowship had been successful, we can only speculate about his life at Oxford or at another university as a permanent member of staff.

Soon after leaving the Slade School of Art Gershom visited the Alps to draw and paint, mainly at Chamonix below Mont Blanc staying at the Hotel d'Angleterre. This visit shows that he was intent upon art as a career at this time, following in the footsteps of his father, Prout and Ruskin, although a letter from the Alps to his father concerned mainly his applications for fellowships. Montenvert above Chamonix, a popular place for travellers on the Grand Tour, was visited and a day was spent drawing. He arrived in Chamonix over the Col de Balme from the Valais area of Switzerland so he spent many hours of rough walking as well as sketching.

After leaving the Slade in the summer of 1877 he struggled for three years before enjoying any success, when a portrait he painted of his father was exhibited at the Royal Academy. Though Gershom never achieved greatness as an artist he did exhibit at the Academy a further four times during the 1880s while based near Windermere.

With little hope of a fellowship, the idea of a more secure future in academia was behind him and a very insecure future lay ahead. Introductions to established artists also became crucial at this time and John Ruskin, well known to prominent artists and respected by most of them, introduced Gershom to Edward Burne-Jones an artist associated with the second phase of the Pre-Raphaelite Brotherhood. This introduction led to Gershom acting as tutor to the Burne-Jones's son Philip; for the next two years, he spent time in a charming room at 41 Kensington Square surrounded by the art of Philip's father. Burne-Jones proved to be a good friend for around twenty years until his death, though unlike Ruskin he cared little for mountains. People who love mountains tend to look for kindred spirits among those they meet and Gershom was no exception, but Burne-Jones provided considerable support during those difficult years in London.

Gershom had no difficulty fitting into the Burne-Jones family; his association with Professor Ruskin was shared not only with Edward (Ned) but also with his wife Georgiana (née Macdonald) who had visited Ruskin at Brantwood in 1873 with her six-year-old daughter Margaret. Georgiana first met Ruskin in the basement of the National Gallery when he was busy cataloguing drawings of the Turner bequest; later with husband Ned she joined Ruskin on a tour to Italy. Mother and daughter came to know the Professor very well at Brantwood during days spent indoors away from heavy rain. Ruskin, adept at amusing young children would have made a wonderful father. Later in 1884, while Gershom was working with Ruskin, Georgiana spent another week as visitor to Brantwood. With children grown up, Georgiana, a socialist, was active with social reform so had much to discuss with Ruskin. The Burne-Jones family also had close association with

William Morris who was to have an influence upon Gershom. There were summers while in London, that Gershom was tempted to visit the Lake District and took the opportunity to visit Ruskin and this led, in the Autumn of 1881, to an invitation from the Professor to join him as an assistant.

## Joining Ruskin

In a letter to his father (AH) in 1881, he described early days working with John Ruskin. Gershom stayed at Low Bank Ground a house next to Bank Ground Farm near Ruskin's home at Brantwood and received board, lodging and salary. He sent for his things from a cottage at Gillhead and told his father that he expected to be there through the winter and to save a pretty penny and that he would be able to repay him some of the money borrowed earlier. He had no means of knowing whether the work for Ruskin would extend beyond the winter months. Gershom also wrote that he had no prospects in London, suggesting that he was beginning to give up hope of being a successful artist; if he had no prospects as an artist in London, where could he have prospects?

A close working association with Ruskin began that autumn when a breakdown in Ruskin's health brought Gershom to his side to help progress various projects, but only became firmly established in 1882 when Ruskin recovered and together they went on a tour of France, Switzerland and Italy. Initially, this early association with Ruskin was an extension and further opportunity in his aim to become a recognised artist, despite any earlier misgivings while in London. Ruskin made a serious study of draughtsmanship and during the tour he produced drawings that in Gershom's view could be compared with Samuel Prout. Ruskin was his own most severe critic, in a letter home to his parents when on a tour as a young man he wrote of his art, 'it isn't Turner and it isn't Corregio, it isn't even Prout, but it isn't bad'. He felt that fine art is a worshipful thing, far beyond him to be appreciated (and that alone is worthwhile) after a course of training, but never to be attained unless by birth-gift.

Before going on tour with Ruskin in 1882, Gershom began work, in January of that year, to produce a painting of the Professor in his study at Brantwood.

## Painting Ruskin at work

Gershom's finished work is possibly the finest picture of John Ruskin (and there were many) working in his study at Brantwood. Generally, Ruskin disliked sitting for portraits, yet during his lifetime around 330 images were produced either as photographs, caricatures, drawings, sculptures or paintings; possibly why Gershom chose to paint the portrait while Ruskin was not at Brantwood, he would know well Ruskin's aversion to sitting for portraits. The picture measuring 30 by 21 inches (76 by 53 centimetres) shows the Professor seated at his desk in the study at Brantwood. Ruskin's health had been poor during the previous year and he was recuperating at a house near London at Herne Hill. Gershom planned the picture as a surprise and enlisted the help of Laurence Hilliard to sit as a model; he was a secretary at Brantwood. Gershom wrote about this work in a letter to Edith (Dorrie) Isaac[23] more than a year before they married:

> 'I'm working vigorously. I'm doing a drawing 21" x 30" of the Brantwood study seen from the fireplace showing the bow window and the Professor's table where he writes and Coniston Old Man out of the window in the sunrise, and the old man at his table. And if the water colour is successful I'll do an oil from it for the Academy. Hilliard who is such an actor is going to sit for the Professor, and I'll do the face out of my head, I think I can. Also the favourite cat is in the armchair. I think that will be a good picture. Mr Ruskin is coming on the 25th and I want to get it done before he comes'.

Gershom wrote a descriptive account of the setting for this picture:

> 'In the picture, the sunlight has just caught the snowy top of Coniston Old Man, seen through the window; while the lake and tall chimneys of Coniston Old Hall below are still in shade. Inside the room, the candles on the table have been put out, but the fire shines on the armchair in which the tortoiseshell cat is taking her ease. Mr Ruskin wears a blue coat and grey trousers, blue stock and creased wristbands, with a long gold chain; the costume familiar to his audiences at Oxford and elsewhere. He writes with a cork penholder, the paper flat on the table, and the rough notes of his subject there also. Slips of proof and sheets of paged revise are on the floor, and the spent copy is in the waste paper basket. The accessories are all accurately represented as they were at the time. On the left of the picture a Turner drawing of Florence from Fiesole stands on the chest of drawers, behind a row of selected minerals illustrating his theory of Agates. The open drawer holds the St. George's Guild business papers (in connection with which he was then at work). Below it, on the velvet cushioned top of the case for framed Dürers is a favourite MS bible of the fourteenth century, which he used to read as a beginning to his day's work; and against the chair is a portfolio of drawings for the St. Georges Museum. The cabinet behind it is that which held Liber Studiorum prints; beside it is a roll of lecture

---

[23] Letter, W.G. Collingwood to Edith (Dorrie) Isaac. 1881. Abbot Hall.

Figure 7 Ruskin in his library by W.G.C. 1882 (Ruskin Museum Coniston)

diagrams; above which are two sketches by Prout, to the left of which is the 'Geology' bookcase, the celestial globe, the mineral cabinet hardly seen behind the Turner Florence. The bookcase in the middle of the picture holds 'Botany'. In the window are some of his own books in the Ruskin purple calf bindings: grass of Parnassus in a tumbler of water, and a box of early daguerreo-types of Venice. In the shelves on the right are a vase and archaic figurine of a horseman from Cyprus, cases of coins, books, and a terrestrial globe on the floor. In the fender, much foreshortened, is the once famous Ruskin shovel, he designed and had made by the Coniston Blacksmith.'

The painting (Figure 7) eventually found a home at the Ruskin Museum in Coniston.

Janet Gnosspelius noted (CACU) that eldest daughter Barbara sold prints of this painting to Yanks for three shillings and six pence.

## On Tour with Ruskin

Gershom gave a comprehensive account of the tour in 1882 with Ruskin in his book Ruskin Relics (Chapter IV). Ruskin knew already of Gershom's draughtsmanship and would be pleased to have him produce images in addition to those he had time to create. Recognition by Ruskin was much sort after by aspiring artists and indeed by many established artists and this opportunity to spend around five months, working with Ruskin among mountains and architectural splendours of Europe was a dream come true. Gershom was not the first student of Ruskin to accompany him on a European tour, a John Bunney toured with him in 1863, and Arthur Burgess in 1969. Both men were artists, Bunney an accomplished topographical painter and Burgess a draughtsman and engraver.

While on the tour, Gershom would be thinking about a young lady back in England, Edith Isaac from Maldon in Essex had become part of Gershom's life, they were very close and both longed to be married; the months apart had to be endured if Gershom was to establish himself more firmly and become a worthy husband for Edith.

Ruskin as an only child travelled with parents who gave him a love of touring European cities and mountainous areas, and in adulthood, he made frequent visits across the Channel. On August 10, 1882 with valet Peter Baxter and Gershom as general assistant Ruskin travelled from his home at Herne Hill to Dover then to Calais heading for the mountains. Peter Baxter was the third manservant to accompany Ruskin on his travels, the first, John George Hobbs was succeeded by Frederick Crawley, but Gershom was the first to be taken on a tour to help with drawing, and geological work even though like Ruskin he had only an amateur's interest in geology.

When writing about the tour, Gershom described them travelling from one French town to another, and drove over the Jura and through Savoy in pre-railroad style. Throughout their journey Ruskin talked about similar tours made with his parents. From W.G.C's diary,[24] the tour starting at Calais visited Laon, Reims, Troyes, Sens, Avallon, Dijon, St. Cergues, Geneva, Sallanches, Geneva, Annecy, Turin, Genoa, Pisa, Lucca, Florence, Pisa, Aix-les-Baines, Annecy, Talloiries, Annecy, Geneva, Dijon and Paris, arriving back in London December 2. Although Gershom's perceived role on tour was as an artist's assistant, this was possibly the first opportunity he had to show his versatility by being able to collect sufficient material and make use of his own drawings to write a book with a forward by Ruskin. The book 'Limestone Alps of Savoy' was published in 1884. Ruskin intended this book to be a supplement to his earlier work 'Deucalion' published in 1879, in which he discusses the landscape and structure of the Alps and Jura; Ruskin had shown a strong interest in structure of the Alps of Savoy since 1863. To gather details of formation in the Alps of Savoy Gershom carried a sketchbook, which he filled with numerous drawings. Writing the book prompted Gershom to reflect upon the subject of geology and of history:

---

[24] W.G.Collingwood, Diary 1882. Collingwood Archive, Abbot Hall, Kendal.

'We do geology a wrong if we think its tale ends where history begins. Wars and rumours of war, revolutions and reformations, they do not make history; the people and their feelings, aspirations, passions, culture, they make history; of which , battles and sieges, councils and codes, are only as the barometer is to the weather, merely the indications. And, once again, the people are swayed by the thinkers, and the thinkers by their nature, little though they know it; and especially by the sublime in nature; and most vigorously of all by these limestone mountains.'

Savoy has a complex geology and a complicated history, both aspects of the area would fascinate the two travelers. Between the middle ages and mid nineteenth century the area was held variously between France, Italy, Switzerland and the Kingdom of Sardinia; at the time, Ruskin and Gershom studied the geology, control of the area visited by them was held largely by France. Ruskin had declared the wish to be a geologist and Gershom developed an equally close interest in the subject but both men had to be content with an amateur's approach to the study of rocks and their formation. Eventually, both men knew more about appreciation of scenery, especially mountain, than most geologists did, and both knew more about geology than most artists did. Ruskin was elected to the Geological Society in 1840, when the subject was in its infancy.

Apart from study of the subject and writing about geology when abroad, the immediate area around Coniston was of special interest to the geologist lying as it does between the Borrowdale volcanic rocks of the higher central fells and sedimentary Silurian flags and slates of the lower southern fells. If they had decided to follow a geological path more closely, Ruskin and Gershom would have become embroiled in dispute after dispute about the forming of different structures, possibly to the exclusion of all other interests. Gershom eventually came to realise that any book written about geology would soon be out of date and lose value, apart from throwing light on the development of geology as a discipline. Their decision to keep a distance by acting the part of interested amateur geologists was to their benefit and our own.

During the tour of 1882, Gershom described his role as a 'man-jack-of-all-trades'. The main task was to help Ruskin gather geological data. Ruskin could still climb Wetherlam or Silver How in Lakeland, and even the Langdale Pikes but needed a younger and fitter man to reach difficult viewpoints in the Alps. Ruskin knew of his young assistant's extensive hill walking and climbing and of his invaluable help when they worked together on the retreating Glacier des Bossons below Mont Blanc. They realised that glaciers were like a viscous fluid, flowing like a river of thick honey; not long before this work glaciers were thought (wrongly) to be static. At only fifteen years old in 1869, Gershom crossed glaciers in the range

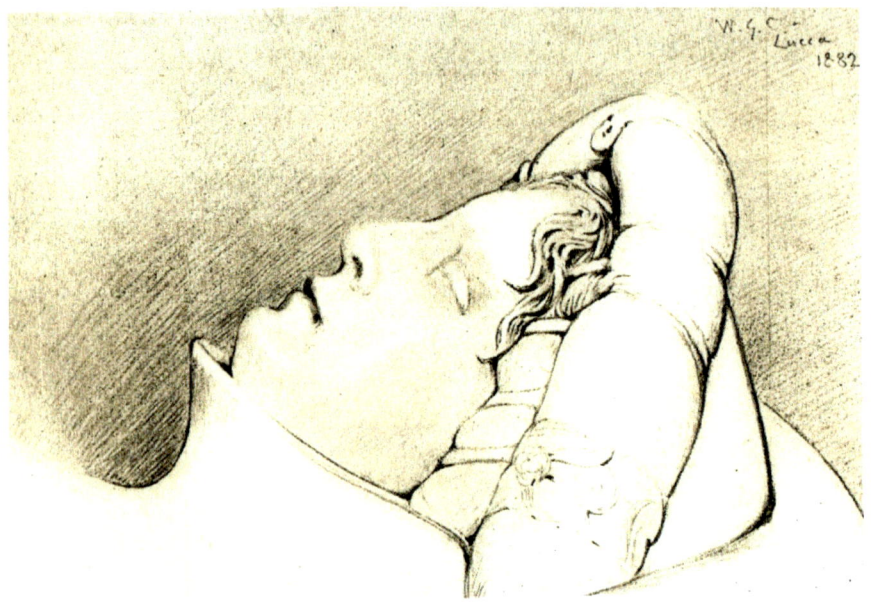

Figure 8 Lady of Lucca by W.G.C.

of Mont Blanc with his father and a Swiss mountain guide but even with close attention from the guide his father would not venture to more adventurous places; he realised that his half-Swiss son was much more capable when moving around mountains; something Ruskin was to discover.

They spent days in a number of towns and cities on their way to the Alps. Local people became used to seeing this Englishman [Ruskin] with his servant holding apparel and various items of a painter's craft, seated in a square painting. Gershom when describing parts of this tour in his paper for 'The Critic' in 1902[25] wrote about a typical painting day for Ruskin:

> 'On his camp stool in the square, manipulating his drawing board with one hand and his paint brush with the other; Baxter, his valet, holding the colour-box up for him to dip into, and a little crowd of chatterers always looking on'.

---

[25] Collingwood, W.G. 1902. 'Ruskin's Ilaria.' The Critic, vol. 40, number 4.

Two works painted by Ruskin of the façade of St. Marks in Lucca are particularly fine. Gershom wrote that Ruskin never did better work in his life. Whenever Ruskin saw architectural details or natural scenery, especially mountains, of interest to him he would sketch them and ask Collingwood or 'Collie' as he called

Figure 9 Ruskin in Troyes by W.G.C.

him, to draw particular places worth recording; typically Ruskin would write, '*left Collie sketching in Pisa*'. The party left Pisa by carriage in style by coach and horses, when they reached the gate leading into the walled town of Lucca the coachman shouted '*English family, nothing to declare*' and the officer at the gate bowed in an unquestioning manner. Ruskin remarked how it was so much nicer than being bundled about among trucks and all the hideous things they heap around railway stations. In a few minutes, they were at the Hotel Royal, where Signor Ruskin was expected. Ruskin kept Collie busy when in Lucca sketching the marble figure of Ilaria di Correto, known as the Lady of Lucca who died in 1405 (Figure 8).

He drew the head of the effigy side-faced, full-face, three- quarters, every way possible, normally in pencil sketch but did produce one picture of Ilaria in watercolours. Gershom's task was to capture the image that had fascinated Ruskin for many years, he had drawn Ilaria full length during a tour of 1874, but was fascinated by her head. Gershom wrote that to describe Ruskin's first sight of the marble Ilaria as falling in love was not an exaggeration. Since a young man, in 1845, the effigy captivated Ruskin. Ilaria's husband Paolo Guinigi commissioned the greatest sculptor of the age Jacopo della Quercia to create the marble figure around eight years after his wife had died (we can only assume that the sculptor had earlier drawings of Ilaria as a guide). Gershom described the figure as having the '*best qualities of mediaeval art, its severe symbolism and decorative effect, with all the best of later classicism; its reality, softness and sweetness.*' Another task that demanded all Gershom's drawing skill was detail from the early thirteenth-century porch of St. Martin in Lucca. Other notable works by Gershom while in Italy with Ruskin were Pont Vecchio in Florence and part of a pillar at the Baptistery in Pisa. He captured a scene of John Ruskin standing in a street 'in contemplation of a mediaeval town' (Troyes), it was Ruskin who added this title to the drawing, dating it wrongly as 1884 instead of 1882 (Figure 9).

The drawings were Gershom's record of the tour because unlike Ruskin he did not keep detailed notes. When, one day on the tour Ruskin was discussing something rather confidential, Gershom said '*Never mind I'm not Boswell taking notes*'. Ruskin replied '*I think you might do worse*'. Ruskin kept up his daily habit of working at his writing, drawing or painting in the morning and afternoons went on walks; it was during these walks that he would have long discussions with Gershom (Collie), building a close friendship that would endure until the Professor's death.

Gershom gives what he described as a fair example of an afternoon spent with Ruskin and servant Baxter at Lucca:

> 'A biting scirocco [sic] was blowing, but we started in the usual carriage driven by the boy with the red tie. As we left the hotel an army of beggars hailed the Professor [as they called him at home] who solemnly distributed

Figure 10 Ruskin, centre, with Collingwood (left) and Randal

pence, to lighten his pocket and his mind. We scampered through the streets, which are all pavement, and none broader than Hanway Street; but everybody drives furiously in them as a point of Lucchese and Tuscan honour, and nobody seems to be run over. Out through the city walls you are in the country at once. Indeed, I can't help thinking of the town as a garden where houses are bedded out instead of flowers; they are so closely packed, so varied and pretty. But out at the gate it is a wide stretch of plain with mountains all round, and bright cottages, cadmium-yellow in the stubble-fields and cane-breaks, for they thatch the maize-heads over the roofs by way of storage. Out of one quite decent-looking farmhouse a decent-looking woman came rushing and gesticulating after the carriage. The Professor called on the driver to stop; and the woman, out of breath, declared she was the mother of five and wanted charity. He gave her a note; notes you know can be a great deal less than five pounds in Italy. At the foot of the hills, south of Lucca, we left the carriage and walked up the road; Baxter, too, while the dutiful servant with coat, umbrella, campstool and geologist's hammer as usual. The road goes up through chestnuts and under vines, till you get to some farms and a church on top of the buttress-hills, with a splendid view of Lucca and the valley, behind rich slopes of autumn colours, and a monastery with its cypresses in the middle distance. Then we dived into a valley and across a marble quarry, for all the stones here are marble; the road is mended with marble, and the pigstyes [sic] are built of marble; and then we scramble up the main hill. There is a sort of track through chestnut and myrtle and arbutus with scarlet fruit against the sky. Girls were gathering chestnuts and arbutus berries, such a picture. So with an hours scrambling we came out through a wood of pines to the top, a sort of marble platform. The scirocco [sic] had blown us up fine weather; the Carrara hills were clear, and the Apennines for miles; fantastic peaks, all sorts of gables, pyramids, cones and domes. The sea was ridged and beating hard on the shore of the Maremma; the bay of Spezia in the distance, and little Lucca, tidy and square below, tucked into the four walls like a baby in a cot with a patchwork quilt. I stayed ten minutes to get a sketch, while the Professor and Baxter howked out a particularly contoured bit of marble.'

As the party arrived back at the gate, the officer asked 'Have you anything to declare gentlemen?' 'Nothing Sir' 'Felice sera, signori' (Happy evening gentlemen). The walled city of Laon provided both artists with fine buildings and landscapes, particularly the west front of the cathedral, which Ruskin drew while 'Collie' sketched other notable buildings. In contrast, they passed over Reims quickly. Ruskin describing the cathedral as 'confectioner's gothic', and looking now at contemporary drawings and photographs Ruskin's comment seems particularly apt. The tour continued through Avallon, Geneva, Sallanches, Turin, Pisa, Florence, Lucca by Mont Cenis, back to Geneva, Paris then home.

Ruskin helped artists he admired and did what he could to encourage them in their work; in addition to Baxter and Collingwood, he employed Italian artist Angelo Alessandri after their first meeting in 1876 when both were in Angelo's native city Venice; patronage for the Viennese artist lasted nine years. Other artists: Henry Roderick Newman (American) worked for Ruskin in Tuscany and visited the touring party when in Lucca during the tour of 1882 and Frank Randall who was in Avallon working on a series of drawings for The St. George Trust. A drawing, believed to be by Frank Randal's brother Charles (Figure 10) shows John Ruskin centre holding the hand of Frank Randal to his left and holding Gershom's hand to his right; Ruskin as can be seen trimmed his own beard. (Note a steam train in the background).[26]

The artwork done for Ruskin, and subsequently producing landscape pictures or illustrations for books and journal papers provided Gershom with a modest income but major success in this field eluded him. Over the years, many students,

---

[26] Dearden, J.S. 1999. 'Ruskin: a life in pictures.' Sheffield: Sheffield Academic Press.

particularly of archaeology, derived considerable value, and pleasure, from Gershom's pen and ink drawings of ornamental stone crosses, and artifacts.

The tour with Ruskin had been stimulating, but back in London he still lacked direction. It seems reasonable to assume that the motivation to build some kind of career came as a result of meeting Edith Isaac. They were made for each other and Edith coming into his life was Gershom's greatest good fortune.

# Chapter V
# Edith Isaac (Dorrie) and Marriage (1877-1884)

## Young Edith

Edith was small, slim and pretty; she was described as a very nice girl with considerable artistic and musical talents (Figure 11). Edith was born to a prosperous middle-class family in Maldon, Essex. Edith's father Thomas Isaac was a corn merchant with business based in Notting Hill, London and her mother Sara née Prentice came from Stowmarket in Suffolk. When Edith was six years old, the family moved their home, still in Maldon, to Fullbridge House a substantial building with a large garden; Edith's sister Annie was born in the same year.

The family left Maldon in 1868 when her father decided to start up a business at Clifton in Bristol but after investing in shares of sugar refining with his two brothers they all lost money and the family returned to Maldon to live in what Edith called a dear old house, Cromwell Hall. Apart from this venture, Edith spent her childhood in Maldon.

Parents Thomas and Sara Isaac had four sons and two daughters; when Edith was born there were two brothers in the family, one child, the first, had died as a baby: Thomas born 1853, Sydney born 1855 then Edith born 1857, Arthur born 1859, Stanley born 1861 and Annie born 1863.

Edith went to a Dame School around 1862 attended by her two older brothers. An interview, given to E.V. Powell at Reading in 1910[27] was transcribed by daughter Barbara from pencil notes, and typed by Janet Gnosspelius in 1970. Edith recalled events at school during that time showing a curious turn of phrase, she recalled *'a very naughty little boy called Willie Stamper who was always being told to stand in the corner. He was massacred in Russia'*. Another naughty boy told to hold his tongue would say *'can't Miss Smiff* (Smith) *it's too slippy'*. Edith found most children to be 'nice' and often had parties where the main delight was a drink made of wine, whey and milk straight from a cow; they called the drink 'Syllabub'. When the owner sold the school it ran into difficulties and closed, Edith had a governess while her brothers went to a grammar school. Her brothers at a day school often brought other boys to the house, Edith described them as nicely behaved except

---

[27] Powell, E.V. 1910. A fragment of autobiography recalled by Edith Collingwood in Reading, transcribed from notes by Barbara Gnosspelius. Cardiff: Collingwood Society. Collingwood Archive, Cardiff University.

Figure 11 Edith (Dorrie) Collingwood

Figure 12 Envelope addressed to Edith by W.G.C.

one who tried to kiss her on the stairs and *'I boxed his ears'*. At home, Edith had a black mare of 16 hands, which she said had *fought in the Crimea*.

During a visit to the Collingwood home her Aunt Polly suggested that Edith should go to a boarding school in London, at this point Edith met the Collingwoods for the first time. Frances Collingwood, wife of Gershom's eldest Uncle Samuel ran the school 'Northbourne House' Adelaide Road in St. John's Wood. Miss Georgina Isaac (Edith's Aunt Polly) assisted Frances Collingwood at the school. Edith found it bewildering to be in a school with 34 other girls and no boys; she had little experience of girls her own age at home. Physical activity was encouraged and all students went up Primrose Hill after breakfast and before lessons began. From time to time father offered release from school by coming to collect her to go with him to the City, there she saw various people at work and having lunch with her father in Bishopsgate Street was one of many treats. She played hide and seek among the wharf sheds where grain was stored. Sometimes they went to the National Gallery, which possibly sparked Edith's lifelong interest in art. Another much-loved trip was on a Thames boat to Greenwich. On one occasion, that Edith would never forget, her father stayed at the school overnight and both went to Covent Garden Market at 4am; they brought back strawberries and roses for the whole school. Learning art or any other subject was not a strong feature of life at that school; lessons in two subjects thought to be important were 'how to entertain' and 'deportment'. Aunt Polly would shout from an upstairs window *'ten times around the garden and keep your head up'*.

Edith stayed at the boarding school until 1873 which included one of the coldest winters on record 1870-71 at the time of a war in Europe. Her recollections of the Franco-German war and being at school were closely associated, especially when one teacher, believed to be German, had a cousin Fritz Korte a soldier in the fighting. The girls were fascinated by this teacher because she had fingernails that grew longer and longer. When asked why she did not cut them her answer was that she would only do so when Fritz returned safely from the war. Edith wrote:

> 'Alas, she was not faithful to Fritz a rich merchant came along and stole her young affections; when Fritz did come to claim her he found her married. My Aunt Polly was most sympathetic; Fritz was a very handsome and attractive young officer in the Prussian Guard and in the end Fritz and Georgie (Aunt Polly) married, so he became my very dear Uncle Fritz'.

While at school, Edith became a close friend of Selina Collingwood a daughter of Samuel and Frances living in Kensington at 162 Lancaster Road. Later, while at the home of Selina, also an art student, Edith met Gershom who was visiting his Aunt and Uncle. Edith attended the West London School of Art and while there stayed with Selina's family. On the 1881 census Edith is listed as a boarder at the house in Kensington, though an envelope addressed simply to Miss Isaac Maldon Essex was sent by Gershom from Gillhead during that year (Figure 12).

Edith became a water colourist specialising in the painting of miniatures, mainly portraits on ivory. Later, it is believed that, a portrait of daughter Barbara, led to her election to the Society of Miniaturists in 1901, and annually she paid her two guineas membership fee to the Society.

That Edith also became an accomplished pianist was due largely to 'a darling music-master' called Koenen from Holland, a great pianist. Under his tuition Edith practised five hours each day. Unfortunately, Edith did not get the same inspiration from her first teacher in art a Mr Nightingale *'smelled horrid and was mostly half-drunk'*. Edith joined a sketch-club called The Polygraphic Society she called 'Polywog' and found membership of this club far more helpful than working with Mr Nightingale. Edith kept her membership long after she was married. Edith's music progressed too; in addition to many hours practise on the piano her father and brother Sydney playing violins meant they could enjoy music evenings together. Father Thomas also had a fine singing voice, much like Gershom the man

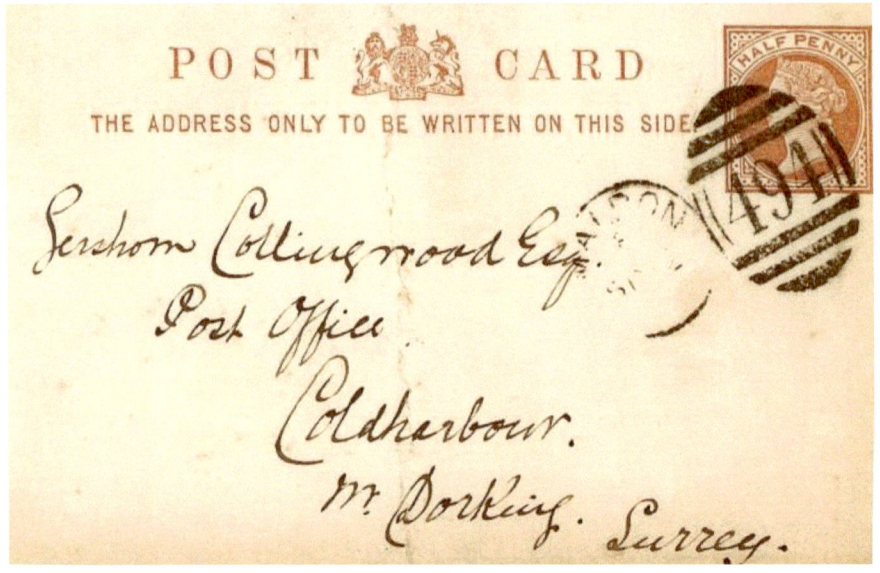

Figure 13 Postcard to W.G.C. from Dorrie

Figure 14 Reverse Runic side of Postcard
Collingwood (R.G.) Archive Cardiff University

she was to marry. Her father shared a love of music with two of his children, and he conducted a Choral Society in Maldon.

Edith displayed a child-like innocence into her adult life; one grandchild recalled that she was more like a big sister to her children and sometimes even a younger sister. The family felt that sometimes she did the oddest things like asking a partner of her daughter Dora when he was going to get married, in Dora's presence and she felt herself going scarlet. The family adored Edith and Gershom was indeed a lucky man when she agreed to be his wife.

## Courting Edith

In meeting Edith, Gershom was following the example of his father William, though quite by accident. Meeting Edith at Uncle Samuel's home in London was similar to Gershom's father meeting Marie Imhoff from Switzerland while she stayed with the Collingwoods in London.

Given the background of his father and the years Gershom had spent helping him with painting in watercolours, followed by his own education in art at the Slade School he and Edith would find much in common. In addition, his fine singing voice could go well with her piano playing. He did not like the name Edith '*horrid and thin*' was how Gershom described it and gave her the name Dorothy or Dorrie. During their relationship (April 1880) in a letter to Gershom[28] Edith Isaac signed herself Dorrie and in a footnote to a letter during their engagement and time apart wrote '*You can't think how I miss being called Dorrie.*'[29] Earlier, on the last day of 1879 Gershom wrote a letter to 'Dorothy saying that '*in sending congratulations for the New Year I ought to be more respectful than to call you Dorrie, so I have adopted the more dignified term of address.*' Edith would sign her artistic work EMDC or EMD Collingwood (In the 1911 Census return she is Edith MD). When not referred to as Mrs. Collingwood, the name Dorrie was most commonly used, even by John Ruskin who, while in Italy at Lucca, lifted a glass for a birthday toast saying, '*Here's to St. Michael, and Dorrie and All Angels*'.

There were times, leading up to their marriage, when Edith and Gershom were apart for long periods especially during 1882 when Gershom was on a tour with John Ruskin.

They liked to communicate by writing letters or post cards using the runic alphabet, first used by Irish Celts, a first use dated to first century AD. All runic

---

[28] Letter, Edith (Dorrie) Isaac to W.G. Collingwood, 1880. Collingwood Archive, Abbot Hall, Kendal.
[29] Letter, Edith (Dorrie) Isaac to W.G. Collingwood, 1880. Collingwood Archive, Cardiff University.

characters contain only straight lines, which made it easier to carve them in wood, bone or stone but for Edith and Gershom runes ensured a high degree of confidentiality; they used the Old Norse version. The postcard (Figure 13) is addressed to a post office but not in Edith's handwriting, she arranged for a friend to address her correspondence to Gershom to disguise the sender.

They achieved further confidentiality by writing in runic (Figure 14).

With the introduction of postcards (cheaper than letters to send), many people did not like the idea and refused to use them. John Ruskin on hearing about the new idea of postcards asked why some people used Runic writing, when told it was to ensure confidentiality, replied *'Isn't language given you to conceal your thoughts?'*

Any objection to a marriage, any marriage, would come normally from the bride's family, but not in this case. Edith (Dorrie) wrote to Gershom on June 6, 1880[30] saying that Mother and Papa on learning of their engagement were both pleased. In another letter from Maldon, Essex three years before they married, Edith wrote to Gershom that *'mother says I am to send her love'*; it appears no objection came from the Isaac family it was Gershom's father who raised objection, feeling that his son had insufficient income and prospects to support a wife and possibly children. William Collingwood's objection to his eldest son's marriage may have been rooted in the disappointment he felt about Gershom rejecting a life as preacher and possible leader within the Brethren, or his objection could spring from a genuine concern for his son. Gershom wrote to Edith (Dorrie):

> 'We must make an effort to be happy without being certificated sweethearts with a diploma from friends and relations including everybody and signed Mrs. Grundy as Home Secretary. We may always love each other but we may never live together. Meanwhile I must work hard and you will come and see me when you go for a walk sometimes – and I will come and see you – tomorrow night.'

A number of letters to Dorrie (1880) from Gershom expressed regret that they would have so little time to do all they wished to do together. The wished-for time together was 40 years, which Gershom thought still too little (they had 45 years of married life). The letters at this time between Edith and Gershom show a mixture of emotions and can be revealing about the relationship between them. Gershom only three years older than Edith could be rather patronising but at other times could be giving father-like advice, at other times Edith especially would write as someone very much in love. After Gershom had written in 1883 about being ill, Edith replied, *'My Darling If only I could come to you instead of writing for I do believe I*

---

[30] Letter, Edith (Dorrie) Isaac to W.G. Collingwood, 1880. Collingwood Archive, Cardiff University.

Figure 15 Nursing baby Dora at Gillhead Cottages by W.G.C.

*could make you better- do you know what I would do. I would put my arms right around you, make you put your head upon my shoulder and I would kiss you all over your forehead and eyes, then you would go to sleep and wake up better –then I'd come away'.*

At another time, Edith (by now addressed as Dorrie) wrote of being in a muddle with her drawing and wished Gershom was with her to '*tell me what to do*'.

When Gershom was unwell, he wrote to Dorrie in 1883 saying he was not worth anything and she replied:

> 'I think of you every minute and if you were well I should give you a great big scolding. Dear, you mus'nt, you mus'nt say you are'nt any good and that your love is'nt worth anything, of course it does'nt make any difference to me because I know just how good you are and what a lot of good you will do all the time you are in the world. Only it is so bad for you to think like that. How could we all love you so much if you weren't a darling'.

In the early days of their relationship, in 1880, Dorrie wrote about an incident that showed an adventurous spirit and an ability to cope with harsh conditions. She offered to help her brother Sydney moor a boat to its buoy when the weather was not promising. After mooring the boat Sydney and Edith had to struggle against wind, tide and rain in getting back to land, Sydney rowing the punt with oars and Edith with a canoe-type paddle. '*The wind blew away my grumpiness, it nearly blew away the breath out of my body too, but I liked that,*' Back home Edith was wet through and very tired but seemed to enjoy the experience.

Only after his son's successful translation work for Ruskin, lecturing at University College Liverpool and a Continental tour in 1882 with Ruskin did William appear happy about a possible marriage.

**Early-Married Life**

In December 1883, William Gershom Collingwood and Edith Mary Isaac married in Kensington Registry Office. Soon afterwards, the couple moved north to spend most of their lives in the Lake District. Childhood memories of spending holidays with parents William and Marie whenever possible in a cottage beside Windermere would make Gershom chose this as a home for his wife and any children they may have.

When they heard, shortly before their wedding that a cottage at Gillhead was vacant and to rent they wasted no time in moving from London. 'Gillhead, Cartmell Fell' was the address given on their marriage certificate. From a painting done by Gershom it can be seen that two cottages were in a short terrace fronted by a rough cart track leading only to a gate giving entrance to woodland. The image, painted in 1886, shows a lady by a cottage entrance holding a baby that was Dorrie holding their eldest child Dora then only a few months old (Figure 15). Later, they lived in the second cottage to accommodate a growing family; parents with baby Ursula in one cottage and Harriett as nursemaid with the older children in the other cottage.

The young couple had plans originally to live in or near London, which would offer the best opportunities for their artistic work, but for Gershom especially the possibility of a move north would bring back happy days of childhood spent in the cottage of William Alexander the local professional fisherman. Dorrie did have an offer from a friend Sydney Bentall to use his house in Orpington, Kent rent-free for five months while he went abroad, but she expressed concern about what could follow the five-month period. Before this offer, Dorrie had written about finding a little cottage far away from the smoky grey place that was Liverpool, possibly fearing that they would live in or near Gershom's old home. The chance to live in Lakeland at Gillhead could not be missed.

Married life for Dorrie and Gershom was always going to be an adventure; could it be in Kent near Dorrie's family, in Liverpool near Gershom's father, in Switzerland given connections of Gershom's mother or one of numerous possibilities? Good fortune stepped in when the cottage at Gillhead in the Lake District became available.

# Chapter VI
# Life at Gillhead Windermere (1883-1891)

**Home at Gillhead**

In a letter to her mother in December 1883 (CACU), soon after moving into the cottage at Gillhead, Dorrie described the interior of dark wood cupboards and shelves, and the unpacking they had to do, but still Gershom and Dorrie could not resist scrambling up a nearby hill Gummer How; in the letter, Dorrie described the view:

> 'When we got to the top the view was grander than anything I ever imagined, such colours, and such mountains, range after range with the setting sun lighting them with exquisite tints, and the lake flecked with white waves, an intense blue, I never saw anything that come up to it, and the thought that we have such a view within a quarter of an hour's walk from our house makes one feel very thankful, and almost overwhelmed.' They were also a short walk to a boathouse on Windermere.

If Gershom wrote a letter from Gillhead to a member of his family he would feel no need to describe the view, all would know it well. For Dorrie this was a new exciting experience; hills and mountains of Lakeland provided a scene so different from the mud flats near Maldon in Essex. Some people (flatlanders) would miss the large open skies of East Anglia or Kent, but not Dorrie.

Settled in their cottage beside Windermere, Gershom was now only around six miles (9.7 km) from Ruskin's home at Brantwood, but only as the crow flies. To reach Brantwood from the cottage at Gillhead they rowed a boat across to the west bank of Windermere, around half a mile wide, before walking through a twisting route between low hills, which led to Brantwood. The final part of the journey was along a lane on the east side of Coniston Water, a total journey of around ten miles of between three and four hours depending upon the weather. Crossing Windermere appeared to be a safe exercise but a serious accident did happen in October 1635, a ferry crossing the mere sank and 47 people lost their lives. Gershom crossed in a boat regularly during the seven years spent in the cottage at Gillhead, giving little thought to any possible dangers.

All four children were born in the cottage, Dorothy (Dora) Susie 1886, Barbara Crystal 1887, Robin 1889 and Ursula Mavis 1891. Life for Dorrie would be little different from mothers with young children in rural communities at that time. Running a household of husband and four children with no energy-saving devices so common today, was a full-time occupation, but to help family finances Dorrie also painted miniatures whenever possible. Over the years Dorrie, arguably a more accomplished painter than her husband could claim to contribute more to family income from her artwork. In the 1880s, and for many years afterwards, it was the man of a household who earned money, keeping the family housed, fed and clothed, a role referred to as sole breadwinner, especially in middle-class households. To earn money Dorrie painted miniatures mainly of women from prosperous families. There is no reason to suppose that Dorrie regretted her move north from the family home in Essex. Among her papers, after she died, was a newspaper cutting *'There's nowt caps Coniston. If Coniston is not actually peerless it is, by common consent, hard to beat.'*

## Earning a Living

These years from 1883 to 1891 spent at Gillhead were very different from memories of a carefree childhood in the same place enjoyed by Gershom. As size of the family increased, Gershom became more concerned about his ability to make a living as an artist. The seven years at Gillhead proved difficult if enjoyable for both Dorrie and Gershom. Dorrie continued to express delight at living in such a beautiful place and Gershom was at last living in an area that had absorbed him from boyhood. Yet, a living had to be made, rent and bills to pay and a very young family to care for, all in a remote place. Art was the subject uppermost in both parent's minds whenever the subject of earning money arose. Dorrie continued to be more successful than Gershom in this respect. Gershom became an authority on the works of Ruskin and could make use of his experience at Brantwood by giving talks, which included his work with minerals done on Ruskin's behalf. By the end of his period at Gillhead (1891) Gershom had become one of the most accomplished and respected interpreters of John Ruskin's work. He had found something close to a vocation in lecturing; with a fine speaking voice he was able to offer lectures of interest in art and geology as well as about Ruskin.

Gershom delivered talks not only in venues locally but also in Oxford and London. When agreeing to a series of lectures as part of a University programme, as at University College Liverpool in 1883, he was paid a fixed fee otherwise he earned around £5 for each lecture. During their time at Gillhead, Gershom and Dorrie exhibited in Kendal where some pictures were sold, which gave them encouragement to continue painting. Princess Louise daughter of Queen Victoria opened the exhibition, which was organised by Arthur Simpson a Quaker and prominent figure in the Arts and Crafts movement in Lakeland. He had his own distinctive style of furniture made in Kendal. He also collaborated with Gershom in giving a series of lectures, his on woodcarving and Gershom spoke about minerals.

While the last two years at Gillhead was a period spent worrying about income, Gershom studied and researched for the writing of a book, one of his finest, 'The Art Teaching of John Ruskin'[31] a work of scholarship published in 1891, which for many years remained the finest writing in existence on this aspect of Ruskin's life. Gershom was not an art critic but more out of respect for Ruskin than anything else, he wrote the book to reflect at least a consistent theory of art. To do this he concentrated upon the teaching of John Ruskin, the foremost art critic in the country; he used lectures, books, and conversations he had with Ruskin about the subject. The book was well received, though people who saw art as primarily promoting and helping to sustain religion, questioned Collingwood's 'art for art's sake'; he would not accept that art was the handmaiden of religion but did accept that a connection between art and religion was a historical fact. When Gershom's father was beginning to make a career in art, most artists were not ashamed of being in the service of religion and morals, but Gershom had sensed a change in attitude towards art being in the service of religion. Gershom's writing dealt with theory and practice of techniques used by artists: thoughts about drawing, painting and in particular the importance of acute observation, as shown in Ruskin's drawings, were all of value to many interested readers.

In a letter to Ruskin in 1888 (CACU), Gershom wrote about their uneventful life at Gillhead:

> 'We are very well and happy in our quietness, but that means that I have nothing in the way of news to bore you with.'

Despite this comment, life was a very productive one of writing, and painting of which four pictures were accepted by the Royal Academy all done during years spent living at Gillhead cottages. His first book, 'The Limestone Alps of Savoy' published in 1884, based on his tour to the Alps in 1882 with Ruskin, was followed by enormously detailed work when asked to edit the writings of the late Rev. William Slater Calverley, a book not published until 1899. Many hours of work were spent on this book with any payback coming only years later. The book contains around 77 hand-drawn illustrations by Gershom. He also added an Afterword to the book, reviewing early Cumberland Art in seven stages: (1) post-Norman development of pre-Norman forms, (2) the Norman period, (3) the Viking Age,

---

[31] Collingwood, W.G. 1891. The Art Teaching of John Ruskin. London: Percival.

Figure 16 Mist on Mickledore Scafells by W.G.C.

(4) the 'Spiral' school, (5) the Anglo-Classic school, (6) the British period and (7) the story of Cumbrian independence. Organising and writing this edited work helped Gershom form ideas about Pre-Norman Northern England, to make him eventually an authority on the subject.

Other works, published during years spent at the cottage, were: 'A book of Verses', 'On the Lake Basins of Windermere'; 'Astrology in the Apocalypse'; 'A short biographical outline of John Ruskin' and edited two volumes of the 'Poems of John Ruskin' (Appendix A).

From December 1883 when Gershom moved to Gillhead he became more firmly established as general assistant to John Ruskin, normally spending two days per week at Ruskin's home Brantwood, which meant the difficult journeys across Windermere and along tracks, with one overnight stay before making the return journey. There is no evidence that Ruskin 'employed' Gershom on a full-time basis during these years at Gillhead; only after settling nearer to Ruskin in 1891was there a record of being paid quarterly the sum of £25, sufficient to pay the rent.

Figure 17 Dorrie's Drawing of Baby Ursula

## Hill Walker

The description of Gershom's life beside Windermere could be of a typical nineteenth century academic closeted away among his books but Gershom was an active walker and climber until shortly before he died. He climbed no major mountains (defined as peaks over 13,123 feet or 4000 metres in height normally with glaciers), but like Ruskin he loved being among them, and climbing modest mountains (peaks over 2000 feet or 610 metres), and hills (below 2000 feet) where they could be idolised, studied, sketched or painted. Gershom had come to love the mountains and hills of Lakeland from the time spent on them as a young boy with his father and sometimes alone; every minute spent working at Gillhead or Brantwood surrounded by that wonderful, (as yet) unspoiled country would lead to frustration for the young man. Later when more in control of his time Gershom roamed the Lakeland hills and mountains extensively, dressed in a tweed jacket and knee-length climbing breeches; he climbed rocks alone, some that in time would become climbs done by others and recorded in climbing guidebooks, published by The Fell and Rock Climbing Club of the English Lake District. During

Figure 18 Lanehead, based on photograph by H.J. Taphouse

this hill walking and climbing he claimed to have swam in almost every suitable tarn. Gershom would describe himself as an enthusiastic hill walker but not a mountaineer. He did venture into the highest places in England, often alone, such as between the summits of Scafell and Scafell Pike with all his equipment to paint a scene of 'Mist in Mickledore' (Figure 16) a gap between the summits of Scafell Pikes and Scafell.

The picture shows, from below the summit of Scafell Pikes, the cliffs of Scafell exaggerated through the mist. Though exaggerated, it is what can be imagined in the mind's eye when mist is swirling around what are formidable crags, making them even more dramatic.

Gershom normally welcomed the opportunity to draw geological structures and there are none finer in England than the north-facing crags of Scafell, but by exaggerating what he saw through the mist the result bore no resemblance to the actual rock structure of that fine mountain.

Both Ruskin and Gershom were elected to The Alpine Club for their writing and artwork in portraying mountains, rather than the more common entry qualification, climbing of routes on major peaks in the European Alps or other mountain ranges. Gershom also joined The Fell and Rock Climbing Club of The English Lake District and contributed papers to the club's journal, which reflected his interest and love of Lakeland fells and modest mountains.

## Move to Lanehead

By 1891 two small cottages at Gillhead had become home to Gershom, Dorrie and four children, the youngest Ursula then a baby (Figure 17). Moving, while desirable was not essential but there is every reason to believe that John Ruskin walking near his home noticed that a large house called Lanehead (Figure 18) was available to rent, and suggested to Gershom that his family could move from Gillhead. Ruskin would see such a move to his advantage because, by that time (1891), Gershom had become a valued and trusted assistant and he would be living along the road only a short walk from Brantwood.

The previous occupants of Lanehead, from 1876 until 1891, had been a wealthy widow Ellen Melly née Grieg and her daughter Louisa from Liverpool.[32] Ellen's husband André Melly had been a prosperous Swiss merchant, who served as Member of Parliament for Stoke-on-Trent for seven years beginning in 1868. It was during this time that he was reported to have walked and talked politics with Ruskin not long after he arrived at Brantwood. In contrast, the Collingwood family was poor and far

---

[32] Viljoen, H.G. 1971. The Brantwood Diary of John Ruskin. New Haven and London: Yale University Press.

removed from affairs of state. The quarterly sum of £25, a form of retainer Gershom received from Ruskin paid only the rent on Lanehead. That the agreed rent was £100.00 per year, £50.00 less than paid by the previous tenant is curious, especially when Ruskin paid Gershom exactly that amount each year. A receipt dated August 12, 1891 stated, *'received from Mr Collingwood sum of £25.00 being a guarantee of a year's rent of Lanehead House Monk Coniston due to the Rev. A Starkie this day; signed the Agent.'*

# Chapter VII
# Working with Ruskin
# (1881-1900)

## John Ruskin

When Gershom became firmly established as a valued assistant to Ruskin in 1882 the Professor was already famous and had accomplished most of his best work. The sculptor Conrad Dressler visited Ruskin at his invitation in the spring of 1884 and spent two weeks at Brantwood beside Coniston Water; both men shared an interest in the Arts and Crafts movement. Ruskin sat for Dressler who completed a small bust the following year. This is possibly the finest image we have of Ruskin as an older man. Plaster casts were made from the original modelled in clay, and one given to Ruskin. A bronze was produced, signed by Dressler and dated 1888, this was presented to the National Portrait Gallery in 1924. Dressler also produced a fine bronze of William Morris.

Dressler was indeed fortunate to spend many days working on the bust with Ruskin, which he described in a letter to M.H. Spielman on June 18, 1890: seated in the coach house at Brantwood; taking breakfast with Ruskin and in the evening as the sun set over Coniston Old Man, he had many opportunities to learn a great deal. At the time, only Gershom and Ruskin's cousin Joan Severn had such a privilege of discussing with the Professor at length alone. Dressler in a letter written in 1919 reminisced about those 'golden' days:

> 'I felt that Ruskin had given up his battles and was dwelling wistfully on the work accomplished. He would stand gazing at Coniston Old Man through the window as the sun was setting in peaceful repose. Like everyone who approached him, I came away converted to his views. After all these years (34 years after the visit), I still feel that they are the sound doctrine which can alone save a world in turmoil. He taught us to love nature, to respect tradition, to take a joy in our work, and to seek our pride and reward in its honest accomplishment. Unfortunately, to their misfortune and undoing, the opposite doctrine is now being preached to the working classes'.

In Ruskin, Gershom had found a soul mate, though he would never attempt to compare himself with the Professor. Ruskin had numerous interests and accomplishments: art critic, Artist, antiquary, Epistolographer, Philanthropist, Employer, Social Reformer, Amateur Geologist, University Lecturer, Writer,

Figure 19 Brantwood showing the Turret Room
Photograph by John McClelland

Academic and Hill Walker. Some of his followers would argue that he wasted years as art critic that would have been better spent on his social reform work. So too, Gershom developed an equally long list of skills and interests.

**Relationship with Ruskin**

In a book 'Philosophy of Ornament', written by Gershom, based upon eight lectures on the history of decorative art given, by invitation, at the University College Liverpool, he thanked John Ruskin in the introduction. *'But beyond all I am grateful for the teaching and encouragement of my best friend and kindest patron, Professor Ruskin; though the reader will not hold him responsible for the sayings and doings of his self-willed scholar.'* This throws some light on the relationship between the two men. The book, published in 1883, consists of eight chapters beginning with the use of ornament in Palaeolithic time through Egyptian, Asian, Greek and Gothic to the nineteenth century.

Early in his relationship with Ruskin, he made a comment about life in the nineteenth century and in particular about peoples' attitude to art, that was close to Ruskin's heart: *'people of the present day become more and more unashamedly and universally distinguished into idle capitalists or mechanical drudges. The age is doing its best to make each person into one or the other.* This work was followed soon afterwards by a book about the Savoy Alps; Ruskin became fascinated by the structure of the Alps since seeing magnificent peaks and an impressive glacier during his visit to the Bel Alp in Switzerland (1849) at the age of 30. The Bel Alp was a little-known part of the Alps at that time but became one of the main centres for Victorian Mountaineers. Research for this book was done during the tour with Ruskin in 1882 and most of the writing was done while helping Ruskin at Brantwood. Gershom grew up with wide interests and in Ruskin met a man who could help him cultivate these interests to the full and add even more.

Ruskin was elected to a range of societies: Geological, Zoological, Architectural, Horticultural, Anthropological and Metaphysical, and to clubs the Athenaeum and Alpine, they show the breadth of his interests, which proved to be of great help to Gershom. Ruskin was also a man with enormous energy, filling every day from first light with intellectual or practical activity, though Gershom when writing an article for The Critic in June 1902 recalled that Ruskin said *'when you have too much to do, don't do it'*. Gershom found Ruskin a hard taskmaster, *'so exacting and so indulgent, spoiling you and slave driving you at once.'* Gershom remarked that unless you were ready for everything you could not work with him for long. He was always eager to teach all he knew and to learn all you knew.

**Brantwood**

John Ruskin's Lakeland home 'Brantwood' stands on a steep (brant) wooded slope looking out over Coniston Water. He bought Brantwood at Easter 1871, which later became an important part of Gershom's life. When John Ruskin bought Brantwood, it was a small rather basic cottage. He bought it from William James Linton, an admirer, after meeting him in Covent Garden, London (when told of its location, while in London, Ruskin could visualize the view so bought the house unseen). His first visit to the house was not until September, and he did not settle there until 1873. Many years earlier (1837) when on a tour of the Lake District Ruskin had sat, as a young man of 18 years, sketching beside Coniston Water not far from Brantwood. A scene he drew was across the Water to Coniston Old Hall and a mountain Coniston Old Man, not realizing that an old cottage behind him would become home for the latter 29 years of his life.

Ruskin appeared to give little thought about reaching the cottage from London or for people wishing to visit him from other parts of the country, or even from abroad. The nearest mainline railway station, Lancaster, was 45 miles (72 km) by horse and trap; a journey preferred to local trains that ran from Lancaster to Coniston stopping at numerous smaller stations. Eventually, the service was improved; the whole journey from London to Coniston was preferable by train stopping at Crewe, Preston, Carnforth, Barrow, Foxfield and finally Coniston; leaving London Euston at 9.45 a.m., arriving at Coniston 6.55 p.m. (it is no longer possible to travel from London to Coniston by train).

The man selling Brantwood, Mr Linton, was a wood-engraver, poet and author who had married Elizabeth Lynn from Keswick and both moved into Brantwood with seven children from Linton's previous marriage.

Elizabeth Lynn was the first female professional journalist in England, as well as a successful novelist, and highly controversial campaigner; among her causes was to support the movement *against* womens' suffrage. When the couple separated, Linton took his children to America and his wife went to live in London.

Ruskin moved into Brantwood, to make it his permanent home, at the time he was established as the most influential art critic in the country. He had written and published the highly successful 'Modern Painters'; completing the five volume work by 1860. In Gershom's words, *'He excelled at draughtsmanship and inspired readers of his work with fine language and poetic description. He had built a theory of art and thrown light on the Middle Ages and renaissance.'* Over the years at Brantwood John Ruskin was responsible for the building of a coach house and added the turret room, that can be seen clearly in Figure 19 (the room where John Ruskin died); in addition a new roof and enlargement to the cottage overall were made. Enlargement was done mainly to accommodate his cousin Joan Severn, her husband and their growing family, by 1883, when Gershom worked regularly at Brantwood, five children of the Severn family lived in the house: Lily aged ten, Arthur nine, Agnew eight, Violet three and Herbert one. Most visitors to see Ruskin stayed in or around Coniston. While Ruskin was normally pleased to welcome people into his home he did not hesitate to persuade any able and willing visitor to work on developing the surrounding hillside into a garden with greenhouses, an icehouse and at times a small farmstead. Originally, 16 acres of land went with the cottage but over the years Mrs. Severn extended the estate until it was very much larger, more than twice the original acreage.

Brantwood was visited during Ruskin's time by well-known figures from the arts, sciences, literature and academia, among them Charles Darwin and his family who stayed at the nearby Waterhead Hotel for one month in 1879 (shortly before Gershom arrived to work at Brantwood), artists Sir Edward Burne-Jones, Holman Hunt and illustrator of children's books Kate Greenaway. Other visitors included

Figure 20 Susannah (Susie) Beever by W.G.C.

Professor Jowett Master of Balliol Oxford, and writer Coventry Patmore, all came to see Ruskin during the time that Gershom worked at Brantwood. Added to these names of people prominent nationally were Ruskin's local friends like Mary and Susie Beever, artist Harriette Rigbye and writer Harriet Martineau plus ex-students of Ruskin and local craftspeople such as boat builder William Bell and gardener David Downs, the house was often full of people. Downs had worked for Ruskin over many first in London then supervising the road building at Hinksey near Oxford, while Ruskin was in Italy. Downs also worked on various projects for the Guild of St. George. Bell had more business with Lawrence Hilliard, who designed boats, than with Gershom but all three had a close interest in anything to do with boats. One of Gershom's favourite books was 'The Falcon on the Baltic' by E.F. Knight; story of sailing a converted P&O lifeboat. William Bell enjoyed a special relationship with John Ruskin. Writing in 'Ruskin Relics', Gershom described a meeting in 1879 when Ruskin paid a visit across Coniston Water to talk politics with a 'carpenter'. Debate was between the views of Conservatives and Liberals. The Professor had respect for the carpenter's [Bell] craftsmanship and became intrigued by his views on society. Canon Rawnsley, writing in 1901, recalled a typical meeting between the two men:[33]

> After one long session talking politics, Bell clapped Ruskin on the shoulder and said 'well to my ways o' thinking, for aw your conservative talk and writings and what not, thoos as radical as t'best on us'. Ruskin looked up with a smile clasped William's hand and said 'well, well, you're not so far wrong efter aw'.

After Gershom's occasional meetings with Ruskin at Oxford in 1872 he visited the Professor at Brantwood with his father in summer of the following year; Ruskin recorded in his diary of 1873, Friday August 8, *'Thomases and their children at lunch, Mr Collingwood and his son afterwards. I much tired, but a useful day'*. By 1891, Gershom had become a well-established aid to John Ruskin. The tasks were hugely varied which no doubt laid foundations for the remainder of his life. Among many varied tasks, he produced with Ruskin's design and his guidance, a diagram of the sky which helped children at Coniston School study the stars, it was in the form of a celestial globe that children could enter and see stars as luminous points against a blue background. He positioned the globe in the schoolyard at Coniston. Gershom needed the help of local tradesmen to carry out parts of his design; the globe revolved on rollers so that the position of the stars could be seen roughly at any time of the year. Unfortunately, this aid to studying the night sky did not survive. With further encouragement from Ruskin, Gershom made a model of Coniston and its neighbourhood at a scale of 6 inches to the mile, representing an area around Coniston of 4 miles by 5 miles (6 x 8 km); roughly 28 inches (71 Centimetres) square, which was placed in Coniston Museum. Geological survey work was done at Ruskin's request that allowed Gershom to use his drawing skill when illustrating rock formations and in making geological maps. Maps fascinated Gershom all his life, whether drawing maps of Norse settlements, wilderness areas of Iceland or relief maps of Lakeland, some he made from papier-mache by boiling paper. Crystallography was another interest he developed while recording Ruskin's mineral collection. Proofreading Ruskin's work and helping a secretary deal with a large amount of correspondence kept him fully occupied.

## Daily Routine

Each day, at Brantwood, Ruskin would be sitting at his table by candle light before dawn working at his writing without any disturbance. Breakfast around three

---

[33] Rawnsley, H.D. 1901. 'Ruskin and the English Lakes.' Glasgow: MacLehose and Sons.

hours later would break his concentration he would then talk with any friends visiting the house, and always with Gershom if he had arrived from Lanehead. More writing would be done until lunch; given suitable weather, he would have a session of wood chopping before the meal and the afternoon would be spent doing work that was more practical. Making places to sit in the grounds added to a variety of tasks; on one occasion, Gershom caught a viper (adder?) Ruskin recorded in his diary of October 9, 1881 *'Collingwood caught a viper with his bare hand'*. He gave it to Ruskin who found a place for the snake in a greenhouse. Ruskin developed a theory about how snakes moved after careful observation, and liked to make friends with the creatures. This attitude towards animals he held throughout his life; he became an enthusiastic supporter of any new organisation created to help protect animals but he felt that to this aim should be added *love* of animals, which led eventually to him resigning his Slade professorship at Oxford in 1878 because they were planning to introduce vivisection.

A major task at Brantwood was developing the steep wooded hillside behind the house: draining, planting and experimenting with crops. Gershom played a full role in doing this work. Ruskin asked the Beever sisters, Mary and Susanna (Susie), to help him by planting grains of corn in their own ample grounds to watch the stages of germination, which helped him to study root and blade growth. Ruskin described Mary Beever as more worldly and interested in politics while Susie was a far more homely person who loved animals, though in a letter to Ruskin she commented about having a fund of love she could not spend. Susie produced beautiful drawings of flowers and birds. Hundreds of letters passed between Ruskin and Susie over the years, even when Ruskin was travelling abroad. In one letter to Miss Beever, Ruskin wrote; 'I write to *you*, one of the true loves left'. A selection of this correspondence has been published in a book 'Hortus Inclusus'.[34] Susie inscribed a copy of this book to Gershom (1887).

Both sisters lived at a large cream-coloured house called The Thwaite, positioned on the slopes of Guards Wood near Coniston village. The Beever family had lived in the house since 1827 when father, a Manchester Merchant, moved there with his two sons and four daughters. Ruskin knew three surviving daughters but Margaret died soon after he arrived at Brantwood; one sister, a well-known local botanist, Susie Beever (Figure 20) was especially close to Ruskin.

Susie Beever also provided considerable help to Gershom and Dorrie from the time they arrived at Gillhead in 1883.

After some years at Brantwood, Ruskin developed among the grounds a smallholding with hens, lambs and young pigs. The nearest conventional farm was up the hill behind Brantwood called Lawson Park where the Stalker family

---

[34] Ruskin, J. 1887. 'Hortus Inclusus.' London: G. Allen.

farmed until 1883. To reach the farm from Lanehead, the Collingwoods walked the road towards Brantwood, to where a rough track led upwards to the left and on the way to the farm passed above Brantwood. The Wilkinson family took over the farm from the Stalkers, the farmer, Wilkinson, had been a miner and well prepared for hard farm work but during the early days the family experienced great misfortune, a son died aged only six, cattle died and their only horse became lame, then a gale destroyed their crop. During the next year (1884), Ruskin started an appeal for the family with £5 of his own money and raised 35 pounds 5 shillings (£25,470 in 2013 by retail price index, income value). The one daughter of the family Jane Ann Wilkinson worked for Ruskin as a shepherdess and became a regular companion, bundling sticks for firewood as Ruskin chopped them, and made sure a basket by the fire was kept full of wood in his study. According to Arthur Severn, recorded in a memoir of him by J.S. Dearden, Ruskin called her 'Pigwiggina'. For Gershom, Jane Ann was a familiar figure around the grounds and the house and he made sure she was acknowledged when visitors came to stay, so a wide range of people including ex-students of the professor came to know Jane Ann.

Gershom adopted Ruskin's habit of devoting mornings to academic subjects and afternoons to practical tasks with his own family, which gave each day structure and balance appreciated by most adults and children who took part.

Evenings at Brantwood were spent reading aloud from a variety of books, if the choice was left to Ruskin it would be something from Walter Scott or, if not reading, someone would play the piano and Gershom or Joan Severn would be asked to sing. The Collingwoods when living at Lanehead a short distance along the road would go home, while sleep for Ruskin was in a small single bed in a room with walls covered with paintings, most by Joseph Mallord William Turner, purchased by Ruskin.

Before sleeping, Ruskin would look closely at these pictures holding a candle in one hand while shielding his eyes with the other. According to Arthur Severn, Gershom and Alexander Wedderburn were staying at Brantwood and one evening Wedderburn, thinking Ruskin had gone to bed, imitated the Professor with candle in one hand shielding his eyes with the other, he stood in front of a Turner painting to the amusement of Arthur Severn, Gershom and others. Ruskin suddenly returned and said '*now Master Alec, I'm not going to have you imitating me.*'

**Severn Family**

When Gershom began working at Brantwood on a more regular basis from 1883, he found there a number of people attending to the various needs of the Professor. Most important was Ruskin's cousin from the Scottish side of the family Joan Severn née Ruskin Agnew who had lived there for ten years and continued to look after him until the day he died. When his father died John Ruskin arranged for Joan to travel from Scotland to Denmark Hill to stay one week with his mother, and she stayed for seven years. The Ruskin family home at Denmark Hill in London stood in 7 acres of garden, orchard and shrubbery. Eventually Joan married a civil servant Arthur Severn who aspired to be an artist. As a wedding present, Ruskin gave the couple his house at Herne Hill. J.S. Dearden in editing the memoir of Arthur Severn, claims that the Severn family became more or less dependent upon the Professor because while Arthur exhibited as an artist in some London and provincial galleries he had difficulty supporting his family as an artist.[35]

Children of the Severn family were brought up at Brantwood where they had a live-in governess Miss McClelland from the Isle of Skye. Joan continued to manage the household after Ruskin's death until her own death in 1924. Arthur Severn then returned to London to live out his remaining days, he died in 1931. The Severn family inherited Brantwood, manuscripts, pictures and all household effects in a Deed of Gift executed by Ruskin in trust for his lifetime, then for the Severns and their heirs. This would be in recognition for all the work done by Joan in looking after Ruskin. Towards the end of John Ruskin's life, from around 1895, he needed a good deal of care with dependence upon laudanum and responsibility for this care fell mainly to Joan Severn and Gershom, both wrote letters on behalf of Ruskin for ten years at the end of his life, he wrote nothing after 1890. When Ruskin did write letters it was normally to people some distance from Brantwood, the one exception being to Susie Beever living just outside Coniston, very little correspondence passed between John Ruskin and Gershom, he much preferred face-to-face dialogue. Letters passed between Gershom and Ruskin only when Gershom lived at Gillhead. When Ruskin was away from Brantwood Gershom wrote occasional letters, relying upon Sara Anderson, Mrs. Severn's secretary, to forward any correspondence.

Despite relationships between Gershom and both Severns being at times rather strained he was invited to join them and Ruskin on a trip to Seascale in June 1889, or rather Joan Severn took Ruskin to Seascale and her husband and Gershom accompanied them. Ruskin did not like being beside the seaside; he did his best to write his book Praeterita but according to Gershom it was a struggle and heart-breaking to see the Professor lost among his papers, and he suspected that Ruskin knew how he felt at witnessing this decline. Being on the west coast of the Lake District, they were in easy reach of Muncaster Castle, and spent a night at Wasdale Head beneath Scafell and Great Gable, but even these excursions did not please Ruskin. The 'holiday' was cut short at Ruskin's insistence; so ended the Professor's

---

[35] Deardon J.S. 1967. 'The Professor: Arthur Severn's Memoir of Ruskin.' London: Allen and Unwin.

last journey from Brantwood. In this year (1889), Ruskin sketched Langdale Pikes, possibly his last drawing.

### Lawrence Jermyn Hilliard (1855-1887)

It would be wrong to describe Gershom's time with Ruskin as a working partnership because the young man was very much in the 'assistant' role but one difficult to define clearly, not a secretary doing well-defined tasks but nearer to what we now call 'personal assistant'. Gershom joined Ruskin as an 'assistant' in the autumn of 1881 with the title of 'Geological Surveyor and Draughtsman' and worked on the landscape surrounding Coniston.

For six years up to 1882, Ruskin employed a conventional secretary Lawrence Hilliard, referred to by Ruskin as Lollie. Lawrence Jermyn Hilliard appointed Secretary mainly to take care of the Guild of St.George business correspondence and served as chief secretary from 1876 to 1882. Hilliard was described by Ruskin as an admirable draughtsman, painstaking and able to handle boats, his knowledge of boats and the design for specific purposes was to prove of great assistance to Ruskin when he wanted a craft to use on Coniston Water. Gershom could not replace the skill of Hilliard in this respect, even though he had a strong interest in small sailing craft, but was effectively taking his place administratively and bringing with him additional skills, especially those of research and accomplished writing to help support Ruskin's work. Hilliard's failing health caused him to resign in 1882 but he continued to live close to Brantwood at Low Bank Ground farm where his brother and sister rented a house. Hilliard died from pleurisy in 1887, aged only 32, while on a friend's boat in the Aegean.

### Sara Anderson (1854-1942)

Lawrence Hilliard and Gershom provided 'secretarial services' in addition to many other duties but the supreme secretary was Sara Anderson, though Joan Severn claimed that Sara was her secretary. Sara was the same age as Gershom. John Ruskin was extremely fortunate to have the help of Miss Anderson from 1882 to 1891; roughly, the same period that Gershom helped Ruskin while living in a cottage near Windermere. Sara Dunlop Anderson was the cousin of James Reddie Anderson a pupil and disciple of Ruskin, the Professor knew her since the early 1870s.

Her first task was to transcribe the Psalms of Sir Philip Sidney in support of Ruskin's work 'Rock Honeycomb'. Anderson was described as a super-secretary and super- friend; Gershom could not hope to match Sara in administrative work. After leaving Brantwood, Sara helped Sir Edward Burne-Jones then became secretary to Rudyard Kipling. Both Ruskin and Kipling placed Sara on a pinnacle; Kipling remarked that she was a class by herself. In a letter to Dorrie in 1881(AH) Gershom wrote, '*our nice, good Miss Anderson went away yesterday and left us all like sheep without a Shepherdess*'. Gershom maintained contact with her and many years later, in 1919, met Sara and her mother in London for what he called a 'crack'. Sara Anderson knew many secrets, but never broke confidentiality. She lived in retirement with music, literature and friends until her death in 1942 aged 88; an obituary notice written by Sir Sydney Cockerell appeared in The Times newspaper of October 30.

Another notable member of the Brantwood staff was Marion McClellan who came to Brantwood from the Isle of Sky in 1882, aged nineteen to act as governess to children of the Severn family, she was a great help to Gershom and Mrs. Severn during the early years of Ruskin's declining health. Ruskin thought highly of 'Clennie' as he called her and would frequently be comforted by her calming influence and softly spoken voice; she shared her time between the schoolroom and caring for Ruskin and left Brantwood around 1892.

**Guild of St. George**

When Gershom began the task of helping Ruskin he inevitably became involved with The Guild of St. George, helping Lawrence Hilliard handle the considerable correspondence; the control of funds and keeping of accounts was done by Joan Severn. The Guild was a charitable organisation founded by Ruskin around ten years earlier, with a personal start-up contribution of £7,000 (£573,700 in 2013 by retail price index). The overall aims of the Guild were set out in Ruskin's published work Fors Clavigera, a collection of letters addressed to working men between 1871 and 1884. Much earlier than this Ruskin had papers published in the Cornhill Magazine of 1860 giving his ideas on the economy and in particular the treatment of industrial workers. Ideas heavily criticized at the time, but over the years have become more meaningful and highly relevant. One of his concerns was the plight of young unemployed people and that the government should set up workshops for the teaching of skills where good works could be done. Thirty-three years after Ruskin's death a letter was published in the Manchester Guardian drawing reader's attention to Ruskin's book 'Unto This Last', published 76 years earlier, offering solutions for youth unemployment. Howard Whitehouse (Secretary of the Ruskin Society), The Bishop of Birmingham and Lord Conway of Allington signed the letter. Setting up the Guild of St. George was to provide a model of craft workers paid justly for worthwhile work.

To support this work effectively it was necessary for Gershom to be sympathetic towards the aims of the Guild, which meant supporting major social reform throughout the country. There is no evidence that he entered into this work with enthusiasm, but did what he had to do in respect for Ruskin's ideas. Timothy Hilton one of Ruskin's biographers (John Ruskin: The Later Years) referred to a moment between the two men when Ruskin attempted guile. Ruskin presented Collingwood with a small square bit of pure gold and when thanked for the present Ruskin replied, *'no present this is the enlistment shilling and now you are to serve under St.George: I have caught you with guile'*. Gershom did not officially enlist in the Guild of St. George; he only handled correspondence related to the Guild as part of his work in helping Ruskin. A prominent Liberal Member of Parliament William Cowper-Temple behaved towards the Guild in a similar way, he agreed to become one of the Trustees; not with any great faith in the scheme, but with affection for Ruskin.

Ruskin did not wish to follow the late Robert Owen in searching for a workers' Utopia or the Shaker movement in being a phalanx of like-minded people gathered in only one place. This was to be social reform beginning in small units, located at sites around the country, to spread ideas and practices among all working people, following mainly the principles of socialism. He wanted townsfolk to 'come out of the gutter' leaving commercialism and industrialisation behind to work hard at wholesome worthwhile tasks, as he practised himself, and be given their rightful reward. It can be argued that the so-called depression or 'madness' (sometimes called brain fever) suffered by John Ruskin in his last years was more likely anguish that his ideas on social reform would not be realised either in his lifetime or in the foreseeable future. In a letter to his father (AH), Gershom referred to Ruskin's continual grumblings and looking at the bad of things, and their incurableness has to some extent warped Mr R's mind lately. *'Most people say he is mad. I know that on many points he is more sensible than most of us'*. John Ruskin had become accustomed to the term 'mad' in reference to himself, much as any unconventional or rebellious person in the public eye must endure. For John Ruskin it was in art, his respect and support for painters of the Pre-Raphaelite Brotherhood, and for J.M.W. Turner the artist; also for his economic theories, criticism of politicians of whatever party, agitating for social reform or questioning the establishment with its unrelenting moves towards commercialisation. In art, a common view of Turner, the man, was morose, niggardly and inexplicable. Ruskin also acknowledged faults in his paintings and in his character, but as Gershom pointed out; Ruskin could discern the virtues, which they hide. He was a great admirer and supporter of Turner during the artist's later years. John Ruskin was executor of Turner's will and did considerable work in cataloguing Turner's pictures and drawings for the National Gallery in London.

Gershom understood Ruskin's position knowing very well that madness was not the problem but sheer frustration that all Ruskin had worked for would count for very little when he had gone. Ruskin was possibly the first scholar to have societies created in his name during his own lifetime; despite this, he realised that they represented only minority voice and a stronger voice he disliked seemed to overwhelm him. Much of Ruskin's anguish seemed to come from thoughts about what would happen to his work when he had gone. During a second visit to Ruskin by Lady Georgiana Burne-Jones, the pair were walking on hills behind Brantwood when Ruskin raised the problem of handing on to others all he had learned in life so that those who came afterwards could begin at that point and not have to start all over again. To a certain extent Gershom was addressing this problem when writing the first biography of Ruskin in two volumes, while Edward Tyas Cook and Alexander Wedderburn did a masterful job of editing his collected works in thirty-nine volumes,[36] and finally Ruskin's autobiography 'Praeterita'. There must be a feeling that Ruskin meant more than recording his life and work when talking with Georgiana; he would be shocked how, 115 years after his death, working people can be so terribly exploited, what he recognised as much-needed social reform has not materialized.

Earlier, in 1874, Ruskin visited Barmouth in West-Wales where eight fishermen's cottages stood below steep cliffs that form a backdrop to the town. Fanny Talbot née Browne, a wealthy supporter of the Guild bought the cottages. Supporters like Fanny Talbot shared with Ruskin his concerns about the growth of industrialisation and in particular the negative impact upon working people. The cottages in Barmouth became a site for a social experiment entirely through the efforts of Fanny Talbot who had moved to a house Ty'n-y-Ffynon in Barmouth from Bridgewater after the death of her husband. By developing communities around the country based upon practices of the pre-industrial period, members of the Guild known as 'Companions', could demonstrate that social progress was achievable while remaining free from the shackles of the new industries and industrial capitalism. They were not alone in this respect; numerous public figures hated industrial practices or 'the industrial revolution' as it later became known, and campaigned against the age of industrialisation. Oscar Wilde took away with him from Oxford many socialist ideals, when at Oxford he was heard to remark[37] that all factory chimneys and vulgar workshops should be taken up and placed on some far-off island. '*I would give Manchester back to the shepherds and Leeds back to the stock farmers.*' Around this time, Ruskin was heard to say that he would like to blow up Manchester and Birmingham. He was ridiculed about such comments but the idea continues to be a reasonable sentiment if people were removed safely from these centres beforehand.

Apart from references to industrialisation and relationship to poverty in Gershom's 'Book of Verses', poems written as a young man, there was no evidence

---

[36] Cook, E.T. and A. Wedderburn (eds) 1903. 'Ruskin Collected Works.' London: George Allen.
[37] Atkinson, G.T. 1929. Wilde at Oxford. Cornhill Magazine, vol. 66, May, pp. 561-2.

that he felt strongly about the 'new' industry that some people saw as a threat to society; a view common among academics.

A key aim for members of the Guild of St. George was to re-establish strong rural communities that were in danger of being swallowed up by factories and replace factory life with the practice of rural crafts and a belief in the dignity of labour. Centres were established in the Wyre Forest near

Bewdley, Cloughton in North Yorkshire, Sheepscombe in Gloucestershire, Holcombe near Bath and a farmhouse was bought at Totley Derbyshire to provide workmen with allotments. Ruskin was Master of the Guild but Gershom did a good deal of administrative work in addition to promoting fundamental beliefs of the Guild members, even though he could not help feeling some scepticism.

**Ruskin Biography**

Gershom if asked about his writing achievements would no doubt refer to his biography of John Ruskin 'The Life and Work of John Ruskin' in two volumes, a book read to the present day but not too well received by reviewers soon after publication (1893). There were a number of reviews published in periodicals: Athenaeum, Bookman, Living Age and Spectator. While it is possible, in hindsight, to see reviewers as hypercritical, the comments would be taken seriously by Gershom and possibly upset him at the time. The biography being one of his early books would make him determined to learn from the experience and note any comments he recognised as valid. Later published work after 1893 until 1927 (year of last published book) received more positive reactions from reviewers. Unlike now, book reviewers in Gershom's day could be respected for their scholarship, and overall his writings were well received by them. A more serious error found in the biography of Ruskin was that Gershom either misunderstood the relationship between Ruskin and artist J.M.W. Turner or was careless in checking his sources of information. A reviewer wrote that, '*Mr Collingwood failed to point out that Turner was elected a Royal Academician 17 years before Ruskin was born and he* [Turner] *had painted all his best work and given employment for many years to the greatest landscape engravers the world has known*' (among them Thomas Lupton, George Cooke and Samuel Fisher). *Prints produced from his original work helped make Turner well-known far and wide long before Ruskin made his name as an art critic*'. Gershom's implication that Ruskin played a major part in the career of Turner was seen as an error, as surely it was. A number of errors were detected in a section about artist and poet Gabriel Rossetti, sufficient for a reviewer to recommend that all the pages dealing with Rossetti needed revision. One reviewer found humour in Gershom's comment that Rossetti was 'married and settled in life'. In addition, there was error in the statement that Ruskin tried to get Thackeray to print Rossetti's poems in the Cornhill Magazine, but in vain. Gershom claimed that as editors refused them Ruskin became responsible for the cost of the publication. One reviewer commented that, *'it will probably be news to Mr Collingwood to hear that so far from editors refusing Rossetti's poetry in 1868, they were particularly anxious to obtain it; and he will doubtless be surprised to learn that he has only to look over the volumes of Fortnightly Review, The Athenaeum, The Academy and other periodicals to find Rossetti's poems in abundance.* Further comments of a more serious nature for someone writing a biography were about Mr Collingwood's style being seen as too colloquial and too patronising. There was a feeling that the general reader with an interest in Ruskin and his work could find the book stimulating (and so it has proved over the years), but for scholars with a deep interest in Ruskin, reviewers claimed there was nothing new. For almost three years, it was known that a biography of Ruskin was being written by his 'secretary' W.G. Collingwood. People who had looked forward in eager anticipation to publication of the book were generally disappointed. The book had the full backing of Ruskin, support of his close friends and household at Brantwood so more insight and hitherto unknown details were anticipated by some readers. However, the book was popular, the publisher Methuen brought out an abridged one-volume edition ten years after Ruskin's death.

Despite the book not living up to expectations for some readers, the biography of Ruskin was the best they were going to get many years to come. Gershom wrote the book by 1890 when Ruskin was at the beginning of steadily declining health. The intention in producing this work was to contribute a volume to a series of University Extension Manuals, describing the continuous development of Ruskin's thought. In Gershom's words 'it had the advantage and the disadvantage of being written under his eye; that is to say, he saw as much of it as his health allowed; and it received his general approval'. The biographical part of the book was enlarged only after Ruskin's death to replace text that describes his writings; even more of the text was removed chiefly because it had become more readily available elsewhere. Gershom saw in John Ruskin strong traits of the Scotsman *'a combination of shrewd common sense and romantic sentiment; the oscillation between levity and dignity, from caustic jest to tender earnest; the restlessness, the fervour, the impetuosity'.* These traits he came to recognise in Ruskin the man. The two volumes written about the life and work of John Ruskin by Gershom highlight the man himself, after working with Ruskin for some years.

Gershom wisely made little of the controversy surrounding Ruskin's married life and subsequent annulment; the whole truth may never be known. He could show sympathy for both parties. Writing about Euphemia (Effie), *'the disillusioning of a young girl who found herself married, by parental arrangement, to a man* [Ruskin] *with whom she had nothing in common'.* What he did reveal was the love Ruskin felt for a young lady who refused his offer of marriage because he would not say that he loved God before her. Even on her deathbed when still young, Ruskin asked to visit her, but she refused unless he would state his love of God before her; again, he could not use these words. Gershom claimed that her mother denied that this exchange ever happened between Ruskin and her daughter, but it does appear that different views about faith stood between them and a fulfilled life together. Gershom mentioned two loves of Ruskin's life: Adéle Domecq, the daughter of his father's partner in the Domecq sherry business, and Rose La Touche, thirty years his junior.

Before completing the biography of Ruskin, Gershom wrote a biographical outline, published in 1889, edited by John Waugh of Bradford. Gershom did not attempt the writing of another biography after the two-volume work on Ruskin.

The last ten years of Ruskin's life 1890-1900 put a great strain upon Joan Severn who nursed him day and night; Gershom helped when he could and for periods the nursing was shared between them. During these years Ruskin himself was in need of money, a considerable fortune had gone; he gave most of it away. A decision was taken at Brantwood to re-publish much of Ruskin's work to raise funds. Gershom did most editorial work that this involved; he received a percentage of royalties.

During these last ten years, W.G.C. edited eight works by Ruskin in thirteen volumes. Gershom was also very busy as a writer and made a journey to Iceland, all activity that would have the blessing of Ruskin.

The Professor died in his beloved Lake District, and insisted on being buried at Coniston. Soon after his death, an offer was made for him to be buried at Westminster Abbey but Ruskin's wish was carried out and his grave is in Coniston churchyard near that of Susie Beever.

**Brantwood after Ruskin**

Brantwood, a house that meant so much to Gershom was a meaningful place only while John Ruskin lived there; ideally, the house ought to be dedicated to the art and works of both men, including that of Turner, Prout, Burne-Jones, Rossetti and Holman Hunt. From 1900 onwards, the house was destined to become a museum. After Ruskin's death, Joan Severn continued to look after the buildings until her death 24 years later. After this time, Brantwood suffered neglect and would have become a ruin if not rescued. Ruskin had arranged for a trust fund with money from royalties to help maintain the house but this was not done effectively. From 1924 to 1931, the house was in the possession of Arthur Severn, after his death Brantwood with 250 acres of land was sold to John Howard Whitehouse, President of the Ruskin Society, a Quaker, Liberal politician and disciple of John Ruskin. From that date onwards, the intention was to make Brantwood a national memorial to John Ruskin.

## Chapter VII Working with Ruskin (1881-1900)

John Ruskin enjoyed almost 20 productive years (1871-1890) at his home beside Coniston Water and during this time moved from being an art critic of major influence to a social reformer of even greater influence; Gershom was a close friend and invaluable assistant for roughly half this period. Ruskin spent 10 more years at Brantwood as, in Gershom's words, a worn-out invalid.

# Chapter VIII
# Life in Lakeland
# (1891-1932)

**Family Home**

Moving from cottages at Gillhead to a large house beside Coniston Water was to be home for Gershom and Dorrie for the remainder of their lives, the move took place in 1891. The house 'Lanehead', built in 1848, stood on the site of the Halfpenny Alehouse. Gershom in his book 'Lake District History' refers to artist J.M.W. Turner having a drink at the Halfpenny in 1797 while looking out towards Coniston Old Man, a scene he had to paint and when back in London he exhibited at The Royal Academy a picture 'Morning on Coniston Fells' his first true mountain picture. The picture shows a magnificent view of Coniston Old Man and the ridge leading to Wetherlam, two fine Lakeland mountains. Local people, farmers, charcoal burners and ore miners travelling the road to the east of Coniston Water would welcome a drink at the 'Halfpenny Inn' and no doubt Turner enjoyed his visit too with an opportunity to talk with local people. Gershom commented that a road without an inn was useless, but he lived at Lanehead beside a road with no inn or hostelry, in a house where an inn once stood, and another nearby inn 'The Waterhead' had been demolished around 40 years before he arrived at Lanehead.

(Three years after moving to Lanehead a new Parish Council was formed called 'Monk Coniston' with seven members and Gershom was asked to be the Chairman, which he accepted; from that moment their official address was Lanehead, Monk Coniston.)

Subsistence of the family continued to be paid for with income from the sale of paintings from both Gershom and Dorrie. Throughout the Collingwood family life at Lanehead, they were tenants; from 1891 when they moved into the house until Gershom died in 1932. During this time, there were only two owners of Lanehead, the first, until 1918, Rev. Henry Arthur Starkie living in Clitheroe, Lancashire. After his death, Lanehead was bought for £1,700 by Emma Georgina Holt, unmarried only daughter of a wealthy merchant George Holt living in Liverpool who had interests in the shipping company Lamport and Holt; his brother Alfred founded the Blue Funnel Shipping Company also based in the city (I worked for both shipping lines). Emma was philanthropic all her adult life. The Collingwoods paid the rent of £100 per year for Lanehead to Rev. Starkie until 1918 and it is believed that Emma Holt the new owner agreed to the Collingwood family looking after the house rent-free. Emma stayed at Tent Lodge nearby when visiting the Lake District. Emma's uncle

Alfred Holt was already well known to Gershom through their shared fascination with Iceland and with northern antiquities in general. In 1932, to keep Lanehead for the Collingwood family, the house was bought by Gershom's son-in-law Dr Ernest Altounyan, and eventually inherited by a daughter Mavis (Titty) who sold the house to a Local Authority to be used as an 'outdoor centre'; the wonderful Collingwood family home was no more. At the time of writing Lanehead is again for sale.

Whenever I read of Gershom's life at Lanehead it brought on strong feelings of nostalgia and no little envy; it is difficult to conjure up in imagination a more idyllic way of life. Idyllic in imagination but for Gershom and Dorrie the years there were not without concerns about money most of the time. A lasting picture, in imagination, is of Gershom seated at a large table covered with a Persian carpet, surrounded by papers and books where he would be at work for many hours. Life at Lanehead could be described by some people as Bohemian; certainly, it was unconventional in a setting surrounded by hills and mountains, not unlike the former kingdom of Bohemia. In other respects, there were a number of practical considerations: entertaining people from 'outside', earning a living and though children's education took place at home they were being prepared for a life beyond Coniston. Regular contact with John Ruskin meant thoughts were not too far away from the perceived perils of industrialisation and the necessity (as Ruskin perceived it) of much-needed social reform throughout the nation; in these circumstances, it was difficult to be totally detached from everyday life in a Bohemian way, unfortunately.

The large Lanehead house was draughty and damp but a warm family atmosphere more than compensated for any inconveniences caused by the structure and layout of the building. The day began soon after first light with the sound of a piano played for one hour by Mrs. Collingwood, mainly Mozart or Beethoven. Breakfast followed and afterwards, if a clear sky, the family would gather at the front of the house to enjoy the magnificent view across Coniston Water towards the mountains of Coniston Old Man and Wetherlam. This, one of the finest views in Lakeland was gazed at in the evening too, seated on a grass bank at the foot of the garden called the Lair to see the sun go down over the mountains. Two clear descriptions of Lanehead house at this time comes from Gershom's granddaughter Taqui Altounyan[38] and Arthur Ransome.[39] Walls had original wallpaper by William Morris, which were largely covered by paintings and drawings, especially in the Morning Room. One painting of two angels dressed in red holding musical

---

[38] Altounyan, T. 1969. 'In Aleppo Once.' London: J. Murray.
[39] Ransome, A. 1976. 'Autobiography.' London: Jonathan Cape Ltd.

instruments (similar to Angel playing a flageolet) by Edward 'Ned' Burne-Jones, an outstanding nineteenth century artist immediately caught the eye. Paintings by Gershom and his father William also hung there with watercolours by Mrs. Collingwood (Dorrie) and drawings by John Ruskin (a financially poor family surrounded by artwork worth millions at present-day valuations, and a reasonable amount at the time). The Morning Room provided a good deal of space. Even with a grand piano, heavy carved furniture and a marble fireplace, there was ample room to move around and admire the view through large windows facing west and south. Arthur Ransome recalled how Mrs. Collingwood on coming into a room always looked for a draught, in order to sit in it. There were two doors in the dining room, one opening into the hall and one into a passage, which led to the scullery and kitchen. A door in the passage was open to a flagged yard. The door to the hall was never shut and Dorrie sat in whatever gale was blowing through. Other people in the room looked for shelter. In one of the many rooms, they kept plaster busts of family members and eventually of Arthur Ransome made by Gershom's daughter Barbara; generations of artwork lay in the house. The original kitchen was converted to a dining room but a large black cooking range was retained with ovens on both sides, which had brass handles to the doors. From early morning, a fire burned in the range and at breakfast, a large platter of eggs and bacon was kept warm on the hob. The floor was paved with slate, typical of Lakeland farmhouses at the time. Fresh water they drew by using a hand-pump in a small room next to the dining room. Next, lay the kitchen with a black stove used by Ada the cook who came from Tilberthwaite, around three miles (5 km) north of Lanehead up a steep track; Ada continued to cook at Lanehead after Gershom's death, when the house belonged to the Altounyan family. Beyond the kitchen were pantry, larder and lamp room where oil lamps were cleaned and stored when not in use. The Lamp Room also had shelves where Gershom kept his galley proofs and wood blocks used to illustrate his book 'Thorstein of the Mere'. The shelves also housed boat parts, plaster casts, various rusty metal objects and old copies of the magazine Punch. The room filled with the morning sun and would have been a good place to sit and read; one problem was that the room smelled strongly of paraffin. In the evening at Lanehead apart from piano playing and singing a favourite pastime was reading aloud before going to bed by the light of a candle in a brass holder, or an oil lamp.

Possibly the most evocative image from their life at Lanehead is of Gershom and Dorrie skating the length of Coniston Water at New Year of 1895, year of a great freeze. Many people skated in London on the Thames and lakes nearby but none could compare with this young couple skating in silence, surrounded by hills and mountains.

A photograph taken around 1895, shows Dorrie with the four children, (Figure 21). Around this time, the Collingwood family had become settled at Lanehead; a well-

Figure 21 Dorrie with the four children

composed photograph shows a family group of Dorrie and all four children in the garden. The children were beginning to explore the delights of their home and the sailing on Coniston Water.

**Home Schooling**

When of school age the Collingwood children were educated at home by their parents Gershom and Dorrie. It is possible that lack of income, or regular income was the reason for educating the children at home but fundamentally, the choice was more likely one of preference. From 1891, when all four Collingwood children were very young, The Elementary Education Act was introduced ensuring that all children could have free education up to the age of eleven years.

Each day, the children's programme consisted of theoretical study in the morning and practical work in the afternoon. Gershom may well have had Ruskin's pattern of working in mind when thinking of education at home but he was not alone in adopting this practice. At around the same time (mid-1890s) a well-known writer Lytton Strachey experienced the same education at Abbotsholme, a school in Derbyshire.[40] Head of school Dr Cecil Reddie insisted upon class-work in the morning, manual work in the afternoon and the evening devoted to music, poetry and arts. All very similar to education in the Collingwood household, only difference being that at Lanehead there were four children and at Abbotsholme, forty.

The practice of home education continued into the next generation when eldest daughter Dora married a doctor from Syria Ernest Haig Riddell Altounyan (1889-1962) she found it convenient to teach the children at home in Aleppo and her own experience of early learning in this way proved a great help. Taqui one of the grandchildren reported her mother saying '*I wish my children had the advantages I had*'.

Dora Susie married Ernest Altounyan in 1916. He came from Aleppo in Syria and was at Rugby school with her brother Robin. Ernest was the son of an Armenian doctor and an Irish mother and he returned to Aleppo after the 1914-1918 war to help his father run the hospital he had founded. Ernest went from Rugby to Cambridge University to study medicine, then to Middlesex hospital. In 1915, he served in the Royal Army Medical Corps in France; he won the Military Cross and was severely wounded from which he never fully recovered. Although a medical man, he had ambitions to be a writer and on a number of occasions after the war dined with Leonard and Virginia Woolf, both with plans to be publishers. After the war, Dora and the children lived in Aleppo, while Ernest worked at the hospital. Gershom kept up a correspondence with his eldest daughter in that far-away place and she seemed to miss the hills and mountains of Lakeland. In one letter she referred to a lack of scenery with only low bare hills; Dora did mention that snow-capped mountains could be seen from the district of Aleppo, but around 50 miles distant describing them as 'quite good crinkly shapes'.

When the Collingwood's only son Robin wrote a dedication in his book 'Speculum Mentis' or Map of Knowledge[41] (more or less to state his idealism) it was to: '*My First and Best Teacher of Art, Religion, Science, History and Philosophy*' Gershom is not named, but it is beyond question that Robin was referring to his father. There was a tendency in writing for Robin George to make assumptions about the knowledge of his readers, but he was probably mistaken in thinking that all readers would take this dedication as being to his father.

For the Collingwood children at Lanehead, they had conventional-type schoolwork in the morning for two or three hours; they grew up fluent in German and French and learned Latin and Greek from the early age of around six. Almost every day the children had a direct example of both parents being hard at work.

---

[40] Holroyd, M. 1994. 'Lytton Strachey.' London: Vintage.
[41] Collingwood, R.G. 1924. 'Speculum Mentis.' Oxford: Clarendon Press.

Most children at the time had only a vague idea about how father earned a living or mother if she worked outside the home. Robin in particular appreciated the frame of mind he developed in this way and studied all he could find on the natural sciences: astronomy, geology and physics. Robin George did not acknowledge in his autobiography the part played by John Ruskin in his early education, though John Ruskin's health began its decline the year Robin was born. However, it would be strange indeed, if his father did not impart to his son and daughters something of what he learned from close contact with Ruskin for around twelve years up to that time. Ruskin would approve of 'Collie' educating his children at home; he too received his early education at home, mainly from his mother with help from tutors, before he went to Oxford Both Ruskin and Gershom held the view that for any civilized society the greatest influence must come from the family and not from specialised teachers. An analogy was made with health, if a child has an illness or a bruised knee the parents will attempt to make it well but if not they see a doctor. This view is sound when applied to the education of children, but only if all parents were like, or similar to, Mrs. Ruskin or Gershom and Dorie Collingwood and could practise their way of life.

Normal life, especially in industrial towns, was not like that; if Robin had gone out into the rough and tumble of working life, instead of being first a student then an academic at Oxford, it can be argued that his idyllic early upbringing would have made him ill prepared as a working adult.

Of the other Collingwood children, only the youngest Ursula showed how she could survive 'outside' by working as a midwife in London's East End during the 1920s. A comment made to Gershom about his family was *'your poor children, it is hard on them to bring them up in the Lake District they will never be happy anywhere else'*. Gershom replied that one of his children was very happy in town; she said to a friend *'we have no trams at home, only mountains'*. I can only assume that this was Ursula.

John Ruskin would consider the Collingwood way of life at Lanehead as the ideal approach to work and looking after children but he would also acknowledge the impossibility of such an approach when, for example, both parents worked 12 hours a day in a cotton mill. For this reason, he campaigned to bring social reform so that more families could benefit by being freed from the shackles of industrialisation. The afternoons at Lanehead were also for education but of a practical kind, not normally covered in school, when the four children would be left mainly to their own devices with a parent on hand to offer any necessary help towards learning. Practical tasks of home repairs, cutting wood, sailing, making fires for outdoor cooking, were all carried out dictated only by the weather. Expeditions by the children in a boat on Coniston Water would begin with Mrs. Collingwood giving them a bun loaf, a pot of marmalade and a kettle for making tea.

With a fair wind, they would learn how to tack a boat down Coniston Water to Peel Island about four miles (6 km) from the jetty at Lanehead. The island offered a good level site above a cliff on the east side where a camp was made and fire lit, all cooking and making tea was done over a fire and never on a stove of any kind. Three generations of the Collingwood family treated the island as their own secret hideaway, ever since Gershom and Dorrie made their first visit of exploration in 1892, after their move to Lanehead.

Simple drawings by the youngest child Ursula about the adventures of Puff and Fluffs going in a boat to camp on an island capture the scene well (Figures 22, Cover and 23 Detail).

Puff and Fluffs were cats at Lanehead; Ursula's idea of going on an adventure probably came from Puff the cat that would wander off for days, making Gershom comment in a letter that 'Puff was back again'. This was some years before Arthur Ransome wrote about children sailing boats and camping on an island. Soon after arriving at Lanehead Gershom and Dorrie excavated on Peel Island and found evidence of digging on the south side to form a scarp-like slope. What looks like a natural inlet convenient for mooring boats with rock walls at each side showed extensions by building out both natural walls of the inlet to shelter small boats. In the centre of the island, they found evidence of a ruin and relics, chiefly pottery, nails, an old smithy hearth all on the western side of the island. Later, Gershom eventually came to believe that these finds were from the early middle ages[42] and speculated that it could have been the stronghold of Adam Beaumont and his outlaws in the 14 century. Other finds on the island agreed with this period. Gershom described Peel Island in his book 'Thorstein of the Mere' as he imagined it 1000 years earlier, but he said the description was pure fancy. He commented that no mention had been made of the island as settlement or fort in records kept at Furness Abbey or in any other known records from the Middle Ages. He wrote the book about Thorstein for a child (son Robin) but the story makes delightful reading at any age.

**Religious Education**

In the nineteenth century, religion played a major part in the lives of most families; going to church was almost an automatic activity something you did at least once each week. There is little reference to religious education or church-going practice from accounts of daily life at Lanehead.

---

[42] Collingwood, W.G. 1914. The antiquities of the Doe Crags track. The Journal of the Fell and Rock Climbing Club of the English Lake District, vol. 3 number 2. pp. 15-16.

Puff and Fluffs
adventures
by Ursula. M. Collingwood.

Figure 22 Puff and Fluffs (1) from 'Nothing Much'(AH).

Figure 23 Puff and Fluffs (2) from 'Nothing Much'(AH).

When, in 1902, Robin invited a friend from Rugby School, Ernest Altounyan, to stay at his home, Ernest commented that, *apart from not having to go to church there are many things that were wonderfully different about the Collingwood way of life at Lanehead.* A further clue to the family position in this respect comes from son Robin, who at sixteen years old while at School in Rugby chose of his own free will to be baptised into the Church of England, adopting the middle name George and a year later was confirmed. Robin would know of his father's attempts to gain fellowships at various universities and the strong possibility that his non-conformist background was the main reason for repeated failures. If Robin saw his future career in academia, it would not be surprising that he prepared himself by being established in the Church of England, though it must be said that he probably acted in accordance with his faith than for any other reason. It appears that Dorrie followed evangelicalism, normally linked to Protestant faith.

Members of Dorrie's family were Congregationalists and when a girl, she attended Sunday school and Bible readings given by her father. Church attendance was continued by Dorrie after their move to the Lake District, she attended Matins at Coniston church but Gershom did not join her. It appears that once settled in the Lake District away from his father's direct influence, Gershom had no specific ties to any faith. Janet Gnosspelius, researching the Collingwood family, came to the conclusion that by the time he was married and himself a father, he felt that he had a basinful of religion and that he did not wish to subject his young to what he had gone through; he left them to decide for themselves: eldest daughter Dora had interest in Christian symbolism but was not a member of any church. Barbara too was never a member of any church.

Robin, interested in religion from his time at Rugby school, arranged for his own baptism and confirmation. He viewed religion as indispensable. Ursula was interested in religion from her time at boarding school in Dulwich from 1904 and from close contact with her brother Robin. Ursula and Robin corresponded regularly and their letters often referred to religion. In one letter to Ursula (Robin wrote to Dearest Sossie) Robin referred to the Bible and St. John, writing that there is no trouble he cannot cure. Eventually Ursula married Rev. R.B. Luard- Selby of the high church. Robin, when a student at Oxford wandered around many churches but this is not necessarily any indication of holding a faith; his commitment to religion is to be found in his writing.

At home in the Gillhead cottage or at Lanehead, the only religious influence for the children would come from Dorrie; Robin was the only member of the family to embrace a faith fully but not until he left home to attend boarding school and from that time he was an Anglican for the remainder of his life. Gershom did take an interest in Quakerism otherwise he could not have completed the detailed research necessary to write a paper on 'Epistles of early Friends' read at Furness Abbey Hotel in September 1895. He traced the earliest writing of epistles to a John Spoor of Somerset in 1675 and subsequent writings of this kind that formed a kind of Bible for the then nascent church.

The strongest influence to determine whether Gershom followed a faith came from his father. Well into old age, William Collingwood still held his rather unconventional religious beliefs, in this respect he was to have no influence upon his family of Marie and their children Gershom, Ruth and David; William had followed his father as a Congregationalist so may well have expected his children to follow him too.

William was to experience great disappointment that his eldest son William Gershom, so much like him in many ways, would not follow his steps within The Brethren. Gershom gave some attention to his father's religious work and was baptised by him in 1872 just before going up to Oxford, it appears that Brethren did not approve of baptising infants. From later events, it became apparent that during these years, Gershom was pleasing his father. Finally, Gershom expressed grave doubts about the Brethren using strong words in a letter (AH) to his father on September 25, 1889.

Around 1881, Gershom rejected a life devoted to religion, although this coincided with the beginning of his project- work for Ruskin there is no evidence that the Professor influenced his thinking about religion. Some years later, Gershom contributed an article, in 1903, to an American periodical, 'The Living Age' in which he discussed Ruskin's bibles. In this article, he describes how Ruskin went through many phases of faith, including long periods of doubt; yet at all times Ruskin took the Bible seriously and towards the end of his life he showed clear acceptance of Christian hope. Ruskin's mother was a strong early influence in her son's acceptance of the Christian faith and this remained a dominant theme throughout his life, whether to accept fully Christian teaching or reject certain parts; at one time he was drifting towards agnosticism. From time to time Gershom would discuss the Bible, especially at Oxford as a student and later when working for Ruskin. At one of these meetings with Ruskin, Gershom was having difficulty over the correct quotation of some passage in the Bible, when he said to Ruskin 'haven't you a concordance?' Ruskin replied *'I'm ashamed to say I have; you and I oughtn't to need Cruden'*

(Cruden's Concordance, is a work of reference for serious study of the Bible).

Ruskin was implying that young Gershom ought to know the Bible as well as himself; few people in the country could claim to know the book as well as Ruskin. If Gershom wished to turn his back on religion completely he would find this very difficult, there was Dorrie and her faith, and inevitable questions from the children, which had to be addressed. Gershom, when writing a biography of Ruskin, discovered the strong faith of his mother, and how much she influenced her son John. Towards the end of Ruskin's life, when working regularly with Gershom, his faith was strong but he did not appear to have any influence over his assistant in this respect.

When writing of Ruskin's bibles[43] Gershom recognised that Ruskin came from a line of decent, respectable, bourgeois folk who read their bible, 'feared God, and took their own part when required'. To say that John Ruskin was a religious man throughout his life would be wrong, he moved from religious to agnostic bordering on atheist, then back to religious. Gershom moved from non- conformist to disinterest in any form of religion. Tim Hilton in writing his two-volume biography of Ruskin, referred to W.G. Collingwood as being singularly free of personal and social ambition and cared little for politics or religion.[44] Comments of a 'political' nature came rarely from Gershom, in a letter to son Robin he discussed the Boers in connection with a war at that time (1900) and claimed that all the Boers had to do was say 'pax' (peace) and pax it would be. There would be occasional comments about William Gladstone in letters to his father but mainly because of his Liverpool connection, and Ruskin would draw him into talking politics on their walks but the Professor soon detected a lack of interest from Collie, as he called him. It would be wrong to suggest that Gershom turned his back on religious faith, throughout his life he remained sensitive to the part religion played in other peoples' lives; those around him and people in periods of history that he studied. Writing an Afterword to his edited work of Rev. Calverley's research, he commented that before the seventh century we had Christian teachers in St. Kentigern (sixth century), St. Patrick (fifth century), and St. Ninian (end of fourth century). *'All these were Britons of the North-West by birth; and by tradition, by dedication, and by history they are certainly connected with the early religious life of our district'.*

**Lanehead Magazine**

The Collingwood children had their daily adventures and set periods of learning without any real record of events apart from letter writing until 1897 when, after encouragement from Gershom and Dorrie, they started a monthly magazine called 'Nothing Much' edited by eldest daughter Dora. The whole family contributed features and stories; some by Gershom, which appeared later in 'Coniston Tales' published in 1899. Gershom dedicated the book to the Editor of 'Nothing Much' with the words:

> It was owing to your encouragement that these sketches were attempted; and it is by your help and permission that they are now reproduced from your pages. Accept then, the dedication from our little book from your obliging contributor,

---

[43] Collingwood, W.G. 1903. Ruskin's Bibles. The Living Age, February 1903, p. 441.
[44] Hilton, T. 2000. 'John Ruskin: the later years.' (vol. 2) Yale University Press.

Gershom
Coniston April 1899.

This dedication was addressed to his eldest daughter Dora, aged thirteen, Editor of 'Nothing Much'. Subjects covered in the magazine were many and varied: Ursula wrote about feeding the hens, Robin wrote detective stories, Mother (Dorrie) produced Title Pages and wrote on art, poems from father (Gershom) also about various fell walks, and about maps. Gershom's sister Ruth contributed a poem.

There was the possibility that much of the story-telling in print was triggered by father writing and publishing Thorstein of the Mere. Teresa Smith a daughter of Robin Collingwood in 'R.G.Collingwood: An Autobiography'[45] draws our attention to a contribution from all the children at Christmas 1898, which seems to be a very good reflection of the Collingwood family's idiosyncrasies that, unfortunately, Daddy would not sign:

> We don't go in for prizes, and none of us go to schools
> We haven't got no principles, and we don't know nothing of rules
> But we scribble a bit, and sketch a bit – 'the Rabs take after their Pa'
> We're a dilettante family, we are, we are, we are.
>
> We don't do it for money, and we don't do it for praise
> We do it because we like it, and we're glad of the laugh we raise
> Laugh with us then, or at us – we ain't particular – We're a highly casual family, we are, we are, we are.
>
> Daddy he says it's practice, but he mostly pretends it's not,
> I don't think he can be proud of us – he generly says he's not
> It's Nothing Much, you understand, and it doesn't go very far;
> We're an unsatisfactory family, we are, we are, we are.
>
> So here's our second volume, all our numbers nicely bound
> Wishing a Merry Christmas and a happy New Year all round;
> But to say we'll do it another year would be saying too much by far;
> We're a dis-tinctly unpromising family, we are, we are, we are.

The lines come from 'Nothing Much' magazine, a Christmas edition, there appears to be a good deal that was true of the family seen through children's eyes. There

---

[45] Boucher, D. and Smith, T. (eds) 2013. 'R.G. Collingwood: An Autobiography and other Writings.' Oxford: Oxford University Press.

is a suggestion that 'Daddy' (Gershom) did not approve, which would have been a pity we can only hope that at least he saw some humour in the lines.

Gershom's stories in 'Coniston Tales' reflects the variety of subjects to be found in 'Nothing Much'. He begins close to the beginning of recorded history that is where life in Coniston is concerned. The first tale came from a Roman Demetrius in a letter to a friend Ammonius in AD 85. He writes of Ravenglass as a port during Roman times, where three rivers meet and of the pearls to be found there. Demetrius enjoyed the hospitality of 'natives' (Gadeli) but would be especially cheered by the sound of a Greek or Roman Voice. The sight of mountains also cheered him; he called two mountains Skudau and Elbelin and likened them to Vesuvius with craters holding water (something of an exaggeration in volcanic terms, but he was ahead of his time in seeing mountains of central Lakeland as of volcanic origin). Demetrius visited Hardknot Castle or Roman Fort when still under construction and followed the valley of the Esk. Gershom saw, in accounts of this kind, tales from long ago and in another tale, he wrote about St. Cuthbert at Coniston about AD 680. While acknowledging that there is neither history nor legend of the Saint at Coniston, the whole story is a tale of might- have-been. However, there is nothing in the tale that might-*not*-have- been. One person to write of Cuthbert, who lived in the seventh century, was a Benedictine Monk Reginald of Durham, based there during the twelfth century. Gershom wrote of a visit to Coniston by Cuthbert as would be recorded by Reginald. There is sound evidence from writing of Bede that St. Cuthbert did visit Cumbria having been made a Bishop at the wish of King Ecgfrith; while in the north of the region he visited a hermit called Herbert on an island (now St. Herbert's Island on Derwent Water). Next part of the tale, when St. Cuthbert makes his way to Cartmel in the south of the region, visiting Coniston, allows the imagination to run wild because the journey would be extremely difficult at that time. Gershom imagines the Saint taking local shepherds as guides to cross a pass between mountains before reaching a place called Cuninges-tun (Coniston) a town or village below where copper is dug from the bowels of the earth.

## Collingwood Childrens' Development

On most days, the house of Lanehead would be a hive of activity with each member of the family busy with study or some form of creative work, particularly in the mornings. Gershom researching and writing in his study, most painting he did outdoors, and Dorrie painting in the grounds or in a shambles of a conservatory named the Mausoleum, attached to the house (see Figure 18), the children also used this area as a 'studio' painting or working with clay. Dora, Barbara and Ursula became capable painters, Barbara Crystal Collingwood also became a noted sculptor among her work being a fine head of John Ruskin made posthumously for the centenary celebration (1919) of Ruskin's birth, as a young girl she came to know the great man well and made the head from memory and photographs. Another notable sculpting work, completed in collaboration with her father, was to design and produce a relief map of central Lakeland for the 1914-1918 memorial plaque placed on the summit of Great Gable, a mountain in the Lake District. They produced a relief model of mountains and fells of central Lakeland, cast in bronze by B.S. Harlow who became a member of the Fell and Rock Club committee. The plaque is on the summit cairn, viewed by thousands of walkers and climbers since 1924. In her mid-twenties Barbara exhibited three times at the Royal Academy. With sister Dora, she studied art at Copes School in London for two years until 1905 then at University College Reading for three years during the time that father (Gershom) was teaching drawing and painting, before he became Professor of Fine Art. During the 1914-1918 European war (not called the First World War because there had not yet been a second and strictly it was not a world war). Barbara worked in intelligence at the Admiralty, the third Collingwood to do so along with her father and brother Robin George (see Chapter XII).

Barbara married an English aeronautical engineer Oscar Theodor Gnosspelius of a family with Swedish origins. He pioneered the building of sea planes with mixed results and had too an interest in mining deposits found in the Lake District, which has led some writers to describe him as a geologist. Son Robin married twice and had a family of son William and daughter Ruth from his first marriage to Ethel Winifred née Graham and after the marriage was dissolved in 1942, a daughter Teresa from his second marriage to Kathleen Frances née Edwardes.

Ursula, the youngest of the Collingwood children was high spirited and reveled in the outdoor life at Lanehead, sailing and walking the fells mainly with brother Robin to whom she was close. Later in life, she helped him on archaeological digs; a major dig in which Ursula took part with her brother was at the Ambleside Roman Camp in March and April 1914.[46] Ursula became an artist specialising in the painting of flowers and like her mother painted miniatures. Later she taught art at Blackwell, the arts and crafts centre at Bowness-on-Windermere. Ursula returned from her midwifery work in London in 1925, to be with her mother who was ill and with Gershom no longer the fit active father, she needed to look after both parents. The days when Gershom could stride over hills were over; the shortest of walks tired him.

Back in the Lake District, Ursula married the newly appointed vicar of St. Mary's Church Ambleside Reginald Bertram Luard-Selby, a man very well liked

---

[46] Haverfield, Prof. F.J. and R.G. Collingwood. 1914. Report on excavations at Ambleside Roman Camp. Transaction of the Cumberland and Westmorland Antiquarian and Archaeological Society, vol.14, pp. 433-465.

throughout the area. After Dorrie's death in 1928, Gershom was able to visit the vicarage and found great comfort in still having some of the family around him. Soon after Gershom died Ursula and family moved a short distance to the vicarage at Troutbeck, she kept up her artistic work as well as helping her husband serve the parish, while bringing up two children Sara and Philippa (a third child Richard died aged 3.) Ursula died in 1962, aged 71.

**Arthur Ransome at Lanehead**

As pointed out in the Preface, Gershom is known mainly through his association with well-known personalities, one being children's writer, journalist, and alleged spy (but not at the time) Arthur Ransome. This association was based entirely around life in the Lake District, even though at times Ransome spent much of his journalist-life in London when not in Russia, and some time spent in China. Curiously, Arthur Ransome owed far more to Gershom and Dorrie than they did to him. Ransome recognised this in the last few lines of his autobiography when saying how little had been told of how much he owed to William G. Collingwood. For Ransome the Collingwoods provided a home and support that he was not likely to enjoy without them effectively adopting him when a young man. In Ransome's words:

'The whole of the rest of my life has been happier because of them'[47]

On a summer-day in 1903 Gershom was making his way down the rough miner's track to Coniston village after a day spent painting near Coniston Old Man when he saw a body lying on a flat rock in mid-stream. The stream (Church Beck) coming down from Low Water and Lever's Water flowed swiftly and he thought it may be a corpse washed up there. He shouted and the body moved; no conversation was possible above the sound of the rushing water so the 'body' jumped back across to the track. A young man named Arthur Ransome, then only 19 years of age, shook Gershom's hand and this chance meeting proved to be one of enormous good fortune for Ransome; in his autobiography he wrote about the chance meeting with W.G. Collingwood as, '*one of the greatest pieces of good fortune that ever came to me*'. At the time, he was on holiday from working at the Unicorn Press in London.

His journey north began by walking alone through the imposing stone arch of Euston Station in London to board a train to Coniston. Like Gershom, he knew Lakeland well, especially Coniston Water from boyhood and the first thing he did on arrival was to put his hand in Coniston Water as a form of greeting. On visits

---

[47] Ransome, A. 1985. 'Autobiography.' London: Century Publishing Co. Ltd.

to the Coniston area as a boy he was on holiday with his parents, and each time would 'greet' Coniston Water in the same way. The Ransome family stayed at a farm near the foot of the Water. The holiday of 1903, alone in Coniston was to be spent writing poetry and when he discussed this with Gershom on their walk down the valley to Coniston village, the older man gave him encouragement rather than the off-hand dismissive response of many people when Ransome mentioned his writing of poetry. Gershom would not describe himself as a poet even though he had written some fine poems, which eventually appeared in 1885 as a 'A Book of Verses'; he would be thinking of himself at Ransome's age, a student trying to become an artist. Gershom did write poetry for most of his life with examples appearing among his published prose writing, but unlike writing of prose, books of poetry are not normally written for publication; collections of poems are put together into a book from time to time and for Gershom this happened only once. Ransome was attempting to write poetry, not a book of poems. On parting at Coniston village Gershom invited the young man to visit Lanehead, but when Ransome realised that he had been talking to the author of his best-loved book as a boy 'Thorstein of the Mere' he was shy about making the visit until the end of his holiday. Ransome and his brother and sisters had been introduced to the book by their father Professor Ransome. There has been speculation that Professor Cyril Ransome met W.G. Collingwood some years before the chance meeting with his son Arthur. When on holiday near the foot of Coniston Water, the Ransome family lived only a short distance from Lanehead so it is likely that the two men did meet. In his autobiography, Ransome recalls Mrs. Collingwood (Dorrie) telling him how she and Gershom shared a picnic on Peel Island with his parents, in typical innocent Dorrie style she wondered how such a pretty woman (Ransome's mother) could have such ugly children. Ransome was 12 years old at the time, and one of the children. Cyril Ransome died five years before his son's meeting with W.G.C. so it is possible that Arthur Ransome knew nothing about his father knowing W.G.C.

On the last evening of his holiday, Arthur walked from Bank House in Coniston village, around the head of Coniston Water, to Lanehead. A warm welcome greeted him and Gershom said he must make a visit to Lanehead the first thing to do on his next holiday rather than the last. Arthur Ransome at the time was working at a normal routine job in London while struggling to be a poet or writer of some kind. As the years went by Mr. and Mrs. Collingwood virtually adopted Arthur, who called Gershom 'the Skald', Scandinavian for Bard or Minstrel, and Mrs. Collingwood 'Auntie' and in letters would often refer to himself as 'nephew'. Later, in his autobiography, Ransome wrote that *'Mr. and Mrs. Collingwood were touchstones by whom to judge all other people that I met'*. The Collingwood daughters Dora, Barbara and Ursula were all younger than Arthur Ransome and friendships developed to a point where the young man from London almost became a son-in-law of the

Collingwoods, especially with Arthur proposing marriage to Barbara more than once, but she said 'no' each time.

During Ransome's early visits to Lanehead the only son Robin was at a preparatory school, Podmores at Charney Hall, Grange over Sands south of Lanehead. Robin spent a year at Podmores from the age of thirteen. From information in the Lanehead accounts, it appears that Emma Holt of Liverpool paid the fees for Robin to attend the preparatory school (Miss Holt also contributed to the CWAAS Research Fund). Robin then won a scholarship to Rugby School where Ransome had been a pupil for four years. Gershom happily agreed for Ransome to visit his son at Podmores to talk of life at Rugby school despite the experience being a dismal one for young Arthur.

Robin was to repeat that dismal schooling despite becoming head boy; formal school education could not match his experience of learning at home with two wonderful teachers. In his autobiography, Robin wrote that *'going to Oxford was like being let out of prison'*. Robin's view of formal education changed when at Oxford University where he enjoyed brilliant academic tutoring followed by an equally brilliant academic career, though not of the normal kind: Robin, not unlike his father, followed a varied path through life and avoided specialism. Apart from writing and teaching students philosophy and history, he wrote music, played the piano, sang, became an authority in the field of archaeology especially Romano-British, read and contributed to archaeological journals, took part in Yachting, prolific writer of letters and spoke several languages beginning with his parents as teachers. If asked for his chosen (pet) subject a most likely answer would be 'history of thought'.

When thinking about how peoples' activities hang together R.G.C. felt that there is a central core of convictions a 'ring of solid thought' tough and resistant which everything he or she does is attached. The stronger this ring of solid thought the stronger will be their principles and the weaker the ring the chances are that the person will be weak and untrustworthy. From this we have a central core of convictions, the nucleus of our whole life and helps form our philosophy.

People who frequently change their political allegiance prompt the question, do they have any kind of ring of thought? The answer is most likely 'none whatsoever'. Members of the Collingwood family who wrote and writers constantly associated with the family all displayed cores of conviction, but not always in agreement with each other. Arthur Ransome for example supported the Russian revolution in 1917 and Gershom whom he greatly respected did not, they simply agreed to disagree and their respective convictions that led to differences of opinion remained unmoved.

Ransome's experience as a journalist in Russia left him with strong sympathies for the revolution, which he could not share with Gershom but they remained good friends. Gershom was opposed to all forms of revolution and preferred that Ransome read the Great Russian writers, rather than Lenin.

On a visit to Lanehead in June 1919, Ransome wrote to his mother[48] about Mr Collingwood: *'He knew I knew of his violent anti-Bolshevism, and I think he thought I was avoiding discussion. Well, one day he just walked round the table after dinner and collared my right hand secretly with his left one, and said it was very nice to see me again or something like that.....'the words didn't matter. But the whole incident nearly made me weep.'*

Visits to Peel Island by the Collingwood family most surely triggered the idea for Arthur Ransome to write the book 'Swallows and Amazons'. Inspiration for writing about children of the story was said to come largely from Gershom's grandchildren Taqui, Susan, Mavis (Titty) and Roger three daughters and a son of his eldest daughter Dora and her husband Dr Ernest Altounyan. Later, Ransome was to challenge this idea. In his autobiography, Ransome does say that he had in mind a family of imaginary children, but even imagination has to come from somewhere. It is surely more than a coincidence that 'Swallow' was the name of an old fishing boat used by the Collingwood family when Ransome first met Gershom and Dorrie at Lanehead long before writing the book Swallows and Amazons? Ransome did write that Collingwoods boat the 'Swallow was the first of a long dynasty of Swallows in his sailing life'. Something in the writer's character made him deny a connection with the Altounyan family, when clearly it was there for all to see. Since being a young man in his teens, Ransome was very close to Gershom and Dorrie, how he could treat their grandchildren in this way is difficult to understand. In the story of Swallows and Amazons, the Altounyan children of Taqui, Susan, Mavis (Titty) and Roger were the models for the four characters, the Walker family children; a fifth child Brigit Altounyan (born 1926) was too young to be included in the adventures. Ransome changed the eldest sister Taqui for a boy (John) in the story to have two boys and two girls. Gershom's grandchildren referred to Ransome as Uncle Arthur. When Ransome married a second time to a Russian lady who had been secretary to Leon Trotsky, the children knew her as Aunt Genia (real name Evgeniya).

This was the overall picture presented of the Collingwood family at Lanehead and one firmly fixed in my mind and no doubt in the minds of others, especially avid readers of the book Swallows and Amazons. Reality must have been somewhat different for Gershom and Dorrie; there was always a shortage of money, uncertainty about paying bills, and an over-reliance upon a few wealthy friends like Emma Holt and Susie Beever. Early years at Lanehead, when the children were still young, would bring many joyous times despite various concerns; difficulties

---

[48] Brogan, H. (ed.) 1997. 'Signalling from Mars': letters of Arthur Ransome. London: Jonathan Cape.

mounted beyond 1900 after Ruskin's death when Gershom needed another source of income; he continued to write: journal papers, and books 'Lake Counties' and 'Ruskin Relics', he also accepted the role of Editor for Transactions of the Cumberland and Westmorland Antiquarian and Archaeological Society, which meant organising field trips as well as the normal work of editor. Gershom was fully occupied yet income continued to be a problem, leading to him taking a post as lecturer at University College Reading. This was to be his first and only full-time salaried job. Dorrie worked hard at producing works of art to help the family finances such as portraits of Mrs. William Brotherton of Runshaw Hall in 1902, Mrs. Patrick Richardson (Ruskin's Aunt Jessie) in 1917 from an original miniature of 1804, Mrs. A.P. Brydson and Miss Dodie Brydson both of Water Park in 1916. Larger pictures painted by Dorrie varied in subjects chosen: Portraits of Gershom and their son Robin, various children in garden settings, harbour views in Cornwall and Bristol, buildings in the Tyrol and 'Early Morning in Venice'. Increasingly Dorrie was spending long periods in London caring for her aged parents and she shared with Gershom and his sister Ruth the care of his aged father living at number 8 Kings Parade Clifton in Bristol. In the year that Gershom took up his position in Reading, Dorrie accepted a very attractive assignment in Northumberland at Wallington Hall, home of the Trevelyan family. They asked her to complete panels of flower painting in the Great Hall begun in the mid nineteenth century during the time of Sir Walter Calverly Trevelyan. Ruskin was then a regular visitor and was entertained by Trevelyan's first wife Pauline née Jermyn; during these visits Ruskin painted one or two panels of mainly corn and cornflowers, but most of the work was done by Northumberland artist William Bell Scott. Interestingly, Scott was a close friend of artist Dante Gabriel Rossetti, but most certainly not a friend of Ruskin, they had their differences. Mrs. Collingwood of Coniston made the journey north to paint panels of dahlias and sweet peas. From 1905, after being at Wallington Hall, until 1914, Dorrie spent a part of almost every year in Switzerland or Italy for her painting.

For Gershom, Lanehead had to remain their home even when at times other people took over the rental during winter months. The Collingwood family when they could come together, such as Christmas, met in London or Reading. In 1904, Arthur Ransome, still with a base in London, was asked by his 'Aunt' Dorrie to find a place to rent for herself and Gershom. With help from friends he found a two-bedroom flat, with a small balcony, on the fourth floor of Editha Mansions a large red-brick building off the Fulham Road, SW10, a greater contrast to Lanehead is difficult to imagine. Ransome lived in a small flat around the corner so for him the arrival of the senior Collingwoods was like having a bit of Lakeland in West London.

## Lake Artists Society

Gershom showed a keen interest in the work of local artists, from a boy roaming hills and mountains of Lakeland with his father while he painted landscapes until his own adult life spent painting wild places, eventually led him, in 1904, to propose the formation of the 'Lake Artists Society'. He was one of 21 founder members and agreed to become, temporarily, the Hon. Secretary. At the time of establishing the society, Gershom was reluctant to commit himself to any position of responsibility it was also a time of uncertainty for the family with arrangements being made for living in or near London. In 1932, only three weeks before his death Gershom's daughter Barbara, then Mrs. Gnosspelius, was elected unanimously as President of the Society, following the death of recently elected President Colin Phillip. Most members were active hill walkers, climbers or even mountaineers; all loved high remote places and were prepared to reach difficult viewpoints to get portraits of mountains not normally painted at that time, previously mountains provided only a backdrop to figures in the foreground. Most society members at that time were, like Gershom, professional in their approach to art in that they needed to sell their work.

For such a mild-mannered man as Gershom it is surprising that he entered into argument with anyone, he had a horror of controversy, but during the early years of a society designed to help and encourage artists living in the English Lake District he did have an unfortunate disagreement with a local artist. Alfred Heaton-Cooper (1863-1929) and William Gershom Collingwood became known as 'Coniston Gamecocks'. Heaton-Cooper was born when both his parents worked in cotton mills of Bolton. Through his artistic gifts, hard work and sacrifices from his parents Alfred studied at The Westminster School of Art on a scholarship, instead of taking the expected route into the mills. After art training, Alfred travelled in Europe and settled for a while in Norway where he married Mathilde née Valentinssen. Both left Norway to live in the English Lake District at Coniston where Alfred began to establish himself as an artist, mainly of Lakeland village life and mountain landscapes. He opened a studio in the village. At the time, Gershom was helping to form the Lake Artists Society.

(Jane Renouf wrote a history of the society, published in 2004, to mark the hundredth anniversary).[49]

The young Alfred Heaton-Cooper would have been an ideal candidate to join the small group of founder members, instead he complained about an exhibition to be held by the Society at Coniston in 1905, seeing it as a threat to his recently established business.

---

[49] Renouf, J. 2004. 'The Lake Artist Society.' Ambleside: Lake Artist Society.

After an exchange of letters between Alfred and Gershom, who was writing on behalf of the Society, Gershom wrote an article in 'The Sphere' a weekly illustrated newspaper. In the article, he criticised Heaton- Cooper, describing his attitude as monopolistic, this action brought the subject to the notice of the national press, which while annoying Alfred would have mortified Gershom. He tried to smooth the troubled waters by writing to Alfred. In the letter (from the Heaton-Cooper archives), he wrote, *I don't like the suggestion that you and I are to be considered as Coniston gamecocks, made to fight for the amusement of trippers. For my part, I don't admit the insinuation that I am fighting you, even to the extent of competing by exhibition. Holding some sort of show was always the plan of the Institute, and we held many before you came here. Next year we propose an arts and crafts exhibition; this thing will carry on longer than you or I* (this proved correct) *it is no antagonism to your studio but really an additional interest to the visitor, who in this way hears of Coniston as an art-centre and comes here prepared to see pictures. The Lake Artists Society is a very old idea and seems to have caught on. Several of the members have their own shows, like you, but still don't take up a position of antagonism.'* Gershom ended the letter by suggesting that Alfred join the Society, but he never did and the artist not only refused to join the society but initially declined an invitation to submit work to their annual exhibition, although later, in 1913, he did exhibit. After Gershom sent the letter quoted above it appears that no more was heard about this disagreement; Alfred returned to Norway to live there with his young family before coming back to the Lake District to settle permanently. Arthur's son William a highly successful artist of landscape based at Grasmere, born 1903 in Coniston, joined the Society in 1936 and eventually became President. Some years earlier, from the minutes of the Lake Artists Annual General Meeting in 1922, they elected William to the society but he repudiated this election; he joined the society only after his father Alfred died.

# Chapter IX
# Researching the Past
# (1884-1932)

## Northernness

When Gershom began his study of pre-Norman England his interest at first focused upon Lakeland, then slowly extended to Yorkshire, Northumberland and South-West Scotland; at no time did his attention move south of the Wirral. Curiously, he ignored a large area, The Forest of Bowland that featured strongly in the history of pre- Norman North-West. Gershom was not alone among antiquarians in overlooking this area, which for some reason is largely ignored by writers of northern history. In choosing to concentrate upon other parts of the northern England and part of Scotland, Gershom was unintentionally tapping into a current interest, almost obsession, of some people in Victorian England wishing to know more about northernness.

Northerners, a group of people that could be characterised by that term, possibly first came to prominence at the time of King John (early 13th century) when barons and their supporters from the north plotted against him. From that time onwards each 'half' of the country, north and south with the River Trent as a borderline, is inclined to look upon the other half as almost a foreign country. At the beginning of the nineteenth century this north-south antitheses was increased by the growth of industrialisation; more in one-half than the other half. The port of Liverpool and the city of Manchester in particular became a focus for increasing commerce and production springing from the introduction of machinery. Increasingly, emphasis was upon business and production throughout the north and this continued throughout the nineteenth and well into the twentieth century. The geographical divide of north and south had an anomaly: South Wales with its ports, coal mining and heavy industry had more in common with the North-East of England than with any other area of the country so 'belonged' to the south of the country only in a geographical sense.

Gershom was only one year old when the book 'North- South' by Mrs. Gaskell was published (1855). The book emphasised a difference between people indigenous to an area north of the river Trent and those to the south. The difference was stated as between state-of-mind and style of life. So entrenched did these difference become in the mind of most Victorians that for those living in the south it became easy to stereotype people living in the north to the extent of seeing them as belonging to a separate country and, possibly to a lesser extent, people of the north viewed the south in a similar way. There is no record of Gershom entering into this debate, he did not attempt to compare his own adopted north with the south (he had ample experience of living in both 'halves' of the country) his only concern was in understanding the elements that went into someone becoming a Northerner. Gershom grew up with a clear distinction between so-called Manchester men and Liverpool gentlemen, as described in Chapter II. Mrs. Gaskell recognised a dichotomy between north and south in England, but did not see it existing between cities so close together as Liverpool and Manchester, or even within one county (Lancashire). Gaskell identified typical characteristics of people in the north and south: among the characteristics of northern people, she saw them as independent, practical and rough; people in the south she saw as idealistic, benevolent and romantic.

Over the years if only two words were used to describe stereotypically the divide it would be that North is hard and South is soft; some people attributed the perceived hardiness of the north to people having Norse, or Viking, ancestry.

Gershom did not set out to find support, or to refute, claims of north-south differences. Characteristics of different peoples: Celtic, Roman, Anglo-Saxon and Norse simply emerged during the course of his work. He looked for continuities between different stages and how in the north, societies developed. Tracing ancestry of Northerners can be fascinating and W.G.C. made an enormous contribution to our understanding of the subject.

**Pre-Norman Interest**

From around 1885 when Gershom had been settled in the Lake District for two years he was developing a strong interest in the history of Lakeland, beginning at the close of Roman occupation to the beginning of the Norman period (fifth to eleventh centuries). This was a large, complex subject and Gershom may well have questioned the depth of his historical knowledge about the area, based at that time only upon interest and enthusiasm gathered as a boy during visits to the Lake District rather than on previous scholarship. On the other hand, he was well equipped in his analytical ability practised at Oxford and nurtured later by John Ruskin, a master of analysis and synthesis The main problem was where to begin a study of this kind. This was partly resolved in 1887 by Gershom joining a local society dedicated to the study of Lakeland's past: 'The Cumberland and Westmorland Antiquarian and Archaeological Society' (CWAAS), he was joining the society as someone who, at that only dabbled in local history. As a member of the CWAAS, he found an intellectual home for the remainder of his life. The society, which had been in existence for 21 years, held meetings of members, organised working parties, and published transactions yearly (TCWAAS). The transactions reported actions of the society: excursions and published papers read at meetings in various parts of Northern England. The transactions are published under three series beginning with the Old Series (CW1) from 1870 to 1900; second series (CW2) from 1901 to 2000. Gershom contributed to the first and second series, which have been followed by a third series (CW3) from 2001; now (2017) the transactions are still published yearly. The published work of the society provides a 'gold mine' for anyone interested in the history of the area now known as Cumbria; few peopled places in the world can have such a rich scholarly record of the past. (Curiously, Gershom proposed Mr. and Mrs. Arthur Severn as members of the Society in 1889 and even more curiously, they were elected. Mrs. Severn took a close interest in the work Gershom did for the Society but there is no record of her being actively involved, and the same applied to her husband Arthur.)

Gershom was to become a leading figure in this society, elected Editor of The Transactions in 1900 and President of the Society in 1920 (son Robin George succeeded him in both roles). There was for Gershom the question of funding future research, in particular travel to sites, need for accommodation during some visits and time spent writing papers. Active members of the Society (usually antiquaries) were often churchmen (Rev.) attached to a church and though stipends were small, their income was regular and assured; other members were often of independent means or professional men and women, none of these categories applied to Gershom. Cash books, kept in the archives at Abbot Hall (AH), show small amounts of money earned and spent; under receipts he included: paid written work (one guinea per thousand words was a typical amount), book royalties and sale of artwork. Often the cost of travelling to sites, accommodation and time spent writing was financed by Gershom, leaving the family frequently short of funds. He did wonder at one time whether there was anyone who was so busy for such a trifling return in cash (he may have cited coal miners or mill workers). He was referring to being busy with editing, writing papers, attending sites and meetings, painting and answering correspondence from people asking for guidance or help.

Whenever Gershom wrote of the North West in early days of his research, he was referring to the area of Cumberland, Westmorland and Lancashire North-of-the- Sands. In contrast, the area he referred to as 'Lake District', was defined precisely by Gershom as being totally within a circle of 15 miles radius (24 km), taking Easdale Tarn as the centre point; he called this the 'charmed circle' to include all lakes (Meres, Waters and a Lake) and all mountains and major fells. Lakeland was taken to mean from Carlisle in the north to Furness in the south and from the west coastline to Shap Fells on the east.

Before joining the CWAAS, Gershom published a paper with the Cumberland and Westmorland Association for the Advancement of Literature and Science (CWAALS) about the 'Lake Basins of the Neighbourhood of Windermere' (1885) encouraged by well-received geological writing in his book 'Limestone Alps of Savoy', published the previous year. He accepted editorship of the Transactions, published by the society, and in this role WGC completed what he described as several pilgrimages to several parts of the Lake District. As his research developed, the methodology relied a good deal upon interpretation of place-names and his interest became firmly rooted in historical time rather than in pre-history. Stone circles left in the Lake District by people of ages BC were only of passing interest, confined to the question of how local residents lived before the arrival of Romans and to what extent they accepted or rejected Roman occupation. There was an important exception when Gershom did show curiosity and became actively involved in looking for possible pre-history remains, which led him to excavate a stone circle near his home. In 1909, while working as an academic at University College, Reading he spent time on Banniside Moor below Coniston Old Man;[50] for years, people had seen a substantial stone circle on the moor and much speculation was made about its possible origin. There was limited information available to people who simply walked around and stared, so Gershom decided to organise a dig. From his description of the exercise it appears that they would have benefited from the assistance of a qualified archaeologist; some items found were damaged by the wielding of a pickaxe. During these early days, Gershom in his enthusiasm for a subject could have a rather flippant approach to the need for skills of excavation, inclined to dive in to see what he could find. He never did fully master the painstaking processes of archaeology digs, concentrating instead upon artifacts found above ground level. On this occasion, Gershom used plasticine to help repair the damaged remains. At the Banniside site they found clear evidence of interment, from charcoal and bone ash as well as two urns, one large 12.25 inches high (31 cm), the other medium 8 inches high (20 cm) and one small cup, also one bead and a small flint scraper. The conclusion was that a Bronze Age cemetery had been uncovered, Gershom estimated to be from 2000 to 1600 BC He asked a colleague at University College, Professor Austin, to examine the bone remains and he found them to be of a child 3 to 4 years old.

Other excavations around Lakeland and the north were at Roman or Romano-British sites: Ambleside camp, Harknot Castle and Ewe Close. In July 1907, Gershom spent three days at a Romano-British settlement near Crosby Ravensworth in Yorkshire (Ewe Close), helped by his son Robin George and various other assistants. Robin cycled to Ravensworth to join his father at the Sun Inn, and they walked across the moor to the site at Ewe Close. The site lay beside a grassy causeway

---

[50] Collingwood, W.G. 1910. An exploration of the circle on Banniside Moor, Coniston. Transactions of the Cumberland and Westmorland Antiquarian and Archaeological Society. pp. 342-353.

passing over the moor, a Roman road known as the Maiden Way (The site was the likely home of Urien, famous King of Rheged in the sixth century). The road by that time was obvious only in places but could be seen where it passed near Ewe Close. The site consisted of hut circles within an overall area 1000 feet long (305 metres) north to south; 800 feet broad (244 metres) east to west. The ruins were most conspicuous in the northern section so an area of 350 square feet (33 m$^2$) was chosen for investigation. Cost to the Society was £4.3 shillings, including 10 shillings compensation for disturbance of soil. Dykes across the site caused an immediate problem, why are dykes crossing the road when the site was thought to be entirely of the Roman 'episode' or possibly before. The road was blocked for some reason by the dykes. Gershom drew upon his experience in Iceland to suggest that two places in that country have homes built across a public road to force travelers to stay and accept hospitality, but this was dismissed as a possible explanation for this site in Yorkshire. After further investigation, it was found that dykes obstructing the road were of different construction to those associated only with the settlement. Roman roads in the country were used for many years after the soldiers left, so it was no surprise to learn that the obstructing dykes were much later, of the mediaeval period.

Buildings on the site were round, unlike the typically square constructions at Roman settlements as at the sites of Ambleside and Hardknot. There were features recognisable as Roman, Gershom assumed to be copied from them. There was evidence of floors being flagged and Gershom made a detailed drawing of flagstones in place. No museum pieces could be found, only odd bits of Roman pottery. The main achievement of the excavation was the production of a site plan for use by those who wish to explore the site further. Gershom's main comment about the Ewe Close site was that we can know something of the life of the Britons, how they lived in more remote places rather than in Roman towns and that some of their settlements outlasted the Roman rule. The British continued their pastoral way of life when Romans arrived and when they left and sites like Ewe Close would still be occupied when the Angles arrived. Round stone houses had been found, as against mud-built cottages of a later period. *'Even at their poorest the Britons appear to have been somewhat superior in means of life to the Anglo- Saxon first-comers; and though they had been brought low by invasion and continual attacks of barbarians, they retained some of the culture they had learnt from the Romans'.*

## Gifted Amateur

Gershom's study of Northern Stone Crosses between 1898 and 1930 was described by Janet Gnosspelius, a granddaughter, as a less well-known part of his life. This may be true of people in some parts of Britain but not for historians, antiquaries, archaeologists and other people interested in the history of England's Northern Counties (the work done by W.G.C. in analysing early stone crosses continues to the present day). Also, when studying carved stone whether in the form of crosses, monoliths or hogbacks Gershom achieved some of his most impressive results to the extent of becoming an 'authority' on the subject in Northern England. Now 85 years since his death Gershom's work on carve stonework is still valued highly.

Among his many interests, Gershom being described as an antiquary is based entirely upon research and writing of papers on the subject of antiquities. Equally he can be described as an archaeologist but in this respect as a gifted amateur; there were times on the occasional dig, described earlier in this chapter, that he would have benefitted from having a trained archaeologist in the group, especially at Bannisdale Moor.

Two projects in the same year (1901) illustrate well his active interest as an antiquary and amateur archaeologist; one at Gosforth church in Lakeland and the other on Stainmoor in Yorkshire. Early in that year, the committee of the (CWAAS) received a request for help in excavating the site of an old church in Gosforth, a church that was believed to exist before the nearby Norman church then in use. Gershom, who had recently been appointed Editor of the society's transactions, would often follow up requests of this kind to assess the feasibility of working a site, and decide whether the society

should offer their support. Gershom ensured that work could begin and that labour for a dig would be available. The work began in March when a man and a boy were found to make the first digging (one of Gershom's tasks was to find low-cost ways of completing work for the Society). They dug into an identified mound and soon came upon ruins of a building, a snowstorm halted any further work but Gershom kept a close eye on weather conditions and made frequent visits to the site from his home at Lanehead near Coniston. The weather improved and when further work had been done it became clear to him that the church had been destroyed down to its foundations; fragments of stone could be found lying around at some distance from the church. Finally, a rectangular shape was revealed with walls 2 feet 6 inches thick (76 cm) enclosing an area 33 feet by 18 feet (10 metres by 5 metres) with a door in the middle of a long wall on the south side. The building had been constructed around a well of clear water, called a holy well and this find identified the building as a 'well-chapel'. In June, Gershom read a paper in the city of Durham describing the excavation at Gosforth and in the following year this appeared as an article in the Transactions of the society.[51]

---

[51] =Collingwood, W.G. 1902. Report on excavations at the Holy Well, Gosforth. Transactions of the Cumberland and Westmorland Antiquarian and Archaeological Society. pp. 77-83.

The second project in the summer of 1901 involved no excavation but a re-examination of a possible battle site on the wild moors of Stainmoor. Gershom described initial reports of battle as being in legend and history, but from his reasoning it appeared to be more legend than history. Initially, a date of the battle was given as middle of the fifth century, a time when Angles were beginning to settle in Northumbria and were busy fighting Britons. Outline of the claimed battle in the mid- fifth century is:

*An Angle, Prince Hatheolf who lived in the Yorkshire North Riding faced three Danish Kings from Ireland; two had Gaelic names and one apparently Teutonic, both sides lost a total of 60,000 men and Hatheolf died too.* W.G.C. could find no corroboration of any invading kings from Ireland at that time, not even a century later. Nothing of the kind appeared possible until the Viking Age in the ninth or tenth century. In Gershom's words, '*this tale of Hatheolf has been referred to the fifth century, which is impossible; it is a travesty of tenth century events, and, I suggest, of this invasion by Eric and his fall at Stainmoor*' A historian of the twelfth and thirteenth centuries Roger of Wendover collected information about King Eilric, slain together with his son Henry and brother Reginald in a lonely place *Steinmoor*. Eilric is known to other chroniclers as Eric of York. Gershom reasoned that a battle did take place on Stainmoor but in the tenth century rather than the fifth.

Since earliest movement of people in pre-history Stainmoor provided a convenient pass across the North Pennine moors from the east coast to west or later for various Kings and their men, travelling west to east from Ireland to York. The existence of a stone monument on the site helped him arrive at a possible scenario for the battle, Gershom draws attention to the famous Rey Cross, a pillar of stone set upon a crumbling base and placed on the moor around AD 968 (the cross is now close to a road over Stainmoor). The Rey Cross has always puzzled antiquaries, but as shown in Rev. Calverley's work (edited by W.G.C. pp. 264-268) the cross is one of a series of grave-monuments of the tenth or eleventh centuries. The name 'Rey' had been taken to mark a boundary, possibly from the Scandinavian Rá (as in rá-merki, land-mark) but boundary crosses were all post-Norman Conquest, so it possibly marked a grave. Gershom viewed the stone monument as a pre-Norman grave-cross. If burial of a prominent person could not be in a graveyard a cross of this kind would be erected by admirers to commemorate a Christian burial and not Pagan; most of the invaders to the east of the country around AD 945 were Pagan. If, as we have seen there was a battle here, in or about 954, it is quite possible that such a cross was erected over one of the great men. One who died and buried on the spot. It would commemorate a Christian, not a pagan. Eric Bloodaxe, indeed, was baptized, and nominally Christian.

Gershom speculated that the Rey stone cross marks the grave of Eric Bloodaxe (nick-name for Eirik Haraldsson a Christian), and was set up by admirers of the man who was long-famous as the last King of York; after his death the habitation of York, as for Northumbria, became part of the English Kingdom. Gershom presented his speculation in a paper read at Kirkby Stephen, late August 1901 and published the following year in the Transactions (TCWAAS). Much of Gershom's reasoning about the last King of York was based upon work he had done earlier and presented to the Viking Club in their Saga Book II (1897-1900). The Heims-kringla and English Chroniclers have the same account of Eirík's death, the last king of York. 'Egils saga' (1160-1200) was written at or near Egil's home at Borg in Iceland and included details of Eirík Blódöx. He was driven from Norway by his brother and went to Orkney and finally to England where he met Æthelstan, a good friend of his father, who eventually gave him government of Northumberland, on the understanding that he should become Christian and protect the country from Danes and other Vikings. Symeon of Durham, writing around 1100, dated Eirík in Northumberland as AD 948. Eirík Blódöx (Erik Bloodaxe) died in battle. According to W.G.C., *the fight at Stainmoor was one of the decisive battles of English history 'for it ended the Kingdom of Northumbria and made England one realm'.*

The Scandinavian settlement at Furness (Lancashire North-of-the-Sands) has long been accepted as a working theory on the strength of place-names and personal names dating back to the Domesday Book, but it was the early part of the twentieth century before relics of the Viking age were found. In 1902, attention was drawn to the Pennington tympanum with its twelfth century Scandinavian runes; early in the year the Rampside sword was discovered, and then the Urswick cross, with ornament of Anglo-Scandinavian type, the first pre-Norman stone found in Lancashire North-of-the-Sands.

We owe the find to certain alterations carried out in the church by the Rev. T. N. Postlethwaite, vicar of Urswick. In piercing the north chancel wall to make a recess for an organ they uncovered a carved stone, which had been used as a through-stone. After removal and through Rev. Postlethwaite's kindness it was sent to Gershom for examination and for exhibition by the Society. It was a fragment of rather soft red freestone, measuring 14.5 inches x 11.25 inches x 3.5 inches (37 cm x 29 cm x 9 cm) representing the upper part of the shaft and neck of a wheel-headed cross. Though the stone had been split, so that one side and one edge are lost, enough remained to give clues for the reconstruction of nearly the whole cross. Part of the circumference of one of the four holes, and the spring of the wheel, could be seen, giving the approximate shape and size of the head.

Reconstructing crosses from broken parts became a specialty of Gershom's work. Done mainly through his skill at drawing by showing reconstructed sections in dotted outline, not a new technique but one he used to the full and showed how far it could be extended to a wide range of stone carving (an example of this reconstruction can be seen in Figures 26 and 36).

Although Gershom did not train formally as an archaeologist he became one of the most respected practitioners in the North of England, from south-west Scotland and Hadrian's Wall to East and West Ridings of Yorkshire, and of course his beloved Cumberland, Westmorland and Lancashire North-of-the-Sands. Typical of how well-known he had become occurred when a workman uncovered a carved stone at Urswick church near Dalton-in-Furness, some miles from Gershom's home, and wanted Mr Collingwood to see the stone in its first-discovered state. Gershom took his son Robin to the church and later described his son's presence as valuable. The experience was one of many for young Robin with his father, gradually increasing his knowledge of archaeology. The carved stone was in place as a lintel above a window. The workman decided the stone was of no importance to the structure so it was taken down in the presence of the Collingwoods, the Vicar, Churchwarden, clerk and other interested people. They kindly allowed Gershom and his son to take the stone home where it could be cleaned and carefully analysed. Gershom was able to compare the carving with Anglian crosses and found it to be of late Anglian period; there was no Scandinavian ornament of any kind on the stone, which helped to place the date as pre-Viking.

Putting a date on remains or stone crosses was a preoccupation over many years for Gershom, dating anything precisely became an almost impossible task but Gershom and his colleagues could not be expected to appreciate that at the time. Many years later, Rosemary Cramp in a paper 'The Anglian Tradition in the Ninth Century (1978),[52] writing about Anglian tradition in the ninth century made a clear statement: 'There is no absolute chronological framework for this sculpture.' Also in this paper, Cramp made a strong case for a link between ornamentation on stone crosses and  ornamentation found in manuscripts. WGC seemed to deny that there was any relationship between carved stonework from a mason and the art of the scriptorium, or simply chose to concentrate upon stonework; his chronology of stonework begins with the earliest known stone crosses and considers only stone crosses.

'Collingwood made up his mind that other monastic arts were not relevant, the primacy of architectural sculpture in relation to crosses was not considered'. In addition, he seemed to overlook the point that the Priesthood was the main supporter of art at this time. Up to the ninth century there is no evidence of carving unconnected with religious institutions. Cramp did acknowledge that the history of Anglo-Saxon sculpture before the eleventh century is very largely a history of stone crosses.

---

[52] Cramp, R. 1978. The Anglian tradition in the ninth century, in Lang, J. Anglo-Saxon and Viking Age Sculpture and its context, 800-1066. British Archaeological Report, 49.

W.G.C. in attempting to work out a chronology slowly came to realise that he could only hope to identify phases, normally of a quarter of a century and sometimes from mid-point of one century to mid-point of the next century. Curiously, mid-century dates seemed to be the most significant during Gershom's period of study: English settlement around mid-fifth century; Acceptance (full?) of Christianity around mid-seventh century; Scandinavian settlement around mid-ninth century and beginning of the Norman period, mid-eleventh century.

**Roman Lakeland**

Debate will continue about the extent of Roman influence in North-West England, especially the area now known as Cumbria. Gershom was possibly the first antiquary and still one of few writers to claim that their influence was minimal. Celtic, Anglo-Saxon and Norse settlements can be traced with differing results throughout the area, Roman habitation shows itself only through a few roads (doubtful as of Roman origin, some thought to be Celtic and pre-historic), and remains of a few camps with only one placed centrally in the area. Research by members of the CWAAS provided evidence of Romans using Windermere as a means of taking stone by boat from Dalton-in-Furness to build a camp at the north end of the mere; though R.G. Collingwood when exploring the camp wrote in 1914 that the stone used was local, quarried into blocks.

Gershom stressed that years spent by Romans in the north west of the country could be described as army occupation rather than colonisation. Gershom described the Roman occupation of Lakeland as an 'episode' even though it lasted almost 400 years (from the time of Oliver Cromwell to the present day). Robin George Collingwood seemed to be following his father's lead when commenting about Roman influence in Cumberland when he wrote, '*we are almost at vanishing point in the scale of Romanisation.*' A further comment from Gershom was that 'during the centuries of Roman rule, the people of our district, if they learned little, certainly did not forget much. Gershom claimed that the main legacy left by the Romans (after Constantine AD 337) was the adoption of Christianity as a prevailing religion.

Gershom involved his son Robin in excavation work done at the only Roman base built in central Lakeland, Hardknot Castle, and from this early experience Robin George applied his considerable intellect to the study of Roman occupation to become a national authority on the subject. In 1938, Alfred Wainwright who became a well-known Lake-District guidebook writer was walking the Roman Wall in Northumberland and wrote, '*I settled down to read an abridged copy of Collingwood's [R.G.] Guide to the Wall, which I had bought at Housesteads. I have already said that I found this guide fascinating when I read it before leaving home, but now that I have seen the wall and become familiar with the places mentioned I found my enthusiasm for the book rising to fever pitch. I read it again and again, completely enslaved by the racy narrative and the really splendid manner in which the writer had managed to convey the atmosphere of the wall.*[53]

A review of R.G.Cs guide to the Hadrian's Wall in the Northern quarterly journal 'The Vasculum' (1926) was full of praise:

The merit of this little guide is that, for the increasing numbers of people who in this era of the motor-car, are visiting the Wall without much of an idea of what it is that they are going to see, there is now available, for the small sum of sixpence, a most excellent handbook comprising all the information they require, and this by one of the greatest authorities on the Wall.

It is reasonable to assume that R.G.C's ability to describe life of long-ago so clearly came in part at an early age from contact with his father's work, and in particular his elegant prose writing when re-creating life of the Norse in Lakeland. During his adult years, R.G.C. wrote numerous papers about the Roman occupation of England.

## Anglo-Saxons, Background

Raids by Anglo-Saxons began before the Romans withdrew from England but were confined to areas of the southeast coast and then not extensive. After AD 420 immigration increased and people (Anglo, Saxon and Jute) spread across the country, but not to Wales or Scotland. Not long after the Roman military occupation the north of England was largely inhabited by Anglo-Saxons who were from Germanic tribes that settled as immigrants around the fifth century, initially to the east of the country then steadily west, south and north. There is little documentary evidence of invading tribes before the fifth century when this form of immigration began; Ptolemy and Tacitus both give details in their writing of Angles living in the Jutland area. There is too, some difficulty in tracing any one tribe because they moved around, joining others to become a complex mix of ethnic groups.

Another scholar, who wrote in the sixth century, was Procopius who recognised Frisians and Angles; adding to the confusion. Much confusion existed in tracing the development of peoples who emigrated west to explore the island off the European mainland (Britain). Bede had recognised the Jutes as being among immigrants of the fifth century but Gershom largely ignored them because they occupied land in the south of the island from Kent across to Hampshire. Settlers in this area were effectively from southern Scandinavia.

---

[53] Wainwright, A. 1938. 'A Pennine Journey': a story of a long walk in 1938. London: Michael Joseph.

Key questions about the settlement of these people are, peaceful or hostile, how did they relate to native Britons or Romano-Britons, what form of religion did they follow or were they Pagan? What relics remain as evidence of their settlement? antiquaries asked these and other questions, Gershom among them. Gershom argued that Angles and Saxons did not arrive to inhabit a largely empty land (supported by later evidence) the population left behind after the retreat of the Romans was larger than originally thought. The number of invaders from the east was larger too, in the thousands rather than hundreds in both cases. The initial occupation by the Saxons was brutal and savage with many local people killed. Those that did escape went to Wales or even to Britany.

**Researching Anglo-Saxon**

There has been much speculation about the possible reasons for migration of people from east to west, landing on the shores of England between the fifth and eighth centuries, but Gershom was not concerned with this almost impossible task (speculation about motives, for any activity, are best left alone). He researched only the evidence found in the north of England; the main aim being to learn more about the ancestors of people living there.

From rather scanty bits of knowledge from historical sources, Gershom pieced together a description of life in Northern England during years following Roman occupation. After the Romans departed from the north in the mid-fifth century, the remaining local people faced fearsome raids from Picts and Scots based further north. The devastation was so great that it would not have been surprising if Britons and Romano-Britons ceased to exist. Gershom pointed out that it is not easy to exterminate a whole population. However, their existence was precarious in the extreme and their daily lives became even more frugal. This was the scene south of what became Scottish Border country when groups of Angles and Saxons arrived.

Venerable Bede described what he knew of the period between the fifth and early eighth century. Writing in 'Ecclesiastical History' around 730 he recognised Angles, Saxons and Jutes: Saxons came from Old Saxony the western part of north Germany, Jutes from Jutland and Angles from what we know as Schleswig-Holstein. The Anglo-Saxon Chronicle provided further description but based partly upon Bede's writing. Bede in saying that Angles came from Slesvig (Danish name for Schleswig- Holstein) was later supported when it was found that remains from burial sites in that area corresponded with remains found in Anglian burial sites in England.[54]

---

[54] Collingwood, W.G. 1923. The first English in Northumberland. The Vasculum, vol. 9, pp. 34-39.

Gershom, searching for knowledge about this period, recognised St. Cuthbert as a key figure and chronicler of this time. Bede described Cuthbert's visit to Carlisle in AD 685 the Angles had colonised the area and he found an abbey and nunnery already in place. Place-name study, in which Gershom specialised, reveals that Angles occupied areas immediately south of Carlisle and that initially they came north from settlements near the River Humber. From Gershom's place-name study it appears the Lake District, defined by him as the central mountainous area, was never the home of Angles. The first full occupation of Central Lake District seemed open to dispute but Gershom maintained that Irish-Norse settlers occupied this area in the tenth century and on the available evidence he maintained that this is as certain as a proposition in Euclid. He contradicted a commonly-held belief that the Norse came in long-boats from Norway to reach England's east coast, then moved westward. Gershom gave compelling evidence that Norse settlers were really Irish-Norse, coming from the Isle of Man and in some cases from Ireland to land on England's west coast between the Solway Firth and further south at the Wirral around mid-ninth century at the time of Olaf the White, recorded in the 'Ulster Annals' (AD 431 to 1540). It can be misleading to associate migration from the Isle of Man as necessarily Norse. In 913, Danes under Ragnall (Ragnwald) attacked the island after a naval battle and ruled until his death in 921. The movement of people from Man to the mainland is better thought of as Scandinavian rather than more specifically Norse or Danish.

Most place-names in the Lake District are Old Norse in origin; exceptions being the mountain of Blencathra and the place of Penruddock, demonstrating a survival of naming by the Britons; rivers also had been named and indeed deified by the Britons. While place-name research played a major role in Gershom's work at this time, he turned to evidence from artifacts normally found in burial sites and from what could be seen on carved stone. Carved stonework became a major focus of research, especially after his exhaustive editing of Rev.William Slater Calverley's papers in the late 1890s.

**Artifacts**

When Gershom began to develop an interest in the years leading up to arrival of the Normans very few artifacts from those years had been discovered in Northern England. There were only three places: Ormside (originally Ormshed, the settlement of Orm the Dane) churchyard in 1689, Beacon Hill burial site at Aspatria in the late eighteenth century and Hesket-in-the-Forest in 1822.

The Ormside find was behind the church in the Eden Valley; on the south side next to the hall. They found several vessels of brass (normally referred to by archaeologists as copper alloy) some of which seemed to have been gilt:

Thurribulum or censer (container for burning incense). This censer has three holes at the sides evidently to put ye cords through. It was in height 3 inches (7.6 cm) in diameter alone 5 inches (13 cm). It was of brass, guilded.

A ewer of brass, 7 inches high (18 cm), 3 inches wide (7.6 cm) at ye mouth, 13 inches circumference (33 cm) at ye widest part.

A brazen morter.

A pewter basin, 3 inches (7.6 cm) deep, 8 inches diameter.

A pewter flower pot, 6 inches (15 cm) high. Circumference at belly 10 inches (25 cm).

A cullender of pewter, a case of brazen weights, and two brazen candlesticks of different sizes, two pewter candlesticks, large and small; two pewter flaggons, a lesser and a greater; several plates of pewter and a small lead for boiling meat.

Richard Ferguson, President of CWAAS, wrote, 'no further information as to the circumstances of this find could be found, which is of a miscellaneous nature; including both ecclesiastical and domestic utensils'.

The most impressive find at the Ormside site was the 'Ormside Cup'. In the summer of 1898, W.S. Calverley was unable, through ill health, to complete and deliver a paper about the cup. To avoid disappointing members of the CWAAS, the Editor, Chancellor Richard Ferguson, asked Gershom to make a series of drawings of the Ormside cup kept in the Museum of York, and to provide additional notes. The result was detailed drawings (Figure 24) and well-reasoned notes.

This work Gershom described to Dorrie in a letter home.[55] Apart from adding to the small number of artifacts, the importance of the cup is in the design, which Gershom interpreted as planned overall by an Anglian. By 1906, Gershom had time to consider carefully the finds at Ormside and described the cup in a paper published in Saga-Book Five[56] He described the 'cup' as a fine monument to the Anglian age, though not in stone: '*it is a silver-gilt bowl, beautifully ornamented with repoussé work and filigree and set with jewels. It must have been made at a time somewhat before the Danish invasion.*'

The so-called cup (more like a bowl) was found at Ormside, not necessarily from that area but a sword and other pieces of metalwork were also found there.

Gershom said that the cup was remarkable for the combination in one design of inter-lacing work, apparently Anglian, with exquisite floral design, animals and birds, most delicately wrought in the spirit and with the finish of the finest Greek-Italian craftsmanship. Gershom added that it is impossible to study the Bewcastle cross (discussed later) without seeing that it is the transcript in stone of the art of

---

[55] Letter, 1898.W.G.Collingwood to Dorrie Collingwood. Collingwood Archive, Abbot Hall, Kendal.
[56] Collingwood, W.G. 1906. Some illustrations of the archaeology of the Viking Age in England. Saga-Book 5 of the Viking Club, pp. 111-141.

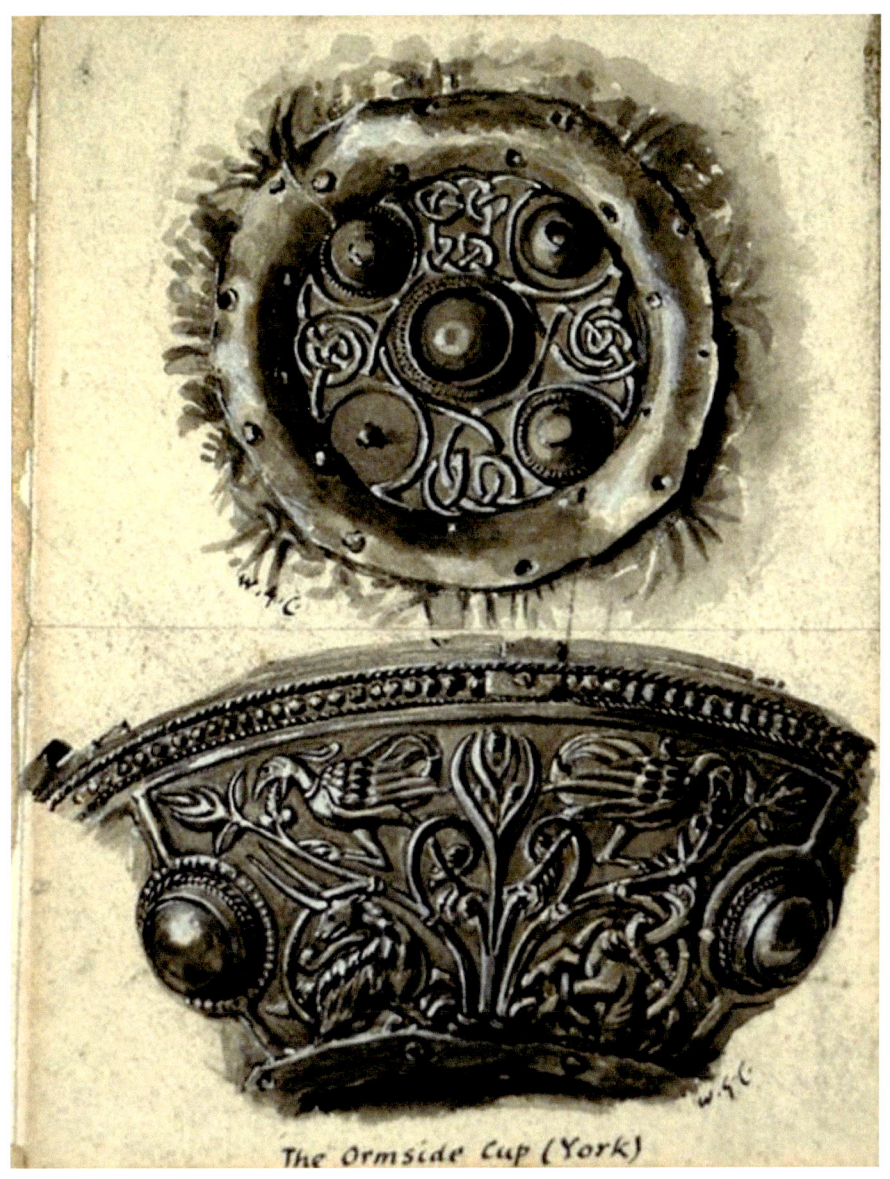

Figure 24 Ormside Cup 1906, Viking Club Saga Book 5.

this cup. Neither of them can be assigned to any age but the age of Wilfrith (seventh and eight centuries), or his immediate successors. With Calverley seriously ill, the Society looked increasingly to Gershom for knowledgeable contributions of this kind.

Artifacts were also found in 1789 by Mr Rigg a surgeon and antiquary of Aspatria who excavated a barrow on the summit of Beacon Hill near the town:[57] a sword, battle- axe, dagger a buckle and various pieces of metal were found. Almost one hundred years later it was agreed that the site was Scandinavian. A re-examination of the site, reported in 2000[58] generally supports the claim that the remains found in 1789 and the *few* remains found during the latest excavation (Mr Rigg was very thorough in his original excavation) are Viking Age.

The third site was uncovered on February 15 1822, in the course of road widening operations on the main Carlisle- Penrith turnpike, within a mile of Hesket-in-the-Forest. Local information, however, had it that when the turnpike was made, about 50 years previously, the cairn had consisted of a very large heap of stones, many had then been used in building the new road, and others taken later by farmers to repair their walls.

By 1822 it appears that the only indication of its existence was a slight deviation of the road, which was to be removed by the road widening. Excavation showed that the cairn had been about 22 feet (6.7 metres) in diameter, and among the stones uncovered by the roadmen were fragments of several querns, one at least being of Andernach grit, which caused the surveyor, Christopher Hodgson, to suggest a Roman date for the burial. He must also, however, be credited with the observation that other features indicated rather a 'Scandinavian or a Tartar' character for the interment. *'The burial is notable not only for the comparatively good condition of the associated objects, accounted for no doubt by their preservation in burnt matter on a peculiarly favourable subsoil, but also for the number and variety of the contents. It provides, indeed, a tolerably complete inventory of the personal possessions of a Norse warrior of the early tenth century, and comprises a sword, an axe, two spear-heads, and the boss of a shield ; a bit and pair of spurs ; a sickle and whetstone ; and a comb complete with case, besides two buckles whose precise application cannot now be determined.'* Finds at Hesket-in-the-Forest were donated by Richard Ferguson to the Tulley House Museum in Carlisle.[59] The museum also housed the Ormside finds and both form prized collections.

---

[57] Rooke, H. 1792, Druidical and other British remains in Cumberland. Archaeologia. vol. 10, pp. 105-113.
[58] Abramson, P. 2000. A re- examination of a Viking Age burial at Beacon Hill, Aspatria. Transactions of the Cumberland and Westmorland Antiquarian and Archaeological Society, vol. 100, pp. 70-88.
[59] Cowen, J.D. 1934. A catalogue of objects of the Viking Period in The Tullie House Museum, Carlisle. Transactions of the Cumberland and Westmorland Antiquarian and Archaeological

Among the artifacts discovered during Gershom's time, one was especially mysterious: a pair of bronze armlets that would have been worn by a lady possibly eleventh century or earlier. Gershom gathered information about the find and wrote:

> 'Two bronze armlets [bracelets] were found in December, 1902, at the foot of Rough Crag, Thirlmere, by Joseph and Solomon Grisedale, while getting material for repairing the road. The site is on the south-western side of the lake, halfway between Hause Gill and Launchy or Deergarth Gill, and nearly opposite Clark's Lowp. Rough Crag is the last of a series of high bluffs on the right hand as you go south from Keswick by the new road past Armboth. After crossing Launchy Gill you skirt the foot of Bull Crag, known by its vertical chimney, and then the road winds into a broad scree gully between Bull Crag and Rough Crag, which advances upon the lower ground so that the road has to take an outward curve to round the precipitous foot of the rock, here more than 400 feet below the brow, with a fall of about one in one. This is by no means vertical, but gives the impression of almost perpendicular height, when seen either from above or below. The armlets were found in the scree gully, less than twenty yards above the road, and close under the rocks. On the six-inch Ordnance Map of 1867 the point is nearly on the 600 feet contour, about one-third of the distance from the R of 'Rough Crag' to the g of 'Bull Crag.' Mr. R. D. Marshall, who acquired the armlets through Mr. W. Hodgson the road surveyor kindly lends them for exhibition. On being exhibited to the Society of antiquaries of London they were pronounced to be of Late Celtic or Early Iron Age. There can have been no interment in the scree where they were found; they must have fallen from above. There is no sign of any tumulus or habitation on the grassy ground above the crag, as on other crags along this side of Thirlmere. But looking up from any point on the road to the northward, you can see a whitish patch in a niche of the rocks, above the birch bushes which fringe the precipice and beneath the actual summit, which is surrounded by a ruinous fence, looking from a distance like a dark curved line overhanging the rocks, with the white patch in the centre of its arch. By entering through the iron gate in the roadside east of Rough Crag and climbing the rough slope, a ledge of rock can be found, leading round the shoulder and across the main face of the precipice, with a well-defined and apparently artificial path, to the niche with the white patch. Here sheep sometimes take shelter, and the path is trodden by them and by shepherds in search of them; but this does not seem to account

Society, vol. 34, pp. 166-187.

for all the aspects of the place. The white patch is a rock face, overhanging a platform about 18 by 12 feet, [5.4m x 3.6m] strewn with stones unlike a mere rock fall. Many fragments seem to have been burnt, and though there is no traceable house wall the ground has all the appearance of a very old inhabited site. One big rock has fallen so as to make a cave, about a dozen feet in horizontal length, and just large enough for a boy to crawl into. From the platform rude steps lead up to a grass slope by which the summit can be reached ; so that, if this were really an ancient stronghold, it could be attacked from below or above only by rather difficult and dizzy approaches. Anything or any person falling from the platform would light at the spot, 400 feet beneath, where the armlets were found. The place resembles Ree Castle in the Watendlath Valley, though on a very much smaller scale, and in its position it is like Buck Castle in the Shoulthwaite Valley, overlooking the country far and wide. It would be more or less visible from below unless the birches, which now stop short of it, once grew in front of the platform; but in any case a small stone bield would be far from conspicuous. From it are seen all the Thirlmere Valley, Legberthwaite, St. John's Vale, Armboth Moor with its many old buildings, and the course of the ancient road beneath. It would make an ideal retreat for robbers or refuge in time of war. As Mr. R. D. Marshall said at the time of the discovery, one can imagine all sorts of romantic reasons for the presence of these bracelets—evidently a pair from a lady's hands—at the foot of that precipice and I think the path and platform above may give us some clue to the mystery.'

Gershom was investigating this find some years later because a letter dated March 1916 (AH) to him from George Abraham at Chestnut Hill Keswick refers to questions asked by Gershom concerning the find of bracelets and a cave above the find. Abraham a well- known photographer and mountaineer explained in the letter that he was not an antiquary but was ready to answer Gershom's questions if he could. Abraham said he got the idea that the bracelets were Elizabethan, from one of the Grisedales who found them and the cave he thought the work of miners. Whatever the date, this was one of the most intriguing finds in the district.

Gershom took his son Robin, in 1903, to see the place where the bracelets were found. Robin wrote to his mother from school describing how they went under Rough Crag near the head of Thirlmere, 'a most awfully steep place' and they scrambled up a narrow winding path to a platform directly above where the bracelets were found, and there a small cave. There were many trips into the hills of Lakeland either walking or seeking out promising places to carry out archaeological digs. Robin was at his first archaeological field trip when only three weeks old, carried by his father to the Roman Fort of Hardknot in a carpenter's bag;

though on that occasion (1889) Gershom was there to paint the site as he imagined it at the end of the fourth century AD.

In his autobiography, R.G. Collingwood wrote that he grew 'up in a gradually thickening archaeological atmosphere'. He also referred to his father as being brilliantly gifted as an archaeologist.

The few remains found from the period fifth to eleventh century offered little scope for antiquaries; fortunately they could turn to carved stonework. The main evidence for Anglo-Saxons and Scandinavians in the North of England was to be found in sculptured stone.

**Early Industrial Archaeology**

Gershom, without fully realising the implications from a study of early industrial processes, was taking part in some of the earliest research in what became known as 'Industrial Archaeology'. He pointed out that Coniston Water provides a good example of how a natural feature can clean and restore itself after earlier ravages by man. Wherever a stream came down a hillside into Coniston Water a bloomery could be found for the smelting of iron ore; charcoal makers worked nearby too providing fuel for the bloomery, and a flowing stream powered a water wheel to help drive air to a furnace. Numerous streams flowed into Coniston Water and especially on the east side there appeared sites of smoky noisy industry. When Gershom and his family arrived in the area (1891) few signs remained of this work and the eastern bank was much cleaner and quieter. In 1897, Gershom with Henry Swainson Cowper excavated Springs Bloomery on the west shore of Coniston Water.[60]

Cowper wrote Report One and Collingwood, Report Two. They had different ideas about dating the period that the Bloomery would be working. Cowper leaned towards Elizabethan time but Collingwood thought the site much earlier because the hearths were small and rude, so unlike those used at a later date. Thomas Ellwood who, in 1886, had presented a paper on 'The Bloomeries of High Furness' (CW1 vol. 8 pp. 85-92) thought the Springs Bloomery to be Scandinavian in age. The subject of 'Industrial Archaeology' was then in its infancy but as the years passed it was realised that this excavation by Ellwood was one of the earliest to be made of industry- based archaeology and it was this field of research that Gershom was entering, but was soon to hand over to enthusiasts fascinated by early machinery.

---

[60] Cowper, H.S. and W.G. Collingwood,1898. Reports on excavations at Springs Bloomery, near Coniston Hall, Lancashire, with notes on the probable age of the Furness Bloomeries. Transactions of the Cumberland and Westmorland Antiquarian and Archaeological Society, vol.15, pp. 211- 228.

While actively involved in excavations of various kinds, Gershom was developing a keen interest in carved stonework to be found around the area; apart from its historical value, the study of stonework also appealed to him as an artist.

**Study of Carved Stonework**

The Scandinavians had virtually no history of making stone monuments or carving in stone when in their native land. Any work of this kind followed on from Anglian practices found already in Britain. The arrived in a land, including Ireland and The Isle of Man, where carving in stone had been practised for centuries, mainly to depict Christian symbols. The involvement of Scandinavians in stone carving seemed to take the subject beyond only the monasteries to a wider public. The practice of stone carving over many years showed a clear continuity from Britons to Angles to Norse, rather than displacement or replacement of people and their skills occurring at each stage. To Gershom, it was obvious that Britons were not swept away by the Angles. *'Otherwise, how could the Angles have adopted so large a proportion of British place names?* Many kept their pre-Anglian titles.

Gershom looking for evidence of continuity across the centuries was encouraged by what he found in his study of stone carvings. Taking a wider view, any claim that any successes of the nineteenth century came from Briton, Anglo-Saxon and Scandinavian roots may be an exaggeration but is an intriguing subject for discussion.

During the transition from Anglian to Norse the form of monuments and carving was copied quite closely. This observation, possibly more than any other made later people question the differences between Angles and Norse. That this continuity exists between Anglo-Saxon and Norse stonework makes it extremely difficult to be sure that work was done during the Scandinavian period or earlier. During W.G.C's lifetime there was no clear tangible evidence of pure Scandinavian stonework in England; this was found at Coppergate in York 45 years after his death when a stone sculpture of animal ornament was found in an unworn state, reports dated the work as early tenth century.

It is of interest that when people walk around a museum or gallery where carved stone-work is on display very few give more than a passing sideways glance, before moving on to more 'interesting' relics in glass cases. In contrast Gershom saw this work as part of our art history and not just bits of carved stone. Although the study involved hours of analysing carved markings in stone, the essence of the work for Gershom was discovering something about the people who lived at the time that stonework was being created. The clues were to be picked up in a number of ways: how methods of carving changed over the years, the use of Runic alphabets, seeing association with the development of Christian religion, identifying links to local folklore or sagas from Iceland and noting similarities or differences in design. It helps to remember that Gershom designed stone crosses in addition to analysing them; he designed around 16 memorial crosses in Lakeland and to this task he brought his artistic training and earlier study of works in stone. Many visitors to Lakeland see the Ruskin memorial on Friar's Crag above Derwentwater, the design and drawing was by W.G.C. carved by a local stonemason. He also produced a considerable number of fine drawings of stone monuments. Writing in 1980 Richard Bailey[61] praised Gershom's papers published between 1907 and 1915 in the Yorkshire Archaeological Journal pointing out that his drawings are still a constant source of information to the modern field-worker, *'and a humbling reminder that since his death, no one has equalled Collingwood's familiarity with the material or his artistic skill in recording it'.*

The ring-shaped head is one of the most distinctive features of carved stone work from the Viking Age (Figure 25).

No rings are to be found on pre-Viking stone crosses. The ring- head can be carved in a number of ways: single ring or double ring, either linking the arms of a cross or superimposed on the front of a cross, or on both sides. Alternatively there can be crossheads, simply a cross at the head of a shaft without ring(s). Gershom made a detailed study of these heads, including those with rings, and found that the distribution of ring-heads matched place names, derived from Gaelic-Norse. This research led him to be convinced that the source of Norse immigration into Lakeland lay on the Isle of Man. Subsequently, a stronger case has been made by Richard Bailey in his book 'Viking Age Sculpture' (1980) for Ireland or North-West Scotland being the source. Bailey gives the example of St. Martin's cross on Iona, Scotland and the South Cross at Clonmacnoise and other ring- heads or crossheads in Ireland at Ahenny, Killamery and Kilkieran. He also compared a ring-head from the Isle of Man at Kirkmichael to show it was not close to those found in Northern England, claiming that Collingwood's argument in this case was difficult to sustain.

*It is almost inevitable that some of W.G.C.'s conclusions would be questioned many years later, especially in archaeology and Antiquarianism, but in writing about his works it is events and ideas of his time that are most important. In this biography I have quoted Rosemary Cramp and Richard Bailey as two of the most respected archaeologists to show how even now Gershom's work is valued, it seems only right to quote them when they express disagreement with parts of his work.* Bailey wrote that, Gershom's book on the subject 'Northumbrian Crosses of the Pre-Norman Age'[62] *'was a magnificent piece*

---

[61] Bailey, R. 1980. 'Viking Age Sculpture in Northern England.' p. 28. London: Collins.
[62] Collingwood, W.G. 1927. 'Northumbrian Crosses of the Pre-Norman Age.' London: Faber and Gwyer.

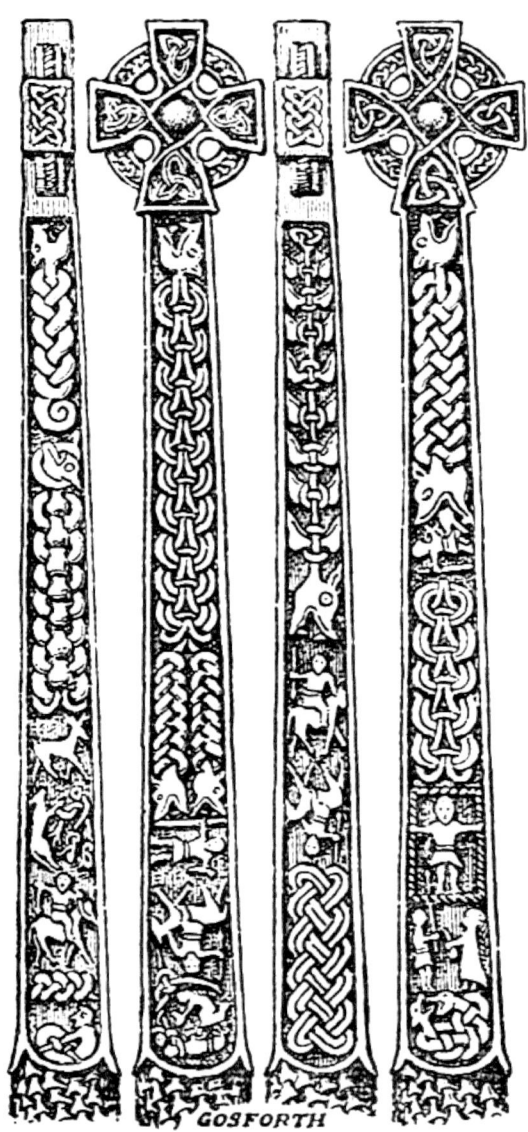

Figure 25 Gosforth Cross by W.G.C.

*of work published five years before he died'.* With more years and in better health he could have worked towards a more definitive record of crosses and other stone sculptures in England. This work is still in progress.

Professor Rosemary Cramp made a significant contribution to the collection of data when publishing in 1984 'Corpus of Anglo-Saxon Stone Sculpture in England'. She cited the work of Gershom as the most noteworthy of regional studies (East and West Ridings of Yorkshire) done and reported in Scholarly papers for the Yorkshire Archaeological Journal: 1907, 1909, 1911 and 1915; volumes 14, 20, 21 and 23 respectively. Much of this work was brought together in his book 'Northumbrian Crosses of the Pre-Norman Age (1927). From Gershom's notebooks at the Ashmolean Museum in Oxford there are indications that he intended to widen, geographically, the scope of this work; Cramp comments that it was unfortunate that he did not complete the work for the whole of England. Gershom's appointment at University College Reading and war work at the Admiralty intervened during years that could have been some of the most productive in his life.

The study of stonework, especially stone crosses, is essentially of the Anglo-Saxon period in history, before the tenth century. The practice of combining Scandinavian carved features with those of Anglian design first occurred fully at the beginning of the tenth century.

Gershom had been a member of CWAAS for five years when he was asked by the Society to produce a drawing of a Tympanum at Bridekirk Church,[63] that had been taken from an older church and re-inserted above the south doorway of the new church in 1868. The sculpture made in soft red sandstone had perished, so it was difficult to pass judgement about origins of the work.

Taking a photograph of the sculpture was not practicable, a solution was to study a carefully drawn image, which Gershom provided and signed, WGC 9.12.92 (1892). He commented *'that general critical feeling tells him that the bas-relief is like others of the eleventh century in France and Italy, but ruder.'* Gershom was possibly drawing upon experience, from a tour in 1882, of these countries with John Ruskin. The sculpture at Bridekirk was 5 feet 9 inches wide (175 cm) and 7.5 inches high (19 cm). Comparison with well-known Saxon manuscripts of early eleventh century shows peaked beard (divided in two each part groomed to a point) which was then in fashion and went out when the Normans came, but returned again in the thirteenth century as alternative to the full beard; this feature alone did not indicate a date. The only evidence to help provide a date for the sculpture was to be found from another Tympanum at Elstow in Bedfordshire, said to be from latter part of tenth century and early eleventh; this example showed the stone carving

---

[63] Calverley, W.S. 1893. Tympanum at Bridekirk Church. Transactions of the Cumberland and Westmorland Antiquarian and Archaeological Society, pp. 462-469.

Figure 26 Giant's Thumb by W.G.C.

in much greater detail than the eroded stone at Bridekirk. The drawing was a first practical venture into the study of pre-Norman stonework for Gershom and his draughtsmanship proved of great value.

His serious study of stone crosses began when Gershom was asked to edit the papers of Rev. William Slater Calverley after his death at the age of 51, in 1898. The request came from Chancellor Ferguson of the CWAAS; prompted by Calverley's widow Constance both thought that W.G. Collingwood was the ideal person to complete the task. He did, and produced a book that no doubt would have made Calverley proud.[64] Part of Claverley's In Memoriam explains how Gershom was chosen as the most suitable person to complete this work:

> 'He [Calverley] did not live to finish the book, which had been in contemplation for many years, the work of completion has been undertaken by his friend, our member, Mr. W. G. Collingwood, who was well acquainted with and shared Mr. Calverley's views on the interesting matters dealt with in the book. Mr. Calverley became a member of this Society in 1877; at the time of his death he was a member of its council; he was elected a Fellow of the Society of antiquaries of London in 1885, and was one of that Society's local secretaries for Cumberland. He was also a member of the Royal Archaeological Institute, at whose annual meetings, as at the meetings of this Society, he was a constant attendant, and his absence from both will be much regretted by numerous friends'.

The book was published in 1899 as volume XI in the Extra Series of the CWAAS and continued to be a standard reference for many years; in 1966 when Nikolas Pevsner was researching in Cumberland for a book 'Buildings of England' he used Calverley's work edited by Gershom as the 'authority'. There was an extensive amount of written work left by Calverley, amassed between the years 1880 to 1897, and to this Gershom contributed his own drawings and where added text was necessary he used a smaller font than that used for Calverley's words. First working contact with Calverley had been in 1892 when Gershom was asked to produce a drawing for a paper, written by Calverley. The main subject studied by Rev. Calverley was of pre- Norman stone crosses and Gershom was well suited to continue this work.

The study of Northern Crosses was an ideal subject for Gershom; he was able to study a subject that combined art, Antiquarianism, history and archaeology

---

[64] Collingwood, W.G. (ed.) 1899. Notes on the Early Sculptured Crosses, Shrines and Monuments in the present Diocese of Carlisle by the late Rev. William Slater Calverley, Vicar of Aspatria. Kendal: Titus Wilson.

covering a period of 400 years between 710 and 1100, although he needed to have some understanding of a longer period, first century to eleventh. This research over the years could best be described as the study of carved stonework, but stone crosses specifically captured Gershom's imagination. Where did they originate? When first introduced? What made people work so hard to create them? Was there a uniform pattern to their design or would he find crucial differences between crosses? What can be learned from carved figures and text, especially the use of runic symbols? Crucially for an understanding of the past, can they be dated accurately? Seeking answers to such questions occupied Gershom, from 1898, when he began the task of editing the late William Slater Calverley's work, until the day he died, 34 years later.

During Gershom's time, stone crosses of around 10 feet high were originally unique to England; there was no known example to be found beyond the British Isles; not even in Egypt where carved stonework was common centuries earlier. Even those found in Scotland, Wales and Ireland were derived from examples in England. Gershom developed gradually a firm idea about how these crosses originated, he felt that the first crosses of this kind were made of wood and erected to mark the sites of battle and that these in turn were derived from smaller portable crosses, Gershom called 'staff-roods', carried by early Christian missionaries as they moved from place to place, smaller but of sufficient length to be erected at a spot where preaching took place. Robin George Collingwood did not doubt the substantial truth of this view, but could recognise an alternative source, which would be much earlier than believed by Gershom. Historian, Gerard Baldwin Brown[65] 'The Arts in England', vol. 5 referred to .

When researching the design of stone crosses, and stonework generally, it was important to take account of their chronology. Placing carved stone crosses within time periods became a major problem that Gershom attempted to solve with some success, first by classifying into groups of: Anglian, Viking and early 11th century up to the Norman period. These three broad classifications almost inevitably involved some overlap of periods. Later Gershom found there was a consistency in design and this offered a more reliable and accurate way of classifying.

Classification into types by analysing designs (Typology) still brought problems when trying to date monuments, it became necessary to use a combination of approaches: study of carved runic text based upon an alphabet in use from the fourth century to late middle ages, comparing with some knowledge of proper names and their origin (Onomastics).

---

[65] Baldwin Brown, G. 1921. The Ruthwell and Bewcastle Crosses and other Monuments of Northumbria. London: John Murray.

A key feature of stone crosses, fully exploited by Gershom, was their weight and difficulty in transporting from place to place; he could be reasonably sure that a cross was made either on site or close to the place of erection. There are exceptions where heavy stone work has been transported: Cleopatra's Needle on the Embankment in London and Egyptian stone monuments also in London, and of course Stonehenge not made of local stone, but most stone crosses in England have been made from local stone by local craftsmen. At times pieces of carved stone often from crosses have been used when building structures nearby, usually as foundations for churches or as lintels built into walls. Finds of this kind could help Gershom and his colleagues set a date roughly by stating that the carved stonework must be older than a building where it was found as part of the foundations, but not how much older. He needed to look for evidence elsewhere before attempting to narrow down to a specific date.

When looking at carved stonework he had to be aware that the stone standing before him may be only a sample of what had been available many years earlier but lost forever. Also that the carved work was not being seen as intended by the designer or craftsman; there was ample evidence that work of this kind was originally painted in varied colours. Carved stone could be found where, not too exposed to the elements, still showed signs of paint. Despite these shortcomings there were sufficient examples to provide a lifetime of fascinating research.

**Gosforth Stone Cross**

A famous stone cross to capture Gershom's interest still stands in the churchyard of Gosforth church. Shortly before Gershom settled in the Lake District and around eight years before he began serious study of early history in the area. A highly significant piece of research was begun by Rev. William Slater Calverley and published two years later by the TCWAAS (CW1) with drawings by Charles, A. Parker M.D.[66] Up to 1881, the meaning of the carvings on the cross was a complete mystery. On a cold damp day in July, 1881, Calverley and Parker stood in the churchyard at Gosforth beside the imposing Gosforth cross (Figure 25). A slender monolith of red sandstone standing 14 feet high (4.3 metres) with at the top a wheel- cross head (Later a cast was made of the cross for The South Kensington Museum in London and a copy placed in the churchyard at Aspatria).

The lower part of the cross shaft is round and represents the trunk of a tree. The upper part is square and each face is carved which together represent a poem of the tenth century, which forms part of the Norse Edda under the title

---

[66] Calverley, W.S. 1883. The Sculptured Cross at Gosforth. Transactions of the Cumberland and Westmorland Antiquarian and Archaeological Society, vol. 6, pp. 372-404.

of Völuspá (see drawing by W.G Collingwood, Figure 35). On that day in 1881, Dr Parker's coachman scrubbed away the already damp mosses using a wet brush and revealed details not seen for many years, possibly centuries. Calverley, excited by what he found, corresponded with Professor George Stephens of Copenhagen (born 1883 in Liverpool, he became a lecturer in English at Copenhagen University then as runologist and philologist, in 1839, made the first complete translation of a Norse saga into English). Calverley is reported to have sent him photographs and drawings of the cross, with the result that Stephens returned to England in 1882 and made a pilgrimage to Gosforth. He declared the cross unique in all his experience and possibly seventh century, which he confirmed after further study. A.Wawn[67] who had made a special study of correspondence between Calverley and Professor Stephens, states that Stephens wrote first to Calverley.) This is understandable because Professor Stephens felt strongly that so-called Anglo-Saxons were Scandinavian in origin and looked for evidence of Scandinavian influence, dated as early as possible, not too surprising that he gave a date for the Gosforth Cross as possibly seventh century. He was hostile towards what he regarded as German military and philological imperialism; he refused to use the German-derived (as he regarded it) term 'Anglo-Saxon', preferring Old English believing the language and literature of pre-Norman England was essentially Old Northern or 'Scando-Anglic' in origin rather than Teutonic. Stephens became a Danish subject in 1855. He is included in the Oxford Dictionary of National Biography, vol. 52 (Andrew Wawn).

Calverley was the first person to attempt an interpretation of what can be seen on each side of the cross. Calverley's interpretation of images on the cross as Norse Edda myths caused a stir among antiquaries. A common belief was that Christian monuments of any kind would show only Christian images especially Calverley; he like many earlier antiquaries, was a man of the church and wished to see Christian symbolism wherever he went but he pointed out that the Gosforth cross showed both Pagan and Christian images. Dr Charles Parker and Collingwood in writing their reconsideration of the Gosforth Cross came to the conclusion that it was impossible to regard it as a purely heathen monument, 'it is Christian with certain heathen allusions.' Parker and Collingwood could take a more independent view of the evidence. Charles Parker was a medical doctor who for 40 years, beginning in 1877, practised in Gosforth and was well-known for his dedicated service to the community in and around the town. He joined the CWAAS in 1878. Collingwood, as already discussed, was ambivalent about religion.

---

[67] Wawn, A. 2004. George Stephens. Oxford Dictionary of National Biography, H.C.G. Mathew (ed.). Oxford: Oxford University Press.

Soon after John Ruskin's death, the work being done by Gershom was best described as that of an antiquary[68] much later to be thought of by many in a pejorative sense but not at the time. The antiquary was concerned mainly with studying evidence from the past found as hard 'facts' from various artefacts that survived in written or non- written form created in history or pre-history, and less concerned with development of theories. A parallel subject of archaeology concerned with the study of landforms to develop hypotheses or theories about how people lived in pre-history mainly from hidden dwellings and artefacts. Excavations are normally needed to find support for the hypotheses or theories. Some archaeologists are less concerned with theories and simply react to discoveries coming often by accident or serendipity, their aim being to see what more can be found, which could be described as fishing on land. Gershom seldom took this approach, he preferred to begin with an idea about what evidence could be found from the past and set out to find support for that idea.

**Giant's Thumb**

Soon after Gershom arrived back at Lanehead from Naval Intelligence in London (1919) he returned to the analysis of stone crosses, a task that clearly absorbed him, mainly because there were still many unanswered questions. In August 1919 he was in Penrith, Cumberland examining 'The Giant's Thumb'[69] (Figure 26).

The cross is nearly complete and Gershom thought it provided material for discussing its place in the history of monumental art. In age, the cross is of Anglian type with Norse motives like the Gosforth Cross; this judgment made initially by William Slater Calverley was taken as being true by Gershom. He added that the wheel-head marks it as not earlier than late ninth century, the type of wheel-head was characteristic of tenth century crosses. Gershom compared the Thumb with the Leeds Cross dated around AD 925 making the Thumb around 920; the date may be later. In the ninth century around AD 880 there were no Scandinavians in the area, the Danes occupied only parts of east Yorkshire and the Norse had only begun their colonisation of Galloway but not in Lakeland, therefore the Thumb's earliest possible date would be at the close of the ninth century or early in the tenth century.

The drawing by Gershom shows the 'restored' head, and patterns on all four sides are made clear. He makes the point that the restorations are not conjectural;

---

[68] Gnosspelius, J. 1995. Notes about W.G. Collingwood. Collingwood Archive, Cardiff University.
[69] Collingwood, W.G. 1920. The Giant's Thumb. Transactions of the Cumberland and Westmorland Antiquarian and Archaeological Society, vol. 20, pp. 53-65.

where the design is entirely effaced by time or weather, this is ignored but all the rest can be inferred from traces of carvings, which can be seen in favourable lights. 'Thus the south side has drill-holes of the intersections of the plait. I have to thank my son [Robin George] for mapping them with great care; and from these the run of the strand is certain. The restoration of the head is obvious; the two remaining holes of the wheel-cross were thought by the late George Watson to have been enlarged when the cross was used, as tradition said, as a pillory'.

The basket plait on the east side with boldly curved straps is also a tenth century feature (the cable is sometimes found with ninth century ornament, but it is frequently tenth century).

These features of wheel-head, drill-holes in the plait and basket plait on the Thumb are common with Danish and Norse ornament.

Gershom made use of what he knew about Cumbrian kings belonging to ancient dynasties going back to the mid-fifth century. With this knowledge, he could make a reasonable claim that the Thumb is named after a King of Cumbria Eugein (Owain). Owain ruled from AD 920 to 937, said to be the most important person throughout the Kingdom of Cumbria. Kings earlier than Owain in Cumbria originated at the time Romano-British people felt threatened by Picts and Angles, after the departure of Roman soldiers. They banded together under 'Cumbri', commonly called Guletic; the line of Kings, from this time, were thought of as representatives of the Roman or Caesarian power that had existed in the North West region in the fifth century. Gershom produced a tree diagram to show the succession of Kings during the post- Roman period.

**Hogbacks**

Gershom's interest and research was not confined to stone crosses; hogbacks were other carved stonework he turned his attention to after spending many hours studying and analysing crosses. He devoted one chapter (Chapter XVI) to Hogbacks in his book of Pre-Norman Crosses (1927). He described hogback as a recumbent tombstone in the shape of a low, long house of which the rooftree is slightly arched lengthwise. Gershom referred to the writing of Bede when he described the sepulchre of St. Chad as a wooden monument shaped like a little house with a roof and hole in the wall, through which people put their hand to gather dust, which was thought to have medicinal use. Gershom wrote a paper on the subject, submitted in September 1907[70] concerning three better- known hogbacks in

---

[70] Collingwood, W.G. 1907. The Lowther Hogbacks. Transactions of the Cumberland and Westmorland Antiquarian and Archaeological Society, vol. 17, pp.152-164.

Lowther Church-yard. When Gershom came to examine them, he found that only one hogback was to be seen clearly; the other two were partly buried by earth. Rev. W.S. Calverley made notes about the clearly visible hogback 20 years earlier, but Gershom was the first to make a serious study of all three hogbacks and extracts from his study are given below:

> 'There is no doubt that Christ's descent into hell was taken as a suitable subject for grave-stones, suggesting the hope of resurrection; as for instance in the Penrith hogback, where a little figure seems to stand on a serpent's head, to signify the victory over death; and this Lowther subject, though not representing Patriarchs, might possibly be a variant of the well-known symbol. The art of this stone is very rude; the carving hacked out with the hammer, and not unlike that of the Penrith hogbacks and other monuments which may be dated tenth century. It is of the type common in the parts of England settled by Danes and Norsemen. The hogback is a development of the shrine tomb, having the ridge curved instead of level. Richard Bailey[71] makes the point that Gershom's drawing was made under adverse circumstances 'and is thus not entirely accurate' but does give the reader unfamiliar with hogbacks an idea of their shape and form. The two hogbacks in the drawing are around four feet eleven inches long (1.5metres) the design in Gershom's words: 'seems to be confined to the Anglo-Danish districts and to the period of the Scandinavian settlements. It is not a Celtic invention, and occurs in Scotland only in Danish or Norse districts. Like shrine tombs in general, it represents a little house with tiled roof and gable ends definitely expressed. The ladies on the two Lowther hogbacks, taken with the boat, the army and the hero, seem to require for their explanation something more than the mere suggestion of saints in Limbo and a portrait group.'

*Considered historically, these monuments are valuable as showing that Lowther was settled in the tenth century by members of the great Danish colony from Yorkshire, Christianized Vikings. If we cannot yet read all that their artist tried to convey without the use of written words, nor give him much praise for his design and carving, there is great satisfaction and interest in adding one more example to the series of unwritten documents which help us to retrace the story of a dark age. Since the meeting of our Society at Lowther we hear with pleasure that these hogbacks, through the kind care of the Countess of Lonsdale and the Rev. T. B. Tylecote, rector of Lowther, are to be placed inside the church for safer preservation. They are well worthy of the honour.* A much later (1979) scholar Dr A.P. Smyth

---

[71] Bailey, R.N. 1980. Viking Age Sculpture. London: Collins.

described Viking-age hogbacks as 'non-Christian in character' and 'thoroughly Pagan in conception'. The reasoned argument about hogbacks used by Gershom in 1927 as being from Christianised Vikings is sustainable. Subsequent writing points to 'nothing Pagan about their form' (Richard N. Bailey 1985).

Gershom emphasises Scandinavian connections, but some Hogbacks were carved and known before Scandinavian settlers arrived, dated around mid-ninth century. Various images are to be found on Hogbacks and one of the most puzzling is that of a snake's head, were they purely ornamental? One idea is that it is meant to scare away evil spirits, but that most images of this kind have the head facing inwards makes this idea difficult to support. Gershom had no clear explanation to offer.

A subject that does not appear to be raised by Gershom or other Antiquities is about how craftsmen planned and carried out carved stonework. Possibly Gershom came nearest when he referred to images in stone being either chiselled or hacked, suggesting that he could identify two methods from inspection of the images. Much later (1980)

Richard Bailey in 'Viking Age Sculpture in Northern England' addresses the subject and refers to the tools of chisels and punches, but for hacking Gershom refers to hammers or even the method of rubbing down cut surfaces with other (harder) stones. It seems that chiselling was the preferred method, producing images of a finer quality.

Present-day students of the subject probably want an answer to the question, who paid for the work? Were there Patrons supporting carved stone? As far as discovered, Gershom did not address these questions and it seems unlikely that answers will be found, or can be found, beyond speculation. It is most likely that the skilled work was done mainly for the Priesthood and highly unlikely that any carved stonework was done independently of the church before the ninth century. The work was done normally by local stonemasons who earned their living with alternative stone working, and that the images were drawn on stone, by the mason, using templates designed by someone with a story to tell that would survive longer in stone than in any other medium.

**Angles and Norse**

Scandinavians settled in the late ninth and tenth centuries: Danes in East Yorkshire and Norse in the North West including the Lake District. Scandinavians did land at places south of the Humber but again, they were of no concern to Gershom. This later period of Scandinavian settlers is commonly called the Viking Age but ethnographically 'Norse' is a preferred term to 'Viking'. The Norse settled in the North West after making the sea crossing from the Isle of Man, a short voyage of only 40 miles (64 km.) to reach the coast at the River Duddon or port of Ravenglass; some made the longer crossing from Ireland, most settling around the Wirral. From Gershom's work in editing the writing of Rev. Calverley and from research by Thomas Ellwood, Rector of Torver in the Lake District,[72] he established from the study of place names, words and phrases in common use recorded over a period of 200 years. That the Norse settled peacefully among the local population, made homes and farmed in an area not too different from their homeland. The Ennerdale valley (Egener-Dalr) is a good example of a place that would be familiar to the Norse and Gershom claimed that only a sparse population of Anglicans lived in or near the valley. The River Liza flows down the valley into Ennerdale Water; in Iceland a river Lýsá means 'bright water' a term that can equally be applied to Ennerdale's River Liza. To quote Gershom:

> 'Before the Normans came, our district was Scandinavian. The Danes burnt Carlisle in 876 and settled in the eastern part of Yorkshire. There is reason to believe, but this is not the place to discuss the whole subject, that Norse began to settle the western parts not much later, coming from the Isle of Man and Ireland. They behaved here as they behaved elsewhere at this period; not as raiders but as colonists. They wanted homes, and settled down quietly.'

Gershom used place names as a primary source to help him explain the distribution of societies in the North of England and in particular the North-West. He became a well-known source of information about place-name research. In a letter to the Journal of the Fell and Rock Club of the English Lake District[73] he referred to correspondence with a man who wished to know the meaning of Pavey Arc, a mountain in the district and very popular with rock climbers, asking Gershom to explain. In answer he said, '*I can't say what it does mean, but I think I know what it ought to mean*'. He went on to explain: a great number of place names contain 'ergh' the same as 'ark' in old forms, which mean 'shieling' or summer dairies of Norse farmers. A dairymaid would make cheeses just as a Sennerin does in the Alps. The words ark or ergh is said in the Orkneys to be equivalent to the Gaelic 'airidh'; there seemed to be little doubt about the meaning of ark. Pavey was more problematic; Gershom suggested 'Pavia' was a common female name in the twelfth and thirteenth centuries. Pavey Ark would be like Langley Park in West

---

[72] Ellwood, T. 1888. Notes upon some of the older word forms to be found in comparing the language of Lakeland with the language of Iceland. Transactions of the Cumberland and Westmorland Antiquarian and Archaeological Society, vol. 9. pp. 383-392.
[73] Letter to Editor, 1921. Fell and Rock Climbing Club of the English Lake District, vol. 5 p.337.

Cumberland, which was Langlifergh, meaning dairy of Langlif and Gershom pointed out that there were plenty of parallels. Pavia's ergh may have been left in ruins somewhere near Stickle Tarn, below Pavey Ark. Gershom added '*A problem which perhaps members of the club might solve by finding the remains*'. He then added, '*short of that, I think this is the most likely guess.*' As can be seen from this example, Gershom used a good deal of imagination and inventiveness to extract meaning from place names, but by finding groups of parallel examples in an area he was able to build a strong case, if not strong evidence. The practice of deriving place names from imaginary roots is fraught with difficulties and W.G.C. worked hard at giving the method some credibility. Nineteen years after his death (1951), The English Place-name Society published volumes 20 and 21[74] followed by a third part two years later; all three covered most areas of Lakeland.

He recommended that place names be used to help clarify the legend of Arthur, when he read a paper to the Viking Club in 1924, on Arthur and Athelstan.[75] Gershom's study was normally confined to England north of the Humber, but he was reminded of a statement made in an earlier book 'Scandinavian Britain' (1908) about tales of Arthur; a statement he said later was made 'in passing' (obiter dicta) adding that such statements come back to haunt you. The statement was, '*Arthurian tales contain many motives of the Viking Age, and confuse the ancient Celtic mythology with waifs and strays from ninth and tenth century history, and from the folklore of the Norse*'. He had been asked several times what this meant so in a paper to the Viking Club he discussed what was known or at least believed about Arthur and concluded that the Arthur of Historia Brittonum, dated around the year 800, is a very different person from the Arthur of romances. '*The place, we have seen, cannot be in the north, nor in the west. But the map of early cemeteries and remains given by Mr. Thurlow Leeds, in his Archaeology of the Anglo-Saxon Settlements, seems to hint the regions where the events attributed to Arthur were possible. South of the Thames valley, where settlements of Saxons were being formed, and some at any rate peacefully, as shown by the evidence of the village recently explored in Berkshire, a little south of Abingdon; west of Kent; north and west of the Sussex and South Hampshire coast, there is a blank space, marked only with barrow interments of men killed in fights on Salisbury Down, and weapons found near Winchester. In that area the Romano-British civilization had been strong, a hundred years before Arthur's time; it is mainly upland country, and dotted over with forts already ancient history to Arthur. That perhaps is the area he defended. And if we do not venture to identify sites, it is because there is a Place-name Society, and it will be their business, when all records are searched, and philology has done its best, to tell us how*

---

[74] Place-Names of Cumberland, 1951. English Place-name Society, vols. 20 and 21.

[75] Collingwood, W.G. 1924. Arthur and Athelstan. Saga-Book of the Viking Club, vol.10, pp. 132-164.

far the names of the twelve battles can be found in that region. Place- names are doing much to lift a corner of the veil which hangs over the scenes of our earliest history. Perhaps, after an age of credulity, another of scepticism, and a third of pseudo-science which has failed to explain him as a sun-myth or a culture-hero, archaeology and philology may give us back a real Arthur'. Gershom referred to comments about Arthur and York, explaining that there was no 'York' when Arthur was said to live: that is a matter of archaeology; the town was destroyed and not re- built until around AD 600. In addition, links are made between Æthelstan (894-939) and Arthur but Æthelstan took York in AD 927.

What Gershom meant in his book Scandinavian Britain was that Arthurian epic is a version of Æthelstan's history: or rather it is built up out of materials from events of the tenth century, not from any real tradition of the fifth or sixth. Gershom went on to suggest that Arthur could have been with the Roman-Celtic name of Artorius who fought the Saxons in 12 battles, winning all and being fatally wounded at the last. Sites of the battles are known: River Glein; Dubglas (4); River Bassas; wood of Celidon; Fort of Guinnion; Urbs Legionis; River Tribuit; hill (mont) Agned and hill (mont) Badon where 'Arthur' died. Various historians have traced these sites and there is general agreement that they are widespread and not confined to south of the Thames believed to be the home-area of Arthur; so widespread in fact that it is difficult to see how one man could take part in all twelve battles in one lifetime. However, the legend and romance of King Arthur intrigues people over the years, Gershom was no exception.

Gershom delivered a paper, 'The Angles in Furness and Cartmel' at Urswick Church in 1923. From carving and runic inscription of a cross-shaft found in the church he deduced that the settlement of Urswick in the ninth century had a flourishing Anglian population. There was further evidence that when the Norse settled in the Furness area in the latter part of the tenth century no structural changes were made to the chapel; a stone of later date has also been found in the chapel of Anglo- Scandinavian type placed there by newcomers. Although there was evidence of raids along the Furness coast in the ninth century by the time of actual settlement they were, in Gershom's words 'more or less 'Christianised'. The Norse came looking for homes rather than plunder; as plunderers they could rightly be described as Viking, but as peaceful settlers they were Norse.

**Norse Anglo-Saxon Dilemma**

There has been an on-going debate about whether Norse settlers were different from earlier Anglo-Saxon settlers, or the same. A crucial question, possibly raised first by Professor George Stephens of Copenhagen (1813-1895), because a reliable answer would largely determine the true ancestry of English people identified as 'Northerners'. What is possibly more significant is the idea that Normans were essentially Scandinavian after Norse and Danish settled in that part of France in the eighth century, eventually to be colonised by Danish and Norse. The name 'Norman' is derived from 'men of the north'. In Normandy their very character was changed, 'and out of Norsemen the land made Normans'.[76]

Historians of Denmark and Norway have been known to quarrel over the origins of the word 'beck' (stream), a name that Gershom and other antiquaries associate clearly with Scandinavia. Scholars of Sweden supported the Danes in their claim that the origin was Danish. Also, 'bee' was a common termination in Normandy and on the strength of this the Danes argued that Normandy was largely colonised from Denmark. 'Tun' was another word- ending thought by Gershom and his colleagues to be Scandinavian, tun occurred in Sweden and is found in Iceland, but generally speaking it is thought to be a Saxon termination. The implications from decisions made on the basis of 'place-names' are enormous: the History of England would have to be largely re-written if nearly one half of the country was found to have Scandinavian ancestry. Gershom seems to have avoided the question directly, but from various writings it is likely that he looked for possible differences and on balance felt that they were fellow-Teutons with little difference between them (Angles, Norse, Danish and Normans). In the early stages of his study he identified at least two key differences that made it difficult to describe Norse and Anglo-Saxon peoples as the same, in other words from a common Teutonic stock. One is attitude towards religion and Christianity in particular; by the time the Norse arrived in the North West most Anglo-Saxons had become committed Christians while the Norse were essentially Pagan in outlook; in terms of religion most Scandinavians were polytheistic, worshiping multiple deities, only those who had spent some time in Ireland or the Isle of Man were 'Christianised'. Second, they spoke different languages, respectively Old Norse and Old English. Going further back to a time before the Saxons and Angles travelled to 'England', the population would still be partially Pagan, leaving language as the only possible difference between them and the Norse. There could then be the suggestion that little difference existed between them and Norse and by implication Scandinavian ancestors of people who would live for centuries in England. A possible reason for Gershom appearing to skirt around this question is that he seemed to have little interest in national identity. The issue would only become prominent around thirty years after his death when Englishness was at risk of becoming severely diluted.

A crucial factor in determining differences between populations is how they become sectioned off. Boundaries or borders appear to be artificial, but after

---

[76] Collingwood, W.G. 1923. An Inventory of the Ancient Monuments of Cumberland. Transactions of the Cumberland and Westmorland Antiquarian and Archaeological Society, vol. 23, pp. 206-276.

existing for some time it seems that people living on one side of a boundary develop different ways of life, or what is commonly called 'culture' from those on the other side. It can be argued that without the artificial intrusion of boundaries all people are the same; at least over a sizeable area of ground of similar climatic conditions: Northern Europe, Britain and Scandinavia for example. This could well underlie Gershom's reluctance to question differences between Norse and Anglo-Saxon, an unnecessary question. However an intriguing question still exists: were they all Scandinavian as Professor George Stephens claimed?

**Beyond Pre-Norman**

W.G.C.'s interest and research extended beyond the Roman-Anglian-Norse history of Northern England. A failed plot in 1663 was planned in Westmorland,[77] so with its Lakeland connection the case became of interest to him and he researched the circumstances. He described the Kaber Rigg plot, which took place after the restoration of King Charles II. An insurrection of the Republican Party was intended and plans were made for a general uprising all over England and Ireland. In Westmorland the head of the movement was Robert Atkinson of Mallerstag who had been Captain of horse under Oliver Cromwell.

The plot in Westmorland was to capture a key supporter of the King, Sir Philip Musgrave, take Carlisle and Appleby and finally force the King to perform promises: to grant liberty of conscience to all but Romanists and bring to an end certain taxes. Plotters were betrayed and the rising failed; Atkinson was captured and hung, which in Gershom's view put back the clock most sadly for all dissenters throughout Westmorland (a rare display of political feeling from Gershom).

W.G.C. ventured again beyond his main period of interest when he considered events in the seventeenth century. He wrote 'Dutch Agnes her valentine' (1910). The fictitious story is based on the diary of a Curate in Coniston between the years of 1616 and 1663. He fills the pages with a rich collection of characters of an area he knew so well: the Squire of Coniston Hall; Rector of Ambleside; Miners from Germany and of course local dales men and women. The imaginary writing of the Curate shows him to be a man interested and knowledgeable about political as well as religious issues of the day; not only in Coniston but about troubles abroad during the thirty years war. The Curate himself had feeling for the beauty of mountains and fells, reflecting the writer's (W.G.C.) own love of the district. Agnes of the title was a Dutch miner's daughter who befriended the Curate. When W.G.C.

---

[77] Nichols, F. 1911. The Kaber Rigg plot. Transactions of the Cumberland and Westmorland Antiquarian and Archaeological Society, vol. 11 pp. 212-232.

wrote Dutch Agnes he had already, in outline at least, a non-fiction account of German miners in the Lake District.

Culmination of W.G.C's research over the years in his own area was the publication in 1925 of 'Lake District History'. Close examination of this book reveals the breadth of Gershom's knowledge about the district, whether from his own research or writings of others. The first two chapters covering pre-history (Ages BC) and 'Britons and Romans' are written with a good deal of reference to other scholars. The next two chapters 'Angles and Norse' and 'Barons and Abbots he writes from the depth of his own research and knowledge. The next chapter titled 'The Medieval Map' consists of an alphabetical list based upon place-name research and an early map drawn around AD 1300. For the remainder of the book Gershom seems confident in bringing the story up to the Romantic Period, covering 'English and Scots', 'Early Industries' and 'The Statesmen'.

**Collingwood's Inventories**

In the early 1920s, Gershom decided to build upon Chancellor Ferguson's Archaeological Survey produced 25 years earlier and in 1923 published what he called 'An Inventory of the Ancient Monuments of Cumberland'[78] and three years later An Inventory of Westmorland and Lancashire North-of-the-Sands.[79] This second inventory was a continuation of the Inventory for Cumberland and for this inventory Gershom gave special thanks to Mr. J.F. Curwen, F.S.A., for the sight of his MS. collections with regard to ancient roads. (A possible project, similar to this work of W.G.C. if completed county by county, would produce a corpus of Pre-Norman artifacts for England and Wales).

Gershom appreciated that a good deal of work had been done over the past 25 years by members of the Cumberland and Westmorland Antiquarian and Archaeological Society (CWAAS) including himself and son Robin, and felt it was time to up-date Ferguson's valuable work. Gershom made clear that nothing of the kind is final; inspection of the inventory would show how many points need further study in the light of modern knowledge. The inventory describes all sites and remains of historical interest known at that time (excepting documents, church plate and other small movable articles.) They are arranged by parishes, and the

---

[78] Collingwood, W.G. 1926. An inventory of Westmorland and Lancashire North-of-the-Sands. Transactions of the Cumberland and Westmorland Antiquarian and Archaeological Society, vol. 26, pp. 1-62.

[79] Collingwood, W.G. 1926. An Inventory of Westmorland and Lancashire North-of-the-Sands. Transactions of the Cumberland and Westmorland Antiquarian and Archaeological Society vol. 26, pp. 1-62.

parishes are grouped in twelve districts intended to conform to a scheme approved by H.M. Inspector of Monuments for the supervision of our antiquities by local correspondents. A valuable index was included at the end of the inventory that enables a reader to turn up any given place. Gershom's son Robin G. Collingwood supplied the entries relating to Roman artifacts.

Gershom's health was poor during 1923, yet he accomplished a great deal of work, presenting papers, visiting sites and working on inventories. Dorrie too was in poor health at that time so they arranged to spend a few winter months of 1922-23 in the Welsh coastal town of Barmouth. The climate can be mild at that time of year also, in Barmouth John Ruskin began a series of experiments in alternative living as part of what became the Guild of St. George, so Gershom was well acquainted with the town. While there he took advantage of the dramatic hill-country and coastal light to produce works of, in particular 'The Rock Gardens of Barmouth' a scene looking over the town across the Mawddach Estuary towards Cader Idris. Arthur Ransome visited them in Barmouth, where Gershom encouraged him to write about sailing his boat Racundra, published later as 'Racundra's Last Cruise'.

When editing W.S. Claverley's research on early sculptured work in the Diocese of Carlisle (Diocese of Carlisle at that time covered all Cumberland and Westmorland, now Cumbria, including Furness, Cartmel and Lancashire North-of-the-Sands). Gershom wrote a review of early Cumbrian art. He came to understand the development of post-Roman people by the art they left behind. Gershom produced a map showing the distribution of early monuments and from that indicated the settlements of people.

> 'We see the Angles coming in along the Wall to Bewcastle, Carlisle and Ruthwell; over Stainmoor to Kirkby Stephen and Addingham; up the Maiden Way to Lancaster, Halton, Heversham; and over the fells or round the coast to hold the important harbour of Ravenglass with settlements on both sides of it at Irton and Waberthwaite. These places have monuments of the earliest Anglian period. Then in the lowlands of North- West Cumbria they seem to have settled and mixed with the native Welsh, producing the group of spiral crosses, with outliers at Addingham and perhaps Dacre. These seem to be of a secondary age and derivative art lasting into the period of Scandinavian settlement. After 876 the Danes began to flock in from the East, over Stainmoor (settling only in the lowlands, most familiar to them); and a few years later the Norse came in from the Isle of Man and Ireland. Their art is to be seen at Gosforth and along the West Coast; that of the Anglo-Danes (connecting with types more common in Yorkshire) at Halton, Burton, Kirkby Stephen, and generally along the eastern side of the district; and both styles gradually and gently slide into the Normanised through still

appreciably English ornaments of the twelfth century, such as we have seen in Bridekirk font.'

Much of Gershom's reasoning relied upon recognising consistent styles in each period, but typological methods could be unreliable, as his son Robin was to point out in a later paper of 1935 when writing about the Bewcastle Cross. He made an important point that much of the art was imported and not of native origin; foreign workmen came to the country between 674 and 705, and later bringing with them changes, which were assimilated into native styles of art; the Acca Cross at Hexham Abbey is a good example. Another important point was the danger of seeing carved stone crosses as self-contained works of art, in Robin's words: *There were wooden crosses before stone ones; these too were perhaps decorated; and if so, the stone crosses form not a self-contained series but one influenced at each point in its history partly by earlier stone examples and partly by surviving crosses in timber.* Carved wood panels have survived with the twisted worm motif, first noted by a Lake District antiquary Robert Ferguson who found they closely matched Norse artwork. Carved work in wood from this period is rare and confined to panels, such as the 'Kist' found at Satterthwaite in South Lakeland (discussed later). The idea that decorated wood crosses could influence later work in stone can only be an assumption because no timber crosses have survived. The story of Cumbria was W.S. Calverley's aim; Gershom set out to complete this work and justify what he said was Calverley's favourite statement: (remembering that Calverley was a man of the Church) '*that there has been a continuous Church here since the days of the Romans, in spite of all the vicissitudes, and that we have monuments of every period bearing witness to the fact*'.

# Chapter X
# Scandinavian Studies
# (1895-1928)

**Early Interest**

Jens Worsaae (Danish archaeologist) writer of 'Danes and Norwegians in England, Scotland and Ireland' (1852)[80] can be described as the first serious writer about Scandinavian influence in Britain followed by Robert Ferguson's 'Northmen in Cumberland and Westmoreland'(sic) (1856).[81] Worsaae made the journey to Britain between 1846 and 1847 at the request of the King of Denmark to look for evidence of Viking settlements, so his brief was to cover a much larger area than the North of England. The first attempt to describe in detail Norse settlement in Lakeland came from Ferguson who could provide evidence from research rather than rely only upon speculation, though Norse rather than Danish settlement in Lakeland was only a tentative suggestion by Ferguson; he reconsidered the subject after reading the book by Jens Jacob Asmussen Worsaae.

Mathew Townend in his book 'The Vikings and Victorians in Lakeland' claims that Ferguson lacked skill in philology, which led him to make errors; it appears that Ferguson was well-aware of this weakness in his methodology, but not necessarily of the full implications, it was left to Gershom to provide more positive evidence about Norse influence in Lakeland. After much research he concluded, as pointed out earlier, that early Scandinavian influence in Lakeland came not from Danes but from Norse. After much research, some referred to earlier, he concluded that ancestors of people in the Lake District were Norse, coming from the west, Ireland and the Isle of Man, and not Danish coming from settlements in the East of England; this conclusion has been supported by subsequent research. Gershom wrote that only the estimated date for Norse settlement, given by Fergusson, can be questioned being earlier than the late tenth century the period given by the much-respected antiquary Ferguson. Gershom described Robert Fergusson[82] as *'one of the great men on whose shoulders we sit saying, how far can we see?'* Gershom recognised fully that Ferguson had done possibly more than anyone previously to establish Scandinavian influence in Northern England as a subject worthy of

---
[80] Worsaae, J.J.A. 1852. An Account of Danes and Norwegians in England, Scotland and Ireland. London: John Murray.
[81] Fergusson, R. 1856. The Northmen in Cumberland and Westmoreland. London: Longman.
[82] Collingwood, W.G. 1932. The Lake Counties (Revised). London: Frederick Warne.

serious study. At the time Gershom was studying the subject another view was presented by J Gray Fellow of the Anthropological Institute (Saga-Book III 1901-1903, pp 217-234). In his paper, 'Anthropological Evidence of the Relations between the races of British and Scandinavian', he found less evidence than expected for the presence people in Britain with characteristics of Scandinavian people: sizes of heads, eye and hair colour etc. Anthropological data and their interpretation have moved on since Gray's study but this was another perspective at that time.

Gershom was not alone in his Antiquarian work, studying possible Scandinavian settlements in Lakeland: William Slater Calverley, Henry Swainson Cowper, Thomas Ellwood, Robert Ferguson M.P. Dr Charles Arnold Parker and Jens Jacob Asmussen Worsaae all made significant contributions but as Mathew Townend points out[83] Collingwood 'may have been the most scholarly and the most imaginative'. Certainly, he was the most imaginative in his attempt to describe life in Lakeland 1000 years ago.

**Viking Club**

Gershom's interest in Norse influence became stronger when he joined the Viking Club in 1894, two years after it was founded as 'The Orkney, Shetland and Northern Society'; later to become, The Viking Club and later still, The Viking Society for Northern Research. In the same year Gershom wrote a paper comparing the names of Norse origin with names in use in the Lake District, published as 'Some Manx names in Cumbria' published the following year. (Appendix A). Manx names were chosen because the paper was written at the invitation of The Antiquarian Society of the Isle of Man. In comparing Manx names with those in Cumbria, Gershom considered three classes of words: Celtic, Scandinavian and mixed. Of particular interest was the mixed class where he recognised words from Celtic to Scandinavian. A set of words were identified, which are not found in Icelandic use yet are used in Cumbria to leave little doubt that they were brought over by the Celticised Vikings from the Isle of Man.

Shortly before Christmas in 1895 Gershom met Jón Stefánsson when in London to give the 'Vikings in Lakeland' lecture to the Viking Club. Later, he received a letter from Dr Stefánsson suggesting that they translate an Icelandic Saga. Gershom agreed and the two spent most of November 1896 working on 'The Life and Death of Cormac the Skald'. The original book was written between 1250 and 1300 about events many years earlier; a copy of the original text was held in Copenhagen at the University Library. The task of Gershom and Dr Stefánsson was to translate

---

[83] Townend, M. 2007. In search of the Lakeland Saga. In Old Norse Made New, Clark D. and C. Phelpstead, (eds). London: Viking Society for Northern Research, University College.

Figure 27 Kist Wood Panel by W.G.C.

a copy of a book written around 600 years earlier, in the thirteenth century about events in the ninth, or tenth century. Original sagas were not recorded by writing them in runes, but simply passed through the generations by word of mouth. Normally, around 200 years could elapse between events being first spoken about and recorded in writing. This suggests that a good deal of invention and modification could take place over such a long period, but as the translators explain, saga telling was an art and a craft that we no longer possess. It can be said that the written word largely destroyed, or at least hindered, the power of memory and recall. When sagas were told and re-told at firesides, people listening would be quick to notice any slip by the teller of the story; the least incorrect detail would be corrected. Cormac seemed so like the Victorians who read of him, yet a major difference existed. Cormac was Pagan, a Heathen of pre-mediaeval time; so different from later characters in stories that were conditioned by Christianity.

The translators, Collingwood and Stefánsson, described the motive of the book as: *The story of a poet, poor and proud, with all the strength and all the weakness of genius. He loved a fine lady, a spoiled child, who bewitches him, and jilts him, and jilts him again. He fights for her, rhymes for her, and rises for her sake to the heights of all that a man in his age could achieve. Then, after years he has her at his feet, and learns her heartlessness and worthlessness. He bids her farewell, but dies in the end with her name upon his lips.* The story is of real persons and real events, it is not a work of fiction. Cormac is mentioned in the Landnámabók; he is also named among the poets of King Harald Greyfell of Norway (AD 960-65).

## Norse in Lakeland

When Gershom delivered a paper in London about the Vikings in Lakeland,[84] it was to members of the Viking Club; he had travelled around 300 miles from Coniston to London in December 1895 to give the lecture. There can be little doubt that for preference he would have chosen the title 'Norse in Lakeland', but he would be thinking of his audience that evening. By the time of the lecture he had been a member of the Viking Club for only one year, his first book of fiction had recently been published, 'Thorstein of the Mere: a saga-type story about Norse settlers in Lakeland'. His lecture to the club was a first venture into the presentation of scholarly work he had done on Scandinavian influence in Lakeland; in the Saga-Book of the Viking Club it was reported that the lecture was received with great interest, though from a disappointingly small gathering. There was much discussion afterwards and questions were raised mainly over Gershom's interpretation of place names claimed to be of Scandinavian origin in Lakeland.

Full appreciation of this important paper was to come much later; to mark the centenary of the Viking Club (1992) a small collection of past papers from the Saga Books of the club were re-published, which included Gershom's paper 'The Vikings in Lakeland'.

In presenting the paper, Gershom adopted an approach practised in his earlier studies of the past in Lakeland, what now would be call 'triangulation' by approaching the subject from three independent viewpoints. First, by using place-name method further developed by Gershom from studies done by earlier Antiquarians in Lakeland: The Rev. Thomas Ellwood, who was 16 years older than Gershom and an established figure in South Lakeland, inspired Gershom to adopt place-name method. The work of J.J.A. Worsaae done many years earlier (from 1842) was especially valuable: Worsaae listed 13 Danish- Norwegian name-endings as they occurred by county in England. The highest number occurred in Lincolnshire (292) followed by Yorkshire North-Riding (186) then Westmorland (158) Cumberland (142) Yorkshire West- Riding (110) and East-Riding (109). The lack of Scandinavian penetration into Northumberland and Durham was reflected in occurrences of (23) and (22) respectively. Counties with low occurrences were Huntingdonshire (1) Warwickshire (3) Buckinghamshire (3) and Bedfordshire (4). Other counties recorded between 6 and 52. Devon and Cornwall were not listed. The highest concentration lay on a line from Lincolnshire through Yorkshire to Westmorland and Cumberland (now Cumbria).

---

[84] Collingwood, W.G. 1896. The Vikings in Lakeland: Their place names, remains and history. Saga - Book of the Viking Club, vol. 1 pp.182-196.

The second approach by using identifiable remains (archaeology) left by earlier settlers in the area was the least productive, as discussed in the previous chapter.

The third approach was to use what Gershom called 'History' in effect, folklore because so little information was in the form of written historical records; so little exists from early Christian period in the north-west that Gershom was forced to rely upon place-name research and folklore. In the words of a more modern writer Deirdre O'Sullivan: *'Then there is folklore, traditions, customs, superstitions and suchlike which archaeologists, but by no means only archaeologists, tend to fall back on when all else fails'.*

Gershom came to realise that Norse settlers moved from the coastal plains into the higher pastures over a lengthy period. The upper valleys were wild and largely uninhabited but for a few scattered British homesteads. The Norse settlers in Lakeland, as in Iceland, relied mainly upon mountain sheep to provide wealth and sustenance. Like cattle, the sheep were milked, and their wool was highly valued when woven into cloth. Pigs too were raised. Norse methods of 'farming' upland areas were established that were to be practised for centuries in Northern England. When reporting his observations on farming in Iceland, Gershom wrote that they used the Irish approach to farming, *'and if you do not know what the Irish approach is to farming, it is to do as little as possible'.* Certainly, no farmer could do as little as possible on the uplands of Lakeland and survive; which is possibly a reason for Anglo-Saxons and Normans staying away from Lakeland's high country, while the Norse farmers and their descendants thrived.

**Place-name Research**

Gershom in his study of Scandinavian influence upon place names in the North of England and in particular the northwest recognised that many early settlers came from the Isle of Man and he wrote a paper[85] comparing names on the island of possible Norse derivation with those in Cumberland and Westmorland. The Isle of Man contains fine examples of stone slabs with inscriptions from Scandinavian language written in runes, Norse version. The carved images on these slabs are similar to many found in Northern England (but note Richard Bailey's comments, previous chapter). Gershom developed a command of place-name study at this time and applied it well in his research and in writing papers about Scandinavian influence in Northern England.

Working with place names, Gershom drew a map showing distribution of Norse and Danish settlements. He named it 'Viking Settlements' The distribution

---

[85] Collingwood, W.G. 1895. Some Manx names in Cumbria. Transactions of the Cumberland and Westmorland Antiquarian and Archaeological Society, pp 403- 414.

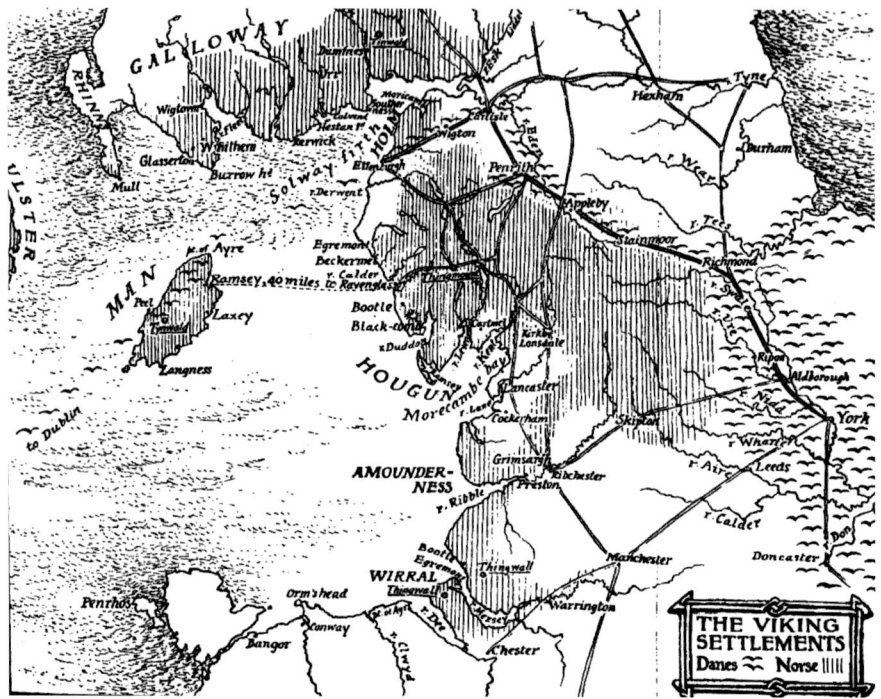

Figure 28 Distribution Map of Norse Danish Settlements

of Danish and Norse can be seen clearly also the position of Thingvellir, in the Wirral and at Fellfoot. The name 'Hougun' south of the map was ancient for the district around Furness, South Lakeland. When complete a line could be drawn running roughly southeast to northwest from York through Richmond, Appleby and Penrith to Carlisle, Norse settlements lay to the west of the line and Danish settlements to the east. Beyond Carlisle, further northwest to Galloway in Scotland, settlements were only Norse. This gave further support to Jens Worsaae's study during the 1840s, referred to earlier in this chapter, though Gershom's findings cover a smaller area.

Study by Gershom of place-names in his own part of the north, Lakeland, showed that settlements were not only Norse but also Irish-Norse. This conclusion came from several Gaelic words embedded in the Norse language, what Gershom called loan words taken from the Gaels. Most of these words appear to have been unfamiliar to Norse on their arrival in Ireland or the Isle of Man, yet there was evidence of a strong Gaelic infusion into the language of Norse by the time they moved into Lakeland. Gershom introduced members of the Viking Club to his own idea that loan words crept into Norse words and all loan-words were of Gaelic origin. These Gaelic names in the tenth and eleventh centuries could be called Gaelic- Viking or Viking-Gaelic because many Gaelic names in the Lake District were introduced by Scandinavians arriving from Ireland or The Isle of Man, or were adopted by them after arrival in Lakeland.

During these early days of Norse study Gershom used as a main reference for place-name study the work of Rev. Thomas Ellwood, he compiled a glossary of words which seem allied to or identical with Icelandic or Norse. His subject of study was the dialect of Cumberland, Westmorland and Lancashire north of the Sands.

Thomas Ellwood came upon this subject of study by chance, as he described in a paper read at Coniston Hall in September 1897, published later in the Transactions (TCWAAS) 'Notes upon some of the older word forms to be found in comparing the language of Lakeland with the language of Iceland'. One day Ellwood was on a visit to Brantwood, at that time the home of Dr George Kitchin Dean of Durham before becoming Dean of Winchester. During the visit Kitchin was working on proofs of an Icelandic dictionary compiled by Richard Cleasby and Gudbrand Vigfusson. Kitchin knowing Ellwood as a local man born and bred asked him if he could find any affinities between Icelandic words and those used in the dialect of Westmorland and Cumberland. In making this request Kitchin, like many people with an interest in Lakeland, would suspect that some links did exist.

Thomas Ellwood, thinking about when Norse first settled in Iceland (around 874) stated that:

> 'The language of the Northmen had been carried to Iceland, and there, isolated and remote from the contact of other languages, it had in great measure preserved its primitive grammar and vocabulary, so that the Icelandic classics of a thousand years ago could with little difficulty be read by the Icelandic peasant of the present day'.[86]

Could any of these words be understood by the native population in Lakeland? The initial request by Dr Kitchin for Thomas Ellwood to compare the two languages led to detailed research for the next 18 years.

When Thomas Ellwood set about his task of finding affinities between words in Westmorland and Cumberland local dialect and Icelandic language he had the

---

[86] Rev. Ellwood, T. 1888. Notes upon some of the older word forms to be found in comparing the language of Lakeland with the language of Iceland. Transactions of the Cumberland and Westmorland Antiquarian and Archaeological Society, vol. 9, pp. 383-392.

advantage of knowing shepherds, farmers and other local people in Lakeland, many he knew from early childhood. Dr Kitchin followed his progress closely over the years and was always ready to offer advice. Up to this time a common image, developed especially by philologists, was that northern settlers were plunderers and that any connection between local dialect and that of settlers must emphasise plundering-type activities. After careful study by Ellwood he came to a very different conclusion. He found a remarkable thing, that matching words reflected mainly a peaceful disposition: farming names, husbandry, management of sheep and cattle, butter and cheese making, knitting and general domestic tasks featured strongly. Another remarkable finding was that corresponding words showed an agreement not only in original meaning but also in secondary meaning derived from them, to show that people of Lakeland retained many of the habits, customs and superstitions common to people of far-northern stock.

In total, Ellwood identified almost 600 words where matches could be identified and made a detailed study of around 100 words. Wild upland-country was called by local shepherds and farmers *fell* the same meaning in Iceland was named *fjall*. The word *valley* commonly referred to in Lakeland as *dale* was in Iceland *dalr*. Name of a well-known Lakeland valley *Langdale* occurs in Iceland as the valley *Langidalr*. Head of a valley in Lakeland is *dale head,* in Iceland *dala drog*. Northern shepherds drove their sheep to the fell along narrow tracks called *rakes,* word for the same meaning in Iceland is *reka* or *rak*, to drive (A Norse verb to drive or drift as in water is *vreka*). A number of places in Lakeland have *ton* in the name, the Scandinavian name for a dwelling place is *tún*. Lakeland sheep 'two winters old' is *twinter* and 'three winters old' is *trinter*, these words for the age of sheep are used also in Iceland. The word *gimmer* is used in the north for a young female sheep before lambing, in Iceland it is *gymber* and in Denmark, *gimmer*.

Some words ceased to be in general use, even in Ellwood's time, an example being a three-legged iron stand used in cooking on an open fire called a *brandrith,* which was being replaced by ovens; when still used in Iceland it was called a *brandreid*. In Lakeland, where three counties meet, a person can have each foot and hand in a different county if standing, bent over, like a three- legged brandrith; a fell top near the mountain Great Gable in Lakeland has three ridges and is called Brandreth.

The work done by Thomas Ellwood in comparing common words in Lakeland with those in Iceland provided Gershom with a sound foundation for his work on place names. As an additional aid Gershom turned to his training in art.

Norse carving in wood and particularly stone provided good examples of their art and this appealed to Gershom the artist. He had already come to appreciate the art of Anglo-Saxon stone working. Examples in wood unfortunately are few; a wood panel (see Figure 27) 10 inches by 7 inches (25 cm x 17.5 cm) shows carving of a typical Norse worm-twist. The panel is known as the Kist from Cunsey, Satterthwaite South Lakeland.

Carved wood panels of this kind have survived with the twisted worm motif, first noted by a Lake District antiquary Robert Ferguson who found they closely matched Norse artwork found in Orkneys and Shetlands Islands. Other examples of worm twisting are found with Norse ironwork; interestingly work of this kind done by blacksmiths of Gershom's time differed little from Norse items found during archaeological digs.

Norse built their dwelling places with wood but these constructions have not survived in the north-west. Gershom can be thought fanciful when claiming that although original buildings have gone the Norse influence in style of home life remained in evidence. He cites both external and internal examples of farms in the nineteenth century where this influence could be recognised by someone, like himself, who was sufficiently sensitive to the earlier period: buildings grouped around a courtyard, porches with high thresholds, heavy oak doors with iron studs, outside stairs leading to loft rooms with small windows, and inside, long wood tables with a bench against a wall, and a stone hearth with peat fire, and above mutton hanging from the beams to smoke for food in winter. Gershom did add that this description of Lakeland dwellings corresponds to descriptions found in the Iceland sagas, but this alone was not sufficient evidence of direct Norse influence.

*Author's note: Many of the stone dwellings in place during Gershom's time were built upon sites of earlier wood construction, an ideal site is an ideal site whatever the year, and the best of features both inside and out would be passed from one generation to the next.* Therefore Gershom may not have been fanciful after all. A later contribution to this subject by R.W. Brunskill (1985)[87] made a distinction between vernacular building for utilitarian every-day uses and prestigious 'polite' architecture. Any Scandinavian influence in Lakeland is most likely found among vernacular building. Brunskill, like W.G. Collingwood much earlier, found it tempting to expect to find evidence of Norse influence in later buildings; he felt that the evidence does not exist, the main reason being that too long a gap existed between the Norse settlement and the seventeenth century when vernacular building fully emerged. Brunskill did not write-off the possibility that one day some evidence may be found; meanwhile we have Gershom's imagination and speculation about the subject.

Much earlier Roman settlements as camps or forts were constructed with local stone and survived quite well in more remote places, but where they have not survived well, in less remote places, is usually because stone was removed from

---

[87] Brunskill, R.W. 1985. Vernacular building traditions in the Lake District. In The Scandinavians In Cumbria. Baldwin, J.R. and I.D. Whyte (eds) Edinburgh: The Scottish Society for Norther Studies.

these sites for building purposes elsewhere. Some surviving stone circles in the north were thought to be doom-rings of the Northmen, but excavations show only earlier British remains.

Old Norse words are to be found throughout the district but mainly as dialect for things and landscape features. The words: beck, force, fell, gill, tarn, scree and thwaite are all based on Old Norse and in use today. Certain words, well-known to locals and to regular visitors to Lakeland, have clear Norse origin: 'beck' for stream; 'force' for waterfall; 'tarn' for small lake; 'scree' for slope of loose stones; 'fell' for rough hillside; 'thwaite' for slope going to the flat. In a later paper, Gershom drew reader's attention to how old forms of names in the north could be transliterated into Norse; names that have little or no meaning in English. He asked, 'what, for instance, does Blawith mean or Claife or Gascow or Greenodd, Ickenthwaite, Greta, Latterbarrow, Satterthwaite, or Sunbrick? These have no meaning in English, nor even in dialect; but when with the help of early mediaeval forms we write them as old Norse, they become not only sense', but thoroughly good sense and appropriate descriptions of the places :-Bla-vidr, Kleif, Gard-skógr, Graen-oddr; Grjót-á, Ikorna-thveit, Látra-bjarg; Saetra-thveit, Svina-brekka. Not only the meaning, but also the grammar of the Old Norse is preserved in these place-names. For example, Osmotherley used to be written Asmunderlawe, for Astmundarljá; Arnside (mediaeval Arne-side) represents Arna-sida; but Rampside (Rammes-heved) correctly represents Hramns-höfdi. The early form of Broughton is Borch, for Borg; but we find the genitive case preserved in Borrowdale, mediaeval Borcheredale, for Borgar-dalr a name given to two valleys from the Roman forts in them.

After further study, Gershom explained pitfalls in using place-names as a guide to previous habitation; not simply the observation made to The Viking Club that only when a word ending of *by* appeared in clusters could it indicate a Danish settlement and that odd isolated use of a name ending could not be interpreted in this way and this applied equally to other name endings. Later he elaborated upon specific places. An isolated Dearham or Brigham does not prove the presence of Saxons. A complication arises with the ending of '*ton*', a group of '*tons*' as in Low Furness (south Lakeland) is a clear sign of Anglian presence, but an isolated '*ton*' as in Colton or Ulverston can be regarded as a Norse settlement. Name ending of '*by*' is common in Norway and Iceland as 'baer' so '*by*' cannot be taken as proof of Danish settlement, but again, a cluster of '*bys*' clearly indicate Danish origin while isolated '*by*' as in Sowerby or Kirkby is not necessarily Danish in origin. The ending of '*ton*' may not be Anglian; in Scandinavia the ending '*ton*', though not widespread, has the same meaning as in Lakeland, not 'town' but ground on which a farm buildings stand. Ancient Scandinavians, like Teutonic people, had no towns as observed by Tacitus. Matches in name endings can be found in unexpected places: ending of '*ham*' is found in Norway with Thrándheimr being Thrandham in English; Medalheimr in Iceland is Middleham in English. A key task for an antiquary like Gershom was to eliminate names that were not coeval with the original settlement, that do not belong to the same age or generation.

The place-name method, as a rough guide to the previous distribution of Celts, Anglian, Saxon, Danish and Norse settlements proved useful when handled with caution. Some members of the Viking Club were able to see a map, drawn by Gershom, when shown as a slide in a magic lantern that shows distribution of Norse and Danish settlements (Figure 28). Gershom was not strictly correct in describing his maps (or charts) of settlements as 'ethnographic' because they showed only the position of settlements in relationship to each other with no description of individual societies and their distinctive features as found in ethnography.

**Mapping Norse Settlements**

In his study of England's northern history, Gershom relied a good deal upon making and using maps. In 1893, while still working with Ruskin and caring for the ailing Professor, Gershom sat in his study at Lanehead and spent summer days of August plotting the Norse names on a map of the district, the names he wrote in runes, Norse version, to help him become immersed in that period. In a letter to his wife Dorrie who was away at the time he wrote that the maps absorbed him completely (even attention from the children could be seen as an intrusion, which suggests all or some of the family were still at home and not with mother).

**Writing the Lakeland-based Sagas**

As Gershom drew his maps, a saga-like story could be coming into his head. Norse settlers coming from the Isle of Man or Ireland did not inhabit an empty land especially in the uplands, where they preferred to live; there they had to confront the native Gaelic or merge with them. The Gaelic had among them people who could claim descent from Romans going back 500 or 600 years (Romano-British). In the absence of written records, Gershom's thoughts would lead naturally to fiction but based on what could be discovered from carved images, folklore and place names that could all be traced to the tenth century, or even earlier.

While plotting Norse and Danish names on a map he checked names leading up his own valley to Coniston Water and a story began to form in his mind about Thorstein the son of a Viking, a young man who explored the rivers coming out of a great stretch of water Thurstan (Coniston Water) nestling among the hills further north from his home. In the twelfth century, the name for Coniston Water was Thorstanes Watter; Gershom pointed out that in Latin this could be Turstini Watra but the most likely source of the name came from a Scandinavian with the name of Thorstein. Origin of the name Thorstein and possible link with a stretch of water was only one example of how the study of place names could make an important contribution to knowledge about the history of an area.

'Thorstein of the Mere' was Gershom's first major venture into saga writing. Through a story of Thorstein Gershom hoped to encourage a perception of and feeling for the idea of northernness and its origins; a sense of belonging to a northern past by knowing more about ancestors. Gershom was a key figure in the promotion of northernness or in encouraging people of Lakeland, his chosen home area to know more of their past. In one review of the book[88] a comment was made on Mr Collingwood's style: *Certain of his images almost hurt by their sharp beauty and every paragraph is drenched in noble feeling for the fells and the dales and the lakes.* To help further this work he became the Lake District representative in The Viking Club. In the saga, Thorstein was a second-generation Norse settler in Lakeland. Father, Swein, settled his family in the south of Lakeland, now Greenodd-on-the-Leven. Thorstein's grandfather, Biorn, had farmed in Norway until forced to escape from King Harald Fairhair and sailed to what they called the South Isles. Thorstein Sweinsson's mother was Unna. From evidence gathered by Gershom of Scandinavian early settlements he describes in detail their living conditions, and type of farming carried out by Thorstein's father.

In writing what could be a first saga about earlier life in Northern England he had to imagine what life for local people would be like around 1000 years before he was writing. Although a work of fiction, the story built upon historical (folklore) evidence available to Gershom through his research over the previous five years. Gershom wrote the book (published in 1895) for a young boy, to help him imagine what life would be like 1000 years ago; the boy was his son Robin, five years old, who took an interest in his father's writing . Gershom dedicated the book to him:

> 'Thanks, Robin: for the wide world o'er
> A writer asks no finer flattery'
> No kinder fate of all in store,
> Than Five-years-old's assault and battery
> Demanding more and more.'

Again, Gershom gathered evidence for the story from three distinct sources: place names, folklore and archaeological remains. Place names he used to describe where Thorstein lived in a Norse settlement while nearby lived people thought of as Welsh (Gaelic) whose ancestors lived there before the Romans arrived, and continued their way of life after soldiers had left the country. Folklore he used to help describe daily farming activity and customs at that time. The archaeological

---

[88] Reviewer, 1930. Fell and Rock Climbing Club of the English Lake District, vol. 8, p. 355.

remains were mainly of stone foundations to show sites of British settlements. The following is an outline of the story as related to Dorrie:

> 'The story begins with Thorstein as a young man settling into a strange area surrounded by even stranger people. The area lay between Ulverston (Wulfherestun) in the south and Torver further to the north. Between these two places were many sites where Britons (Picts) lived; some would claim Roman descent, even though there was little contact with Romans in South Lakeland during their occupation of England. While walking in a wood, Thurstein met a young, tall Pict girl with long auburn hair. He liked the girl and she took to him but once caught up in her tribe he suffered in their hands, he was a fair stranger and so unlike them in many ways. Yet, Thurstein learns their ways and the language and comes to love the girl. Thurstein escapes taking the girl with him but meets only hostility from his own family who treat the girl as their thrall [Servant]. When she was about to become his wife, Thurstein's brothers take her away to be sold. They tell Thurstein that the girl has fled back to her family. Eventually Thurstein satisfies his family by taking a Norse girl as his wife and they have children. The Pict girl returns and murders Thurstein's wife, the children and tries to murder Thorstein but drowns in the attempt. Thorstein is left wondering what to do with his life.'

When Gershom sent the outline of this saga to Dorrie (away from Lanehead recovering from illness), he asked her in a letter (AH) to help him with further writing. The final version of the story had more depth and was rather more complex than the outline; to what extent Dorrie instigated changes, if at all, is not known.

The published story Thorstein of the Mere follows only roughly this outline sent to Dorrie. Thorstein did meet a Pict girl (Raineach) but not in a wood. While wandering far from home, against his father's instructions, to find Thurstan Water he was captured by men with long red hair, men so large they were referred to as giants. Thorstein was only thirteen winters old and they treated him so roughly he needed time to recover. Nursing was done by Raineach a little younger than Thorstein and a friendship developed. Yet, Thorstein still wanted to go home to his family. Knowing the language (Erse) after spending three winters in the settlement he asked Raineach's father to be released. The giant of a man said that if Thorstein would look after cattle upon the fell over one summer and one winter without loss he could go. After much hard work, this was accomplished, but the father insisted upon a second task, to drain a nearby tarn and replace with corn; he was instructed to change blue of the water to yellow of the crop. With Raineach's help, this too was done, but still one more task to build a house from fir trees had to be done before he could be released. On this revised outline Gershom crafted the saga 'Thorstein of the Mere' with possibly some help from Dorrie and in the proof stage, his son Robin. The story is not pure fiction (what is?). Mathew Townend[89] in discussing Dr Charles Parker's book 'Story of Shelagh: a saga of Northmen in Cumberland in the tenth century' (1909) wrote *'this is of course antiquary fiction. But as with Collingwood's Lakeland Sagas, there is nothing in the work that is knowingly untrue, and the re-creations are based on Parker's deep knowledge of the region and its history'*. This last statement is true also of Gershom's writing of sagas; based upon what he knew of early Norse settlements, associated folklore, and limited archaeological remains to provide clues about life in Lakeland immediately before arrival of the Norse. The Norse occupation of what became Cumberland, Westmorland and Lancashire North of the Sands had been a subject of interest to Gershom since boyhood and gradually into adulthood; he recognised a need for Lakeland-based sagas.

**Icelandic Sagas**

Sagas originated in Iceland during the medieval period as narratives of heroes or families. Sagamen, the original tellers of sagas, wrote nothing, but relied upon their ability to tell and re-tell sagas without losing any part of the tale, and without adding new material. Each saga is based upon a story, normally including poetry.

Eventually, Sagamen dictated to a scribe. When a story was derived orally it became known as 'freeprose' and when from written accounts, 'bookprose'. At the time of Gershom's first interest as a boy (1860s) there was no saga-based literature about earlier life in England's northern counties; all literature of this kind came from Iceland.

Probably the first writers to suggest a connection between Scandinavian-based language and that spoken in northwest England were poets Robert Southey, William Wordsworth, Thomas De Quincey and Samuel Taylor Coleridge. Southey followed a Scandinavian theme in his poetry (1795). Wordsworth, in his Guide to the Lakes (1820 edition),[90] referred to *'a population mainly of Danish or Norse origin as the dialect indicates'*. Wordsworth's first edition of his guide (1810) makes no direct reference to Scandinavian influence. De Quincey in the Westmorland Gazette (1819-20) wrote a series of articles in which he gave his opinion that the Lake District dialect was of

---

[89] Townend, M. 2009. The Vikings and Victoria Lakeland: The Norse Medievalism. Cumberland and Westmorland Antiquarian and Archaeological Society. Extra Series 34, p.137.
[90] Wordsworth, W. 1820. Guide to the Lakes. Oxford: Oxford University Press.

Danish origin (rather than Norse). De Quincey had a keen ear for words and knew some Danish, one day sat in the kitchen of a Lakeland farmhouse he heard a woman, feeding her baby, say 'no more patten' he immediately recognised a Danish word for breast. When he questioned the young women about what she meant by patten she was too embarrassed to say, replying that it was just something said to very young children, but De Quincey had recognised a possible Danish connection. On another occasion in Ambleside he heard a woman say in annoyance about a man 'I'll skyander him', noting here a Danish word for 'scold'. That De Quincey, who spent around 15 years in Lakeland, made comparisons with Danish rather than Norse was understandable at the time. He noted, in general, a similarity between certain words in Cumberland and Scandinavia; also he was possibly the first writer to recognise direct links between Scandinavian way of life and that in Lakeland; a step beyond comparing only the use of words.

Coleridge wrote (unpublished at the time) 'Of the Priest Saemundur' based upon what he had read of the man who may have compiled the Edda, loosely a collection of ancient poetry and prose. 'Edda' is a term that frequently appears in works about Scandinavian literature: this Old Norse word has had many definitions from scholars, related to Poetic Edda and Prose Edda. The term 'Edda' appeared first in the thirteenth century in Icelandic literature. However, material goes back to the ninth or tenth centuries. Icelander Eiríkr Magnússon wrote a paper titled 'Edda' to put forward his theories about the name, which was published in the first volume of the Saga-Book of the Viking Club. Magnússon recognised two possible sources of the word as genealogically based or book title-based.

The first use of Edda as a genealogical term occurred in a poem 'Lay of Rigg' where Edda refers to a great grandmother, and took on the meaning of grandmother. Magnússon, after discussing various works of poetry and prose of Iceland in the fourteenth century favours the term being the derivations of Edda as a book title. Gershom appears to use the term as covering ancient prose and poetry from Iceland in an unquestioning way.

Both Iceland and Northern England were colonised by Scandinavian settlers and in this respect had much in common, except in records of their respective history there was a major difference between saga literature of Iceland and total absence of similar literature in the North of England. There were no Lakeland or Northumbrian sagas; a gap or an anomaly? Despite the interest in saga-type prose (and poetry) in Victorian times there was no equivalent literature *from* England. A plausible reason for the lack of sagas in England at the time they were being written in Iceland has been offered by Mathew Townend[91] that the only people

---

[91] Townend, M. 2009. The Vikings and Victoria Lakeland: The Norse Medievalism. Kendal: Cumberland and Westmorland Antiquarian and Archaeological Society, p. 276.

able to write them would be monks at a local Abbey. '*Monks were either Norman or leaned to the Norman party then in power who regarded all Englishmen as barbarians; and not only made little distinction between Norse, Angles, and Welsh, but knew little and cared less for their history and belief.*' Stories were told around open fires at this time to include past heroes or families close to being sagas and passed from generation to generation, but in a less skilled way than the Icelandic tellers of sagas; at times becoming somewhat distorted at each telling until they had the nature of fiction. Although this was not universally true, groups of people listening to the stories were familiar with every detail and would be quick to correct any deviation from the anticipated line as practised in Iceland. When Gershom his sister and brother listened to stories at the knee of a local fisherman, told while in his cottage at Gillhead, the children would absorb early life of people in Cumberland, including those of the Norse period.

Gershom felt he needed to know more about the source of this literature and to do this he needed to talk with someone who knew the country of Iceland or who had at least visited there, this he was able to do when meeting William Morris.

**Lakeland Sagas**

When thinking about why no saga-type tales existed in Lakeland or in the north-country, Gershom recalled the story of John Audland who could form the basis of a saga. He lived at Crosthwaite by the Lyth in the early eighteenth century whose tale could be told in saga-style, in Old Norse. John was known to frequent an alehouse 'The Sign of the Dog' in Dalton-gate Ulverston. He left the hostelry penniless and gave his promissory note by word of mouth, promising to pay what he owed:

> 'I, John Audland,
> Before I gang hence'
> Awe Betty Woodburn
> Just six and two pence,
> And Thorsday' come' sennet
> I'll pay t'auld score,
> And wha kens but I may
> Spend twice as much more.'

Later, John lost a lawsuit and spoke of lawyers; Gershom commented that he rhymed better when he lost a lawsuit:

> 'God mead men,
> And men mead money;

God mead bees,
And bees mead honey;
But t'devil himself
Mead lawyers and tornies,
And placed em i' U'ston [Ulverston]
And Dalton i' Forness.'

Prominent among the early serious attempts to fill this gap of Lakeland-based saga literature was W.G. Collingwood with his two sagas, first sagas of this kind: 'Thorstein of the Mere' (1895) was followed by Bondwoman (1896). There is a possibility that Gershom came across writings about Scandinavia while at Oxford with prompting from Ruskin in the early 1870s. Walter Scott was one of Ruskin's favourite authors and Scott had published in 1814, 'Eyrbyggja Saga', this work of Scott, if introduced by Ruskin, could be read by Gershom, but this is pure speculation.

The work of Scott could mark the beginning of interest in the sagas among some people in the nineteenth century but there was too William Herbert who knew Danish and Icelandic languages and produced 'Select Icelandic Poetry (1804). This had possibly less impact than Scott's later saga-related work, though Herbert continued with his translations that, together, form a corpus of the Poetic Edda. Other notable saga-related writing soon followed translations of Heimskringla in 1844 and Njáls saga in 1861. Publication of an Icelandic-English Dictionary in 1874 and Sturlunga saga four years later were other landmarks in the study of Scandinavian life. Another well-known writer at this time to translate Norse fairy tales, folk tales and a saga 'Burnt Njal' was Sir George Webbe Dasent (1817-1896) Professor of English Literature and Modern History at Kings College London. He saw the Vikings as advanced people well-ahead of other nations in terms of civilization, not unlike the later Empire building of the nineteenth century in Britain; a small island off the north-west coast of Europe.

Possibly the most influential translations (for enthusiasts rather than scholars) later in the century were by William Morris and Eiríkr Magnússon forming the Saga beginning in 1891[92] (William Morris died before they could complete their work). Some years before Gershom visited Iceland a well-known author H. Rider Haggard, the writer of adventure stories, set mainly in Africa, went to Iceland and wrote a saga-type story, 'Eric Brighteyes' published in 1890, which helped fuel still further the interest in Icelandic sagas; though the story was possibly too close to Haggard's own time to be truly a saga. Following on from Gershom's writing of sagas a local

---

[92] Morris, W. and E. Magnússon 1905. The Saga Library: Done into English from the Icelandic. 6 vols. London: Bernard Quaritch.

writer, and close friend of Gershom, Dr Charles Arnold Parker wrote 'The Story of Shelagh Olaf Cuaran's Daughter'. Gershom's book Thorstein of the Mere, published in 1895 was well received, but the sequel 'Bondwoman' published the following year proved controversial among many Victorian readers; the woman of the title was too-easily seen by them as an unwilling concubine, disturbing family life. The book described Oddi Samsson, main male character in the story, as a responsible husband who respected family values. The story revealed tensions between family values and a need for personal freedom and this more than any other aspect of the book upset some Victorian readers, especially those who had difficulty reconciling family values and personal freedom. A reviewer in the Spectator magazine declared that the book ought never to have been written.

Gershom in writing 'Bondwoman' painted a word-portrait of the Langdale valley in the English Lake District; anyone on a walking tour of the area would do well to carry this small book to add interest to what can still be a pleasurable experience. Oddi was one of only three Statesmen in the valley, each being holders of land. Oddi's homestead was at Skelwith, Arni another Statesman was at Colwith and Brand the third was at Walthwaite. A small group of 'native' dwellers, they called 'Welsh' lived at Mickleden at the head of the valley, a cove between the Langdale Pikes and Bowfell. The three families had little contact with these people. The three Statesmen met others of their kind at a meeting place in Little Langdale at Fellfoot where a Scandinavian- type Al-Thing had been established. So Gershom begins the book by describing in detail the Norse settlers and surroundings of their chosen homes.

The story begins with Oddi and his two friends going to Ravenglass, a port on the coast to trade goods for wine and wares from abroad brought there by sailing ships. While on the quay at Ravenglass Oddi and Brand took a liking to some fine lasses who could be bought in exchange for goods. One lass Deorwyn a Saxon woman who became Bondwoman of the title was bought by Oddi for all the goods he had. The three men and two women, the second woman Taté had been bought by Brand, made their way up the Eskdale valley through thick woodland with the river Esk flowing beside them. They had the stiff climb past a disused Roman camp at Hardknot before entering the Langdale valley and reaching home. On the way, Oddi had to think of how he could tell his wife Groa that all he brought back was one lass rather than food or livestock. Deorwyn came from Wessex and Oddi reasoned that she would know many things not known in the north, for example, she could tell tales of King Alfred and how her grandfather has seen him. Oddi did persuade his wife that after some good feeding they could sell Deorwyn for more goods than he had paid originally. Goa felt that it would have been better to bring a horse or swine from Ravenglass. This is briefly the outline of the story's beginning; not too difficult to see how it offended readers in Victorian times with their stress upon family values, especially when Deorwyn settled into the household, but the story needs to be read completely.[93] Subsequent editions of the book were entitled 'Bondwomen'.

## Iceland Early History

The period of first human settlement in Iceland is given by Rev. Joseph Bosworth (1836)[94] who stated AD 861 for the discovery of Iceland. Peter Hallberg 'The Icelandic Saga' (1962)[95] gives dates between AD 870 and 930 for colonisation of the country. Many early colonisers came from Norway, Denmark and some from Ireland. Christianity was officially recognised in Iceland in the year 1000. Christian Chiefs Hjalti and Gizur rode to a meeting place called the Al-Thing at Thingbrekka and appealed to their countrymen to give up idolatry and worship the White Christ, a volcanic eruption made the people at the gathering think the Gods were angry at this appeal, but eventually the religion prevailed. Records suggest that Christianity was known and practised on the island before this time. Eiríkr Magnússon writing in the Saga-Book of the Viking Club[96] stated that Christianity existed in the country a long time before the arrival of Norsemen at around AD 870. Ari the learned wrote in his 'Libellus Islandorum' that Christians had an asylum in Iceland before AD 860. To support this claim of Christians from Ireland settling in Iceland, Magnússon refers to an Irish Monk, Dicuil writing in 'De Mensura Orbis Terrae' of talking to some clerics around 795 who had returned from an island in the extreme north. Their description of the island left no doubt that it was Iceland. Eiríkr Magnússon wrote, *'Christianity, with a revealed ideal of salvation, of eternal hope, was destined to conquer the heart of man; paganism, with no such ideal to lead and to inspire it, was bound to fall back, and eventually to evacuate an untenable position'.* A small number of Christians who did venture so far north, returned to their Irish homeland because they did not want to live alongside Pagans from Scandinavia, and left behind relics and practices from Ireland. The Norse settlers knew these Christians as 'Papar'.

Further evidence that Iceland was inhabited before 860 comes from people who travelled from Iceland to Britain in the time of Bede, who died AD 735.

---

[93] Collingwood, W.G. 1896. Bondwoman: A Story of the Northmen in Lakeland. London: Edward Arnold.
[94] Bosworth, J. 1836. Scandinavian Literature. London: Longmans, Rees, Orme, Brown and Green.
[95] Hallberg, P. 1962. The Icelandic Saga. University of Nebraska.
[96] Magnússon, E. 1890. The conversion of Iceland to Christianity, A.D. 1000. Saga - Book of the Viking Club, vol. 2, pp. 348-376.

For records of Scandinavian settlement around AD 874 we turn to a book of this early period in Iceland, equivalent of the Domesday Book in England, this was 'Landnámabók' (The Book of Settlements) compiled in Old Danish by Ari Frodi (born 1067) in the early 12 century. The book listed people and places connected with the early colonisation of the country around 874. Similar settlements took place in Northern Britain around this time, but in Iceland the early settlers entered an empty land, while in Britain they would come across Celts, Anglo-Saxon and Romano-British. Details of possible Norse settlement in Northern England and Lakeland in particular extended the work Gershom had been doing on Anglo-Saxon stone crosses as part of his study of the pre-Norman period; what he saw as part of art-history could be moved on to include the introduction of Scandinavian influence.

## Land of Volcanoes

Iceland is a land of dramatic coastlines, hot springs and glaciers but above all active volcanoes leading to vast areas of barren wildness; a land that some learned people in nineteenth-century England found fascinating, Gershom among them. For a description of the country and its people, in the early part of the century, they relied upon written accounts from travellers who made expeditions to Iceland and who brought back sketches and paintings; later travellers could add photographs to other images of the country. In addition, they read translations of Icelandic literature, the sagas. Towards the end of the century, this interest was increased by lectures given by Eiríkr Magnùsson and his published writing in collaboration with William Morris. Gershom had the good fortune to meet William Morris and be inspired by him.

## William Morris and Iceland

While in London at the Slade School of Art and soon afterwards, Gershom had almost day-to-day conversations with artist Edward Burne-Jones and eventually met William Morris, a lifelong friend of Jones beginning when students together at Oxford University. Morris was described as: designer, businessman, poet, author and visionary socialist; as a young man, like Gershom, he aspired to be an artist, but was finding another outlet for his creativity in writing poetry, building an arts and crafts business and becoming successful at merging art with business. Gershom, who had already become fascinated by Scandinavian influence upon the history of Northern England, became inspired further by William Morris and his writings, which led to serious study of Iceland and its people.

Morris met Gershom through Burne-Jones but it is not clear whether this first meeting took place while Gershom lived in London or later when Gershom had become more settled in the North of England and was turning his attention, tentatively, to Scandinavian studies. From Gershom's letters there seems to be no clear evidence that he first read of the Icelandic Sagas through works of translation done by Eiríkr Magnùsson and William Morris in the early 1870s while still a student at Oxford. If Gershom did read the translations at this time it would be 'Friðthjófs saga hins frǽkna' and 'Völsunga Saga: the story of the Völsunga and Niblung'. As explained in Chapter II, Gershom could not avoid being aware of Iceland while growing up and at school in Liverpool; first seeds of interest could be planted at that time. Then some years later the meeting with William Morris and his enthusiasm for the country could easily re- awaken in Gershom a desire to know more.

Morris's Iceland companion Eiríkr Magnùsson was born and brought up on a lonely farm in Iceland before settling in England (1863) and from 1871 he worked as a librarian for 40 years at the University Library Cambridge living at Sunnyside, 91 Tenison Road in the city. Gershom was far from being alone or even part of a small group in his enthusiasm for the sagas and interest in Icelandic life; so great was the interest among some Victorians that Magnùsson was in constant demand as a lecturer about Iceland and the sagas, travelling with his wife throughout the country. So great was this interest that he had difficulty in fulfilling his programme of lectures; an interest that has been thoroughly discussed in a fine book by Andrew Wawn (2000).[97] The sagas that appealed to Victorians were stories from Iceland in the thirteenth century, recording family life, Viking expeditions and Norse Kings in poetry and prose.

Apart from both William Morris and Gershom leaving Oxford to have unfulfilled lives as artists, the two men had little else in common; Morris was wealthy and Collingwood poor; Morris was politically motivated, Collingwood had very little interest in politics; Morris was business-wise, again, Collingwood had no interest in business. However, Morris the older of the two had already ventured far north into Iceland and recorded his experiences, which helped foster in Gershom a line of research that would last for the remainder of his life.

Northernness became an area of study among some intellectuals in Victorian Britain, and Iceland became an important part of that study. William Morris wrote possibly the finest account of northern life with his book 'The Roots of the Mountains'[98] written towards the end of his life, the book showed his dedication to the subject.

---

[97] Wawn, A. 2000. The Vikings and Victorians. Cambridge: D.S. Brewer.
[98] Morris, W. 1896. The Roots of the Mountains. London: Longmans Green.

The languages of Old Norse and Old English also became associated with the subject of 'Northernness'. On one occasion, Gershom chatted to a northern farmer and when they were about to part the farmer said:

> 'ye don't look like a north countryman, and ye don't speak like a north countryman; but ye know a deal more than ye should'.

Gershom came into Lakeland from 'outside' (Liverpool/London) yet understood the North Country as well or better than most local people understood.

For both Morris and Collingwood the study of Iceland and the sagas helped maintain an active interest in art, for Morris this was the creation of unique designs and ideas for the writing of poetry and prose; for Gershom an opportunity for sketching and painting in an almost unique landscape.

William Morris began to take an interest in Iceland and Scandinavian influence in the North of England during his time as a student at Oxford, which was reflected in articles he wrote for the 'Oxford and Cambridge Magazine' in 1856. This interest was taken further during the late 1860s, the first written record at this time comes from a work by Morris 'The Earthly Paradise' published in 1868; a story about Norsemen in the fourteenth century. Morris committed himself to the study of Icelandic literature, even to learning the language. In collaboration with Icelander Eiríkr Magnússon, he began the task of translating from the Icelandic, especially sagas from the tenth to thirteenth centuries.

Morris made two visits to Iceland with Magnússon in 1871 and 1873 (while Gershom was still a student at school, then at Oxford). Magnússon, who was to take up his library position at Cambridge University, spent the remainder of his life in England. Andrew Wawn when editing the Iceland journal of Henry Holland[99] included a meeting between Morris and Holland, describing both as 'Icelandophiles'. In 1810 Henry Holland, physician to Queen Victoria, was one of the early travellers from England to explore Iceland and record his experiences. Morris had a fascination with Iceland so meeting Holland before setting out on his first expedition, could only be a dream coming true. He was fortunate to have this meeting because Holland was close to the end of his life when he and Morris met. Eiríkr Magnússon who was to be Morris's travelling companion had already translated some of the sagas. They both met in the London home of María Einarsdóltir, sister-in-law of Magnússon.

Also in the 1871 party to Iceland were friends of Morris from Oxford-student days Charles Joseph Faulkner mathematician and fellow of University College Oxford and W.H. Evans of Ford Abbey, Dorset an army officer interested only

---

[99] Wawn, A. (ed.) 1987. The Icelandic Journals of Henry Holland, 1810. London: Hakluyt Society.

Figure 29 Thingbrekka Iceland By W.G.C. (AH)

in what hunting could be available. The four 'explorers' travelled on Icelandic ponies; beginning in Reykjavík they visited sites of sagas on the west coast. The simple hard life of local people greatly impressed Morris, 'Poor yet contented' he found their lives so different from the divisiveness of life in England; *'the grinding poverty is a trifling evil compared to the inequality of the classes here'* [England]. Morris would be comparing poverty found in Iceland with social conditions found in his home country. When Collingwood met Morris he would be inspired by travels in the north and would get a sense of the social reformer in Morris, as he had done with Ruskin when at Oxford; both men can be described as fathers of the Labour Movement. The next visit to Iceland in 1873 was more adventurous, and arduous, Morris and Magnússon crossed a desolate part of the interior to the north coast at Akureyri close to the Arctic Circle, they crossed a wild volcanic area. Morris again found inhabitants wretchedly poor yet discovered examples of literature and art that were to inspire his own fiction and poetry, it is said that the fine vernacular literature of Iceland inspired some of Morris's finest poetry. Morris had published in 1873 'Love is not enough' based upon his travels. Two years later, Morris and Magnússon published their translation of some Icelandic literature with the title of 'Three Northern Love Stories'. In the next year Morris wrote a long poem based

Figure 30 Thingvellir Icelandic Parliament
by W.G.C. (British Museum)

upon an Icelandic epic; this poem 'Sigurd the Volsung' Morris considered his finest work. Typical of opinion at the time was in a letter from Charles Sayce to Eirίkr Magnusson (1887) 'as a work of art [Morris's Volsung] it is one of the most perfect that I have read'.

Morris's belief in and support for socialism and social reform involved so much effort in public speaking and delivery of party newsletters that it harmed his already poor health, he died in 1896 aged 62. Most of this work was done during formation of the new socialist party 'Social Democratic Federation'. Meetings with Morris and reading of sagas translated with Magnússon inspired Gershom to make the difficult journey to Iceland, one he could ill-afford financially but one he hoped would produce material for a book and cover at least his costs.

In 1910 when May Morris, William's youngest daughter, began editing her father's works (Morris had already one biography and was to have at least five other biographers by 1983) she needed to edit his writings about Iceland. May was close to her father throughout his life and worked in his business as an expert at embroidery and its design, and like her father was a socialist. For volume VIII of Morris's collected works (there were 20) May wrote from his journals of Icelandic expeditions. To help her, Gershom placed at her disposal his collection of water-colour paintings done while in Iceland. This collection helped her over difficulties in map making and was invaluable in supplementing her father's description of the colour of Iceland, helping her to understand his wonder and pleasure over its strangeness. It was essential that, in writing about Iceland, May fully appreciated the impact that scenery had upon tellers and writers of sagas, and Gershom's art helped fulfil a need to feel something of this impact. Another writer to make full use of Gershom's drawings was Olive Bray, editor and translator of 'Elder or Poetic Edda (1908) who appreciated the difficulties a translator had in capturing the graphic style of this work and relied upon the art-work of Gershom to support her writing, both for the cover of her book and throughout the text. Scenery of Iceland was an integral part of the sagas, difficult to put into words so Gershom's art became highly valued for those studying and writing about the subject. While Gershom, through his art, could support text of other writers there was one aspect of the sagas that could not be reproduced, the experience of listening to and, most importantly, seeing a contemporary person deliver a saga. That this was not possible led to difficulties for translators in presenting the true meaning of sagas. Difficulties experienced by various translators during the nineteenth century and into the twentieth have been very well described by Carolyne Larrington in 'Translating the Poetic Edda into English.[100] Also, in March 1897 Gershom spoke

---

[100] Larrington, C. 2007. Translating the Poetic Edda into English, in 'Old Norse made New' Clark, D. and C. Phelpstead, (eds) London: Viking Society for Northern Research, University College.

Figure 31 Altarpiece at Borg Iceland by W.G.C.

most eloquently at The Viking Club about difficulties faced by translators of Scandinavian-related literature.

**Iceland Expedition**

Translation work with Dr Stefánsson, coming so soon after writing his own Lakeland-based sagas, made Gershom wish to see sites of the sagas in Iceland and Stefánsson agreed to go with him. The expedition was planned for the following year (1897). Gershom was to follow in the steps of his friend William Morris who followed the Icelandic coast in 1871; like Morris, Gershom too chose to go in the company of an Icelander. By the time Gershom sailed to Iceland he had written his own Lakeland sagas and helped in the translation of an Iceland-based saga. He was eager to see and record, if possible, the scenes of early Icelandic sagas. Dr Jón Stefánsson who agreed to accompany Gershom was born in a remote northerly part of Iceland at Grundarfjordur in 1862, a Graduate of the University of Copenhagen where he wrote a thesis on Robert Browning. He spent around 50 years of his life in London, much of the time in the British Museum Reading Room when not lecturing about Scandinavia at London University. Dr Stefánsson was a founder of the Viking Society and became co-author with W.G.C. of 'A Pilgrimage to the Saga-Steads of Iceland', an illustrated account of the expedition, published in1899.[101] Dr Stefánsson Co-wrote the text with Collingwood, who also provided the illustrations; Dr Stefánsson called it a picture book, it had 13 colour plates and 140 black and white illustrations. Gershom illustrated the book, selected from his artwork done while in Iceland; in total around 300 works of art were completed. The main aim of the journey was to capture scenes of the sagas which was accomplished, probably the finest book about the country up to that time and still of value now.

The visit to Iceland was seen by Gershom as a pilgrimage, not in the sense of going to a sacred place but because he had an exalted vision of the country and its people, though it would be wrong to think he went for sentimental reasons. Gershom approached the task of studying sites of the sagas in a thorough scholarly way. In addition to his artwork, Gershom produced a map of the island.

In early summer of 1897, Gershom busied himself at Lanehead making preparations for the expedition. He drew £50 from their account, gathered together a number of sketch books together with a pocket Kodak folding camera, though he felt that pencils, paints and sketch pads provided a far more manageable and reliable means of recording images than the use of a camera, which over the rough terrain could too easily be damaged. In addition, after touring with Ruskin, he felt that stopping for an hour or more to draw a scene or building rather than pressing a camera button for only seconds was a far more satisfying way of capturing a journey. Years later, each image would be recalled far more vividly in the mind (Ruskin did make use of a photographic method, the daguerreotype, on early tours, normally taken by an assistant). Gershom also took a plait of Dorrie's hair as a watch chain. His letters home to members of his family were to serve as a first-hand written record of the journey.

Gershom and Jón Stefánsson sailed from Leith in Scotland on June 4 1897. The voyage to Iceland was made on a steam ship called the Laura built in Denmark and crewed mainly by Danes. First ports on the voyage to Reykjavik were in the Faroe Islands, which Gershom named the Fairy Islands (just as he named Iceland, 'Niceland', for a while); both places in the Faroes, Thorshaven and Klaksvig, pleased him and he was sorry to leave. One week after leaving Leith the Laura

---

[101] Collingwood, W.G. and J. Stefánsson, 1899. A Pilgrimage to the Saga - Steads of Iceland. Ulverston: W. Holmes.

entered the harbour at Reykjavik. In a letter addressed to Molly (Dorrie) Gershom described his first impressions of Iceland, which were to be repeated more or less throughout the journey. He wrote of everybody *'looking poor and the place entirely forlorn and heartbroken with bleakness and neglect and apparent depression'* (or so it seemed to him). *'The town is only as big as Bowness'* (beside Windermere in Lakeland) *'but a hundred times uglier and untidier'*.

The Iceland journey began when they joined another steam ship called the Thyra built on Tyneside, England that served as a coastal ship carrying supplies for places in various fjords. During the voyage and throughout travels in Iceland Gershom wrote letters home: to Dorrie and the children separately and to his father and sister Ruth living in Bristol. At the beginning of the journey, letters to Dorrie and the children were sent to Mr. and Mrs. Willink at Burneside, Kendal. Then the family moved back to Lanehead because during Gershom's period away Dorrie attended to some of Ruskin's correspondence. Despite gloomy early impressions of Iceland Gershom did meet some interesting people, mainly friends or acquaintances of Jón Stefánsson. Next day (June 12) they joined the ship Thyra to sail north from Reykjavik; they planned to travel on the Thyra to the Arctic Circle to reach an island on the north coast, home of Grettir the outlaw (Grettir Ásmundarsonar. Saga of Grettir the Strong) and work back overland visiting scenes of other sagas. What became

known as the Pilgrimage really began at Stykkishólm and worked their way through Snaefells-nes then round the Dales to the north and back over Grímstunga-heidi to Borg and Reykjavik; finally making a circular tour in the south, ending at Thingvellir before returning to Reykjavik.

There were places along the coast where it was not possible to dock the Thyra so she lay at anchor; cargo was unloaded and taken ashore on small boats. While the ship lay at anchor Dr Stefánsson and Collingwood could see slopes and cliffs coming straight down into the water, not a place to come for sitting on beaches. During these visits, there was only time for Gershom to sketch from the ship, but at a place called Thingeyri, three days after leaving Reykjavik, he went ashore and made sketches of the harbour. Collecting saga-related images by sketching, painting, photography or in prose was the main aim of the journey; only on two occasions in Iceland did Gershom dig into the earth like an archaeologist. The first dig was described in a letter to his eldest daughter Dora, June 17.[102] He described a journey from a far-north settlement of Stykkisholmur to Helgafell, where with the help of a local farmer he dug into the grave of a Gudrún Osvifrsdōttir who died

---

[102] Lea, M. and K. (eds) 2013. W.G. Collingwood's Letters from Iceland, pp. 42-47. Cardiff: R.G. Collingwood Society.

at the beginning of the eleventh century, said to be the prettiest in the land. They took great care to remove the earth and replaced it in the same order. Remains found in the grave were replaced except for a knife, a bead, some teeth and a small part of the skull; all were deposited with the Antiquarian Museum of Iceland. In a letter to eldest daughter Dora he compared the tomb with that of another lady, Ilaria di Caretto in Italy and wrote that *'it is the most interesting lady's grave to people like Daddy'* He could have added 'Mr Ruskin too'.

A highlight of the journey for Jón Stefánsson was to stay at his father's house by the sea near the Arctic Circle. The small wood cottage roofed with turf at Grundarfjord, surrounded by mountains, was home to his father Stefan Danielsson. While there, Gershom painted the fine waterfall Grundarfoss and visited Hofstadt, where Thorstein visited the great Thor's Temple. Grundarfjord was 100 miles (161 km) north from Reykjavik and they spent four days there, until June 23, before moving to Ólafsvík, where they stayed with a school friend of Stefánsson. From this base they visited the place where Björn the Broadwicker's champion was chased by Snorri and his men, and the cave where he stayed three days in a snowstorm. They went over a high pass, in snow, without guides and descended steeply to the ruins of Björn's house then on across a lava field to a house where they could stay. From the house could be seen a full view of Snaefellsjökull, described by Gershom as 'a sort of Mont Blanc' which he painted in its midnight effect. Both travellers stayed there for three nights and Gershom carried out a second dig of the journey, the tomb of Asmund who was buried in a ship. The grave had not been found before and after they left the area a lawsuit occurred between two landowners; Gershom wrote that he was interested to see whether they would accept his diggings as legal evidence to settle the case.

The next part of the journey meant crossing a high pass of rocks and deep snow, local people advised them not to attempt such a crossing. Gershom wrote that he found Icelanders were afraid of mountains though they lived among them; 'they never climb them, but keep to the valleys'. Dr Stefánsson's father was astonished that they had crossed the pass alone. While on this second visit to Grundarfjord Gershom painted the small cottage with Stefánsson's father standing at the door and horses tethered outside. Next day the travels were resumed by going back over Trollhals and over a lava field heading for Stykkishólm, which they failed to reach that night but stayed again at Helgafell before going to Stykkishólm.

At the beginning of July they were at Herdholt (Hjarðarholt) where Kjartan lived as a boy. Gershom described the place where the Irish princess who was bondwoman, and made believe to be dumb, was overheard talking to her baby and so discovered to be a Queen in disguise. It was here that Gershom recognised scenes featured in William Morris's 'Lovers of Gudrun'. Local people remember Morris and party, around 25 years earlier, camping in tents. There were times at this stage of the journey in Iceland when Gershom could feel himself in the Lake District: Borgardale (Borrowdale), Langdale and Little Langdale. Often in his letters, places are likened to the English Lake District: a high rock like the Pillar in Ennerdale, a track like the Walna Scar Road near Coniston, a pass through the mountains like Cumberland's Sty Head.

By the end of July they were back in Reykjavik and on the evening of July 29, they could return home on the Laura, but with almost half their work unfinished and 'hoping for another time, which may never come' they decided to stay a little longer. With money spent they needed funds to continue the journey. Jón Stefánsson through his contacts raised £10, so with economy they could continue; they had two weeks, before the next sailing, to travel south-east crossing below the mountains of Hekla with its crater and Eyjafell, to see the sites of Njál's saga, then, as Gershom writes, *'north to the Geyser' (Geysir) though this tourist site had no connection with sagas. Then, west to Thingvaller'* sic (Thingvellir). Other sites were passed over quickly, until they reached Thingvellir. At the famous site of the Al-Thing (Icelandic Parliament) Gershom spent time sketching and painting. The whole site is better known as Thingbrekka.

Thinvellir, near Reykjavik, lies at the north end of a lake Thingvalla-Vatn, a large expanse of water twelve miles (19 km) long and seven miles (11 km) wide; Thingvellir is the precise site of an ancient parliament of Republic Iceland; an outdoor assembly set among rocks. Gershom used some of his experience in drawing geological features, gained while with Ruskin in 1882, to produce a his painting of the landscape at Thingbrekka (Figure28), done while visiting the site on August 10, showing only the site of the parliament among rocks and in the distance a church, lake and mountains. The impressive imaginary scene of the parliament meeting painted after the Iceland journey (Figure 30)[103] shows around 130 male Icelanders and one woman attending meetings; the only woman stands arm-in-arm with a man in the foreground of the picture who appears to be hidden (or hiding?) from the assembled crowd. We can only speculate about why the couple are shown and what they were doing; no doubt a mystery that Gershom the artist intended.

Although the scene in the painting is imaginary, from what Gershom learned about large national parliaments of this kind called Al-Thing, the scene can be considered close to the reality of an ancient parliament.

In 1906, Gershom generously presented to the Viking Club this painting of 'The Parliament of Ancient Iceland' an important work that had hung in the Bruton Gallery London. The picture was hung in the Gothic Hall of King's Weigh House

---

[103] Wilson, D.M. 1980. Illustration of Iceland Parliament by W.G. Collingwood. in The Northern World, A.D. 400- 1100. London: Thames and Hudson.

in London, a meeting place of the club. The picture was of interest and value to Viking Club members, not only for its great artistic merit but also for recording a place of interest to all lovers of Icelandic sagas. At the time of writing, the picture has found a home in the British Museum. The painting is often referred to when this parliament is described as the oldest in the world. As expected such a claim is open to serious questioning, the least convincing objection being that the ancient Icelandic parliament was not a parliament in the conventional sense, not being democratic, but originally parliament was simply an assembly of representatives, whether elected or not. Democracy has since been accepted, without question, in Western societies, not too strong a point to say that democracy is worshiped and parliament thought automatically to be made up of elected representatives. For people who give democracy some thought it can be of doubtful value as a concept; the majority are not always wise or correct whether in elections or referenda. The Icelandic parliament operated from 930 AD until 1263 when Iceland came under the Norwegian Crown (A claim has been made that the Isle of Man has the oldest continuous parliament in the world, though not something to get very excited about). After spending time at this evocative place, a good ride along a lonely moorland road took the travelers from Thinvellir to Reykjavik in around 5 hours where they could join the ship Thyra. The ship took them back to Leith, where they arrived on Sunday August 29.

W.G.C. in collaboration with Jón Stefánsson summed-up well their journey to Iceland:

> 'Our one desire was to find the scenes of long ago, to put a background to the figures of history: and this we have done. Though there are a few minor sagas left without illustration, we may claim to have carried out our enterprise. We have seen the homes of the heroes. They are no longer empty names to us, no longer formless dreams; and with their reality the great dramas of old start into life and action. It is as if a curtain had gone suddenly up: as if our eyes were opened, at last, to the glory of the North.'

**After Iceland**

After the expedition of 1897, an exhibition of watercolours by Gershom was held at the Bruton Galleries in London. A Viking-Club member remarked that the pictures were no less memorable for lovers of literature of the north than are Tintagel and Camelot for lovers of Arthurian romance. Another exhibition of Gershom's artwork from Iceland was held at the Alpine Club in London from March 4 to March 25 1899. On the opening day refreshments were available and around 500 visitors attended. Comment from the Alpine Club, in their journal, was that 'his brush is handled, even under the most uncomfortable circumstances of travel, with a delicacy which it is unlikely that any Viking ever attained'. Understandably, from the Alpine Club, came the comment that in Iceland there is apparently more to attract the artist than the climber and perhaps more to attract the saga lover than either. A further comment was that Mr Collingwood was able to bring back a portfolio filled with so many sketches of interest and beauty is alike creditable to his industry and perception. The hope was expressed to see more of his work in the future, but nearer to home.

On his return to Lanehead, Gershom was hard at work putting together illustrations for what became 'A Pilgrimage to the Saga-steads of Iceland. A wonderful travel book, lavishly illustrated with reproductions of Gershom's sketches, some in colour, plus maps and diagrams; the number of colour images to be included was restricted by the cost of colour printing. The book was published locally by William Holmes of Ulverston and after the book's success; the same publisher took the translation of Cormac the Skald and included landscape illustrations. Another work of art by Gershom, related to the expedition, was done for the church at Borg in Iceland, a beautiful altarpiece of 'Christ blessing little children.' The colouring of the altarpiece was tender with sunlight falling through the branches of a vine, which plays effectively upon the head of the principal figure and the infant faces surrounding him. The picture was painted when home at Lanehead where his children could act as models. The picture painted by W.G.C. seemed to diffuse the brightness and warmth of the East throughout the whole building. (Figure 31)

## Reflecting upon Iceland

The overall feeling left with Gershom after the pilgrimage to Iceland was disappointment. Before going to Iceland, he had formed in his mind an image of Icelanders that proved very different from reality. When writing his introduction to Cormac the Scald he saw Cormac with a touch of Viking heredity and that he owed much to his Irish ancestry, like so many Icelanders. *'It was the blending of races that made them a great nation in their prime, greater than the Norse of Norway from whence they sprang.'* After the expedition Gershom came away with an overall impression that the modern Icelander was lethargic. They were descended from bold Viking stock, but over the years had adapted to a barren rather bleak environment. In a letter to Magnùsson, Gershom expressed the depression he felt. The actual contact with contemporary Icelanders had been all too disappointing, they did not live up to the dream he had gathered from the sagas and from Norse mythology, mainly from mediaeval Iceland at a time when Iceland had a thriving population, which possibly explained why Gershom went there with high expectations of his visit only to be totally disillusioned.

We could ask the question, would it be better that Gershom stayed at home working in his study where he could read sagas and tales from earlier travellers in Iceland. The answer must be no, mainly because we would be deprived of wonderful illustrations from his pencil and brush. In a more recent publication, Heather O'Donoghue (2007)[104] put forward a number of reasons for decline among Icelanders, particularly in terms of literary output, there were: climate change, internal instability, colonisation and changing politics of mainland Scandinavia; Iceland became isolated culturally as well as geographically. Valuable texts, a large repository of literature, including mythological texts and treatises, were for a time lost to the wider European world. Iceland had become a Danish colony. O'Donoghue writes specifically about literature when referring to a 'very severe decline' in Iceland and Gershom witnessed the same thing, but the general standard of living and ambition of its people fell well below his expectations too; on the other hand, kindness and hospitality from the people he could not fault.

**Scandinavian Settlements in Lakeland**

Gershom claimed that the 'Thingmount' of Little Langdale was *'the most remarkable monument of the Viking age in Lakeland.'* This terraced mound was first brought to publics' attention in 1889 by Henry Swainson Cowper when he delivered a paper at Fell Foot in September of that year; it was printed two years later in the Transactions of the Cumberland and Westmorland Antiquarian and Archaeological Society (TCWAAS), CW1, volume 11. Cowper was first alerted to the existence of this mound by Dr Alexander Craig Gibson who in 1849 wrote 'The Old Man or Ramblings and Ravings round Conistone'.The mound at Fellfoot, thought to be a Thingmount, stands at the junction of three roads, one leading north connecting to the port of Ellenburgh (Maryport) another west to the port of Ravenglass, and a third to the east and eventually to the gap of Stainmoor, and a possible fourth road, indistinct. This made the mound accessible from many parts of the district and ideal as a meeting place.

The mound is similar to the Isle of Man Tynwald, the main difference being that the Manx Tynwald is round, 240 feet in circumference (73 metres) and at Fell Foot it is rectangular 70 feet x 20 feet (21 metres x 6 metres). Dimensions of the stepped terraces are similar, both rising to around 12 feet (3.7 metres) overall.

---

[104] O'Donoghue, H. 2007. From runic inscription to runic gymnastics in 'Old Norse made New' pp.101-118. Clark, D. and C. Phelpstead (eds) London: Viking Society for Northern Research, University College.

The Tynwald on the Isle of Man is the finest example south of Iceland; 'Court of Tynwald' is still referred to on Man, the island was a dependency of Norway until 1266. A Tynwald exists in Dublin and two further examples existed as far south as the Wirral. After Henry Cowper's article, Gershom became fascinated by the terraced mound and painted a picture of the site. Cowper reported his find rather hesitatingly, suggesting other possible reasons for its existence. At first, Gershom considered the possibility that the mound at Fell Foot could be an old terraced garden, but asked why some of the terracing would be facing north out of the sun? Shortly before his death, Gershom wrote that *'he did not know the theory of a Viking Thingmount can be proved, but nothing so far has disproved it.'*[105]

When Gershom had made his pilgrimage to Iceland, the idea of parliament being conducted outdoors reinforced his about Scandinavian 'Things'; a Thing in Scandinavia is a gathering of people to discuss local affairs, establish laws and administer justice. 'Things' were found in many parts of northern Europe wherever Scandinavians exerted their influence. The sites chosen for people to assemble could be natural features such as a group of trees or mound of rocks. Geological features were often chosen as can be seen in Gershom's painting of an ancient parliament in Iceland at Thingvellir. 'Things' were normally of three kinds, depending upon the level of discussion and gravity of the subjects. The highest or National level was called Al-Thing, portrayed in the painting by Gershom. Where no suitable natural feature could be found, an artificial mound was constructed. Cowper did venture to suggest that *'we have here a Scandinavian 'Lawmount' or 'Thing' belonging to the same period as the Manx example'*. Place-names near the Mound at Fell Foot are mainly Scandinavian in origin. Gershom seems to have accepted the claim that the terraced mound in Little Langdale at Fell Foot was of Scandinavian origin. He referred to it a number of times in his short story about Thurstan at the Thwaite, in his book 'Coniston Tales' (1895) describing how people passed the Thwaite on their way to or from the 'Al-Thing' in Little Langdale. ('Th' is represented by the symbol Þ. Al-Þing or Þingvellir).

Gershom considered history in his study of this subject because in his view we have to ask from history an explanation of any ethnological chart. Alive now he would be likely to point out the origins of people living in the north,

their racial differences and distinctive characteristics, their relationship to one another or lack of relationship; all can be charted but still need explanation. What we do know, or at least knew at the time Gershom was writing, is that by the ninth century Anglian power had waned. The Danes landed at the ports on Humber and

---

[105] Collingwood, W.G. 1907. The discoverer of the Norse in Cumbria. Saga-Book of the Viking Club, vol. 5. Page 140.

Tees rivers to spread inland as far as York; the whole of what we know as Yorkshire East Riding was Dane land.

In 876, further progress was made by Danes when they moved North West leaving on their way names ending in 'by' Appleby, Sowerby and Kirkby. The river Eden was followed to reach Carlisle, through Lazonby, Hornsby, Corby and Newby. Carlisle, for some reason, was destroyed, even though the Danes settled in the area and needed dwelling places. Moving from this base, further travel westward brought them to an old Roman port, Ellenburgh (Maryport). This helped to establish a strategic route from Dublin to Maryport, then to York passing through places established by the Danes; a safer route than going around the south of Lakeland. Like the Anglians, Danes avoided central Lakeland and were happy to leave the hills and mountains to Norse hillmen. Gershom found some support for this idea taken from his place-name studies, very few names of hills or mountains could be associated with either Celtic or Old English before the arrival of Scandinavians. A direct route from Dublin to York, as the crow flies, proved too difficult because they would encounter warring tribes of Mercia. The nearest Danes came to high country was taking a route past the mountains of Skiddaw and Blencathra to Penrith and eventually York leaving behind possible evidence of their passing, close to an old Roman road they would use lies Dovenby and Motherby. Around this period, there is evidence that Norsemen settled along the Irish-Sea coast of Lakeland from the mid-ninth century onwards, eventually to make homesteads in upper valleys among the hills and mountains. This summary of Scandinavian movement around the North of England is more or less, what Worsaae speculated in the 1840s, referred to earlier.

Robert Ferguson put the date for Norse immigration between 945 and 1000 AD. From Gershom doing his intensive research into Norse and Dane movement we need to revise the date to sometime in the ninth century when Norse crossed in boats to reach the seaboard visible from their settlements on the Isle of Man. Once the Norse settled on the coast and moved into the upper valleys, Gershom pointed out that they could have no better refuge from the Danes. Meanwhile in Dublin a struggle went on between Danes and Norse to gain supremacy, but for many years the Danes ruled.

Gershom continued to be an active member of the Viking Club and kept up his Scandinavian studies. In 1911 there was held in London the Festival of Empire, sixty years after the Great Exhibition. Gershom made sketches of Danish costumes, which featured in the Danish Scene as part of the exhibition.

W.G.C. made a vital contribution to the study of Scandinavian life in Northern England; scholars before and after him all made their contributions to what can now be stated with some confidence, that Scandinavian history is part of English history.

# Chapter XI
# Academia and Lanehead
# (1905-1917)

## Reading University College

By 1905, the close Collingwood family at Lanehead, no longer existed they were united only through writing of letters. Daughters Dora and Barbara at Copes Art School in London, Ursula at school in Dulwich and son Robin a student at Rugby School. This must have brought sadness to Gershom and Dorrie even though it is a necessary and unavoidable experience for most families. With children in or near London and Dorrie becoming more successful as a portrait artist, living in or close to the city seemed more sensible. This posed a problem for Gershom, his spiritual home was in Lakeland where his research interests lay and where contact with other scholars and artists associated him with societies in the area. When in October he had the opportunity to take up a position at University College Reading in the Arts faculty a move south became almost inevitable. There was also a need to secure a more reliable source of income. With the loss of a small but regular income from Ruskin and only irregular amounts of money from his art Gershom had little option but to accept an academic position in a Fine Art Faculty.

This appointment brought to an end a few years of great uncertainty for Gershom. He had returned from Iceland to find Ruskin's health in rapid decline, while he was away Joan Severn had taken responsibility for his care and Dorrie helped in dealing with his correspondence. The time was approaching when thought had to be given to the children's possible futures away from Lanehead, especially the three daughters. For a while, around 1900, life went on as normal by Coniston Water, Dora the eldest child wrote an essay about John Ruskin, 'John Ruskin as girls knew him' which was published in 'The Girl's Realm' (1900 pp. 872-577) Robin was the first to attend school in 1902, helped financially by Miss Holt. In the following year Dora and Barbara went to Copes Art School in South Kensington, London funded from the will of Grandfather William Collingwood. The time was right for a move nearer to London, if only temporally, and home at Lanehead was sub-let.

Their first rented accommodation at Abbots Walk, Reading was at the recommendation of the College Registrar, which served them well for over a year before moving to other rented rooms at 16 London Road during the autumn of 1906. The family needed a larger base because there were times when all three daughters Dora, Barbara and Ursula joined their parents in Reading. Dora and Barbara left Copes school to take the Arts Teaching Course (ATC) in their father's department and qualified in 1909. Janet Gnospelius in her notes on the Collingwood family (Collingwood R.G. Archive Cardiff University) suggested that Dora in particular felt stifled at Copes and was pleased to join the Teacher Programme at Reading; we can only assume that Barbara felt the same about Copes. The school in South Kensington had been founded by society painter Arthur Stockdale Cope. Most students were female and there were strict rules about what young women could or could not do, while the few men had much more freedom. Whether at Copes or Reading, both daughters benefitted from being near London with so many galleries to visit, lectures at the Royal Academy and even visits to the Viking Club with Father. Youngest daughter Ursula, still at school in Dulwich, was not too far away and Robin at school in Rugby spent time at Reading, and was at home when the time came for him to attend Oxford for the entrance examination. Art was the main topic of conversation when they walked alongside the Thames at Reading and Gershom was their most serious critic.

**Denmark Lecturing Visits**

Gershom looked forward to his first summer (1905) vacation from Reading (University), to spend the time back in Lakeland but he accepted an invitation to lecture in Copenhagen; almost two weeks were spent in the city based at the Hotel Kong Frederik. Apart from lecturing and socialising, Gershom lost no opportunity to practise his art and produced a picture of the inner harbour of Copenhagen. In addition there was an important wood figure of St. Michael to be seen at Copenhagen Museum that he could compare with images of stone found in England. There was too the association with Professor George Stephens at Copenhagen University, through the late W.S. Calverley, to help facilitate discussion with local antiquaries. Expenses and lecture fees were paid so at the end of August when he wrote to Dorrie (AH)[106] telling her he would visit Stockholm before returning home, he added that he felt he could afford the trip. The lectures on Vikings and on John Ruskin were well received, Gershom told Dorrie that they laughed when they ought to and applauded at the end. So successful was this round of lectures that Gershom was back in Copenhagen for a week in January of the following year. In a letter to Dorrie January 11, 1906 (AH), he said 250 tickets had been sold at three Kroner each, a total of £40.00 *'will liberally cover expenses beside what they give me'*. He returned from Denmark before the beginning of his new term at the University College in Reading.

During these years at Reading Gershom lived in a way much like the years spent at Lanehead apart from the added tasks of preparing lectures and lecturing

[106] Letter 1905, W.G. Collingwood to Dorrie Collingwood. Collingwood Archive, Abbot Hall, Kendal.

to students, he worked on scholarly studies and had 26 journal papers published, two books, three contributions to published books, and translation of a book. From 1911, when he left his post at Reading, until his death 21 years later he produced a further 68 journal papers, six books and four contributions to other published work. While Gershom settled to life as a full-time paid academic he still had duties to perform outside the University, in particular with CWAAS and the Viking Club. In addition to writing numerous papers for Journals Gershom as head of art at Reading made changes, probably with the late William Morris in mind, mainly to encourage an arts and crafts approach to the teaching of art. Art and craft share many things, but art is not craft mainly because craft is always the means to a planned end, this cannot be said of art. Gershom recognised sufficient similarity between the two subjects of art and craft for him to introduce a unified approach. He also removed arithmetic and an essay from the requirements for entry to the courses, putting him somewhat ahead of his time. Dora was particularly critical of her father's decision to drop the essay, she saw it as a means of communicating with the lecturer; of the decision to drop mathematics no objections were raised.

Life at Reading was recorded by Gershom in an extremely brief and sketchy manner in his occasional diary entries (AH). The only consistent entry each year was about where they spent Christmas. During the first two years, each Christmas was spent at Reading. Third year (1907) was a blank but in 1908 Gershom spent Christmas alone at Lanehead because in early January he was working on a Coniston Parish Register followed by serving on a Grand Jury for Assizes at nearby Lancaster. By this stage (1908) Gershom was Professor of Fine Art at a salary of £350 per year. During part of winter 1908-1909, including Christmas, Arthur Ransome and his family lived at Lanehead. In an eventful year (1908) he and Dorrie celebrated 25 years of marriage, and he completed a book, 'Scandinavian Britain'. Earlier, in May of 1906 Gershom was asked to write a book about Scandinavian Britain as part of a history series. The book has remained of interest to people curious about Scandinavian (Viking) settlement in Britain and was re- published in facsimile in 1993, 85 years after first publication. Gershom covered the period from earliest Viking raids 787 to 1069 only going beyond this time to describe re-population of Yorkshire. Gershom provided extraordinary insight into how our society owes so much to Scandinavian influence.

Gershom and Dorrie resolved their conflicting needs as artists by dividing their time roughly in equal portions between London, Reading and Coniston until 1911 when Gershom resigned from the university to concentrate upon research, writing and his art, though there was the suggestion that he left the post because of increasing bureaucracy. The decision for Gershom to leave University College Reading was probably made over Christmas 1910 while they were at Lanehead because he wrote the letter of resignation on December 30. After leaving Coniston

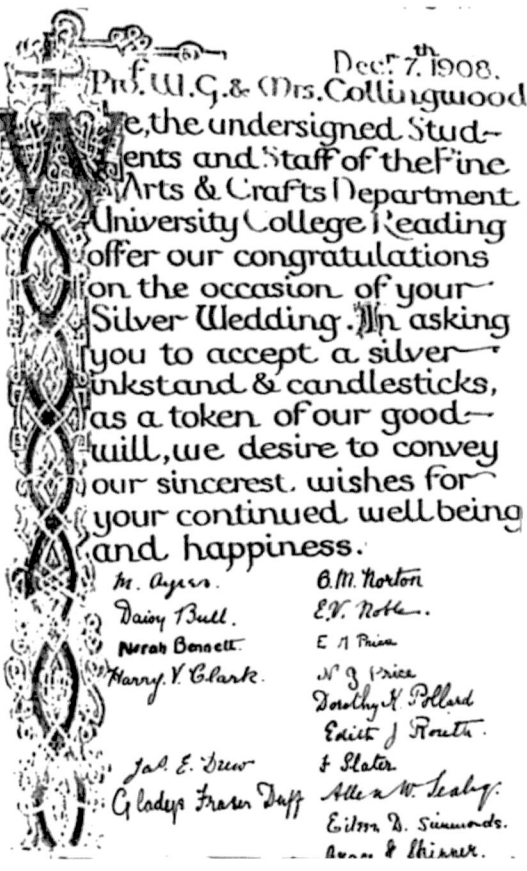

Figure 32 Wedding Anniversary Scroll
Collingwood (R.G.) Archive Cardiff University

for Reading in January, his resignation was accepted in February, and in March he said goodbye to colleagues at University College. Both Dorrie and Gershom were well liked and respected by staff and students at the college, shown by a scroll given to them marking their silver wedding anniversary (Figure 32). During his time at Reading Gershom had not given up any idea of following the life of an academic at a more prestigious University. In 1910, he applied for the position of Slade Professor at Oxford but was unsuccessful; Selwyn Image, who while a student at New College Oxford was strongly influenced by Ruskin, filled the position until 1916.

When W.G.C. left Reading, he left academic life.

## Viking Club President

Whenever Gershom attended meetings at the Viking Cub they expressed delight and surprise, living in Lakeland he could attend so rarely. The move to Reading made attendance much easier and in 1905 became their President. In this role he was called upon to fill diplomatic duties and welcomed explorer Nansen and members of royalty from Sweden, Norway and Denmark.

One of his watercolours, 'Kjartan finds Hrefna wearing the Coif' was bought by the club through subscription and presented to Her Royal Highness Princess Margaret of Connaught on her marriage in 1905 to His Royal Highness Prince Gustaf Adolf of Sweden. She became H.R.H. Duchess of Scania. Gershom in his first year of Presidency made the presentation.

Gershom also designed and illuminated an address, enclosed in an embossed leather case, to be given to His Majesty King Haakon of Norway. The design was of a Scandinavian doorway surmounted by a Viking ship. The address was presented to King Haakon at Buckingham Palace; the wording read:

> 'To their Majesties the King and Queen of Norway. May it please your Majesties: The members of the Viking Club beg most respectfully to offer their greeting and welcome to Your Majesties on this your first visit to Great Britain since your accession to the ancient throne of the Yngling Kings.'

We claim an especial interest in this event, because our Club exists to study and preserve the records of that age, when Norway and the Norse took so important a share in the making of the British race.

Counting among our members natives of Your Majesties' Kingdom, we trust, in studying past history, to strengthen the present bond which links us to Norway by many ancestral memories and natural sympathies. It is our earnest hope and wish that Your Majesties' reign may be long and prosperous, to the furtherance of friendship between Norway and Great Britain.

> '(Signed) On behalf of the Viking Club.
> President.000 W.G. Collingwood,
> Secretary. 00 Amy Johnston, Hon'

Earlier in the year (1906) Gershom, as President, wrote an address to the King of Denmark, on the occasion of his accession to the throne. In the address he referred to the kinship and fellowship which bind together the Danish and the British peoples.

## German Miners

During the summer of 1911 both Gershom and Dorrie would be delighted to settle once more in Lakeland. From around this time a photograph shows Gershom seated on the ground feeding a cat with left to right Robin George, Ursula, and Dorrie looking on (Figure 33).

Dorrie painted landscape scenes around their home, in particular Coniston Old Man from Lanehead garden, from the head of Coniston Water and later the mountain covered in snow. Gershom too settled back home at Lanehead dealing with local matters and writing a book 'Elizabethan Keswick' which was published in 1912. This book was based upon earlier work done while teaching in Reading. In July 1909 he read a paper at Carlisle 'Germans at Coniston in the Seventeenth Century' published in TCWAAS the following year.[107] It was after the publication of this paper that Gershom was told about original account books of the German mining company, David Haug, Hans Langnauer & Co. that still existed. These books, included reports written at Keswick, were sent to Augsberg. From thinking that his paper of 1910 said as much as there was to say about German miners in Lakeland, he realised that this new find enabled him to write a book based on mining around Keswick. The valuable accounts (1569-1577) were placed in the City Archives of Augsberg. Gershom carried out extensive research he sat using these records in what was the hometown of many early German miners. He transcribed and translated extracts from the original account books found in the archives. Before completing this research, the description of mining practices was based mainly on hearsay, and contained a number of inaccuracies.

German miners began working the mines near Keswick in 1565 and Coniston in 1599; in both places they found what they recognised as primitive methods for mining tin, lead and copper (mines of the Lake District had been worked some years before 1565 at the time of Henry III to Edward VI). They came from the German town of Augsberg where mining methods were far advanced.

Gershom pointed out that historically Henry VIII attempted to attract German miners, '*but like so many international measures of the Tudors, they did not become effective until the reign of Queen Elizabeth.*' Foreign miners came to Coniston with encouragement from Allan Nicholson of Hawkshead Hall. Initially the ore from Coniston was taken to Keswick for smelting, causing heavy traffic on otherwise little-used silent tracks.

---

[107] Collingwood, R.G. 1910. Germans at Coniston in the seventeenth century. Transactions of the Cumberland and Westmorland Antiquarian and Archaeological Society, vol.10, pp. 369-394.

Figure 33 Gershom feeding cat with L-R Robin, Ursula and Dorrie. (ULC).

Gershom was outspoken in his support for mining in the district and stressed the value mining had brought to the Lakes, but did overlook that the type of mining did not bring the blight to Lakeland witnessed in other parts of Northern England where mining was being practised. He could see immediate benefits for the area, then and in the future. Some German miners settled in the district and married local girls, providing Gershom with much interest in finding family names of his own time that were descendants of miners who came to Coniston under Elizabeth I and James I, as a branch of German mining at Keswick. The work was reminiscent of his place-name research.

The mines, with improved working methods, generated great wealth until political disputes during years of the Civil War closed most of the workings that had been 'Mines Royal' since Queen Elizabeth's time. Gershom maintained that much of the prosperity of Cumberland and Westmorland during the nineteenth century could be traced back to this growth in mining activity and the wealth it created. Lead and silver mines at Alston had German management in the mid fourteenth century and Gershom remarked that the importing of foreign management had not damaged English trade in the past 500 years, and it need create no fear in the future.

**Surprise Visitor**

After Reading and settled back at Lanehead he and Dorie did not have the number of visitors experienced by Ruskin along the road at Brantwood, and with children grown up and away from home, working or studying, there was little to disturb them. One surprise visitor came on a bicycle the 20 miles (32km) from Keswick over Dunmail Raise. This was Wilfred Owen about to become a famous poet who was attending a Christian convention in Keswick, and decided to visit Gershom to talk mainly about Ruskin as he explained in a letter to his mother[108] (April 1912). At the time Owen was serving as an unpaid lay assistant to a Vicar at Dunsden Vicarage (near Reading) and had a strong interest in the relationship between religion and science so would be drawn to the work of Ruskin; another interest was Rose de la Touche, a close friend of Ruskin who died so young. Owen had a letter of introduction to Gershom from Miss Rayner a colleague of Gershom when teaching at University College Reading; she taught Owen botany during the time he attended a course on the subject, but not as a university student. Owen, young with little reputation at this time would be rather in awe of his host, especially after Gershom's long association with Ruskin. Well-fed and given generous amounts of whisky during a long discussion with W.G.C. Owen got on his bike for the strenuous ride back to Keswick, which would be made with seemingly little effort even though a storm was building up with heavy rain.[109] Back in Keswick 'home' for Owen was a tent outside the town shared with three students from Durham University, a sharp contrast from the Collingwood home at Lanehead.

**Bewcastle Cross**

By New Year 1914, both Gershom and Dorrie were firmly settled back at Lanehead in a house that must have seemed far too large for only two adults. Dorrie still painted and Gershom was occupied with editing Transactions (TCWAAS) and organising various antiquarian and archaeological projects. In July of that year, close to war, Gershom arranged to meet a group of people who were members of the Society of antiquaries of Newcastle-upon-Tyne; most lived in or close to the

---

[108] Owen, H and J. Bell (eds) 1967. Wilfred Owen: Collected Letters. London: Oxford University Press. Also Hibberd, D. 2003. Wilfred Owen. London: Constable. Page 108.
[109] Johnson, P. 2012. A Philosopher at the Admiralty, Vol. 1., pp. 90-91. Exeter: Imprint Academic.

city or from various parts of the North-East, but one lady came from London, a gentleman from Letchworth and another from Enfield. Rain threatened and it was cold, more like a November day rather than July.

They all gathered at Brampton town railway station when the 10.09 am. train arrived from Newcastle. The party of 30 members and friends, including Gershom, had a long drive from Brampton Station to Bewcastle, stopping at abandoned Askerton Castle on the way. The main purpose of this excursion was to visit Bewcastle, its church and ruined castle but most of all to see the stone cross. Gershom stood close to the cross and read to the group gathered there. This was done from a paper he had prepared earlier.

When giving a possible date that ornamental stone crosses were first in use Gershom found he was somewhat isolated from other scholars in the field, he gave reasoned explanation for putting the date as AD 740 rather than earlier at 675 as more commonly thought, mid-eighth century rather than late-seventh century. The current view was that the famous Bewcastle Cross was carved and erected at the beginning of this period around 675. In contrast Gershom gives the date as 790, the main reasons being that the cross at Bewcastle was strongly anglicised in style, which placed it much later than originally thought, and the carving was too skillful and mature to be done at the beginning of the period. This episode in dating one stone cross provides us with a good example of how Gershom would not necessarily follow commonly held ideas, preferring to arrive at a conclusion based upon his research evidence, questioning and reasoning. Later, Gershom had to defend his position with regard to dating of the cross when some scholars gave the date as twelfth century; one writing in the Burlington Magazine in 1912 and a Professor Albert Cook gave this later date.

Previously, Gershom had been guided towards a date for the cross by studying inscriptions. When standing by the cross talking to members of the Society of antiquaries of Newcastle-upon-Tyne in July 1914[110] he spoke of giving up inscriptions to follow instead the development of the art-history of such monuments, thinking that the ornament and workmanship have a story to tell us, quite independently of any reading of the runes. Gershom explained his change of approach: *'I have been looking for methods of classifying the early crosses of this type; and after careful drawing and analysis over 600 of the 800 pieces left in the six northern counties of England, as well as studying what I can of others in this great series, and interlaced work in central France and north Italy, I think it possible to infer some conclusions, perhaps provisional, about this link in the long chain.'* In doing classification he recognised that in the development of knots, scrolls, figure-sculpture and techniques of inscription, shows how the art of

---

[110]Collingwood, W.G. 1914. Bewcastle. Proceedings of the Society of Antiquaries of Newcastle-upon-Tyne, Series 3, vol.6, No 22, pp. 213-219.

the stone carver progressed or declined from period to period, just as in any other branch of art-history. '*I think we can trace back from Norman work to the 11 century, and thence to the Danish and Norse work of the Viking age in Northern England. The Vikings evidently developed their monumental art from what they found here, altering it gradually to their own taste: and the previous work had left abundant examples in its last period (the 9 century), though fewer, but still many of the earlier stage; this earlier stage can be dated in some examples, from such work as the Ormside cup*' (AD 900).

After his father's death Robin George Collingwood debated these conflicting ideas about the Bewcastle Cross[111] and came to his own ideas about its origins independently; he too found support for a later date in the eighth century rather than later in the seventh century.

---

[111]Collingwood, R.G. 1935. The Bewcastle Cross. Transactions of the Cumberland and Westmorland Antiquarian and Archaeological Society, vol. 35, pp. 1-29.

# Chapter XII
# Naval Intelligence
# (1917-1919)

## London Base

Gershom was 60 years old when war was declared in 1914 so could not be expected to play an active part in what was to prove a huge political disaster in our relatively recent history, the first of many to the present day; unfortunately no lessons were learned, other wars were to follow. Gershom's son Robin was a severe critic of the war '*a war of unprecedented violence broke out: and when the belligerents tried to discover what they were fighting for, nobody knew.*' In his autobiography Robin wrote of the war as an unprecedented disgrace to the human intellect. However, in October 1917 while working in his study at Lanehead Gershom received a message from Robin, suggesting that he join him in Naval Intelligence, Geographical Section code-named I.D. 32, based in London at Hertford House. Son Robin had joined this division after being rejected for a commission in 1914 due to poor eyesight and a troublesome knee complaint.

Naval intelligence had been built up by Sir Reginald Hall from room 38 at the Admiralty and was to become the most effective unit of its kind in the world. Hall was appointed Director of the Intelligence Division of the Naval Staff in November 1914; the title changed four years later to Director of Naval Intelligence. He collected around him cartographers, cryptographers, technical personnel and spies. Robin had been with Naval Intelligence since January 1916, at first based at the Geographical Society building in Kensington, where access to maps in their archives proved particularly valuable.

Each day Robin walked across Kensington gardens averting his eyes from the Albert memorial, which showed sensitivity towards art normally associated within the family to his mother, father and three sisters; he felt that the memorial was so bad in every possible way that he could not bring himself to look at it. Robin thought he ought to have more pressing important things on his mind, working for Naval Intelligence, than to become obsessed by what he saw as the ugliness of the Albert Memorial.

The Geographic Section needed more room so moved to Manchester Square to occupy Hertford House which was (and still is) home to the Wallace Art Collection, for protection the collection had been moved out during the war.

During his first year of intelligence work (1917) Gershom still managed to complete the editorship of the Cumberland and Westmorland Transactions

CHAPTER XII NAVAL INTELLIGENCE (1917-1919) 201

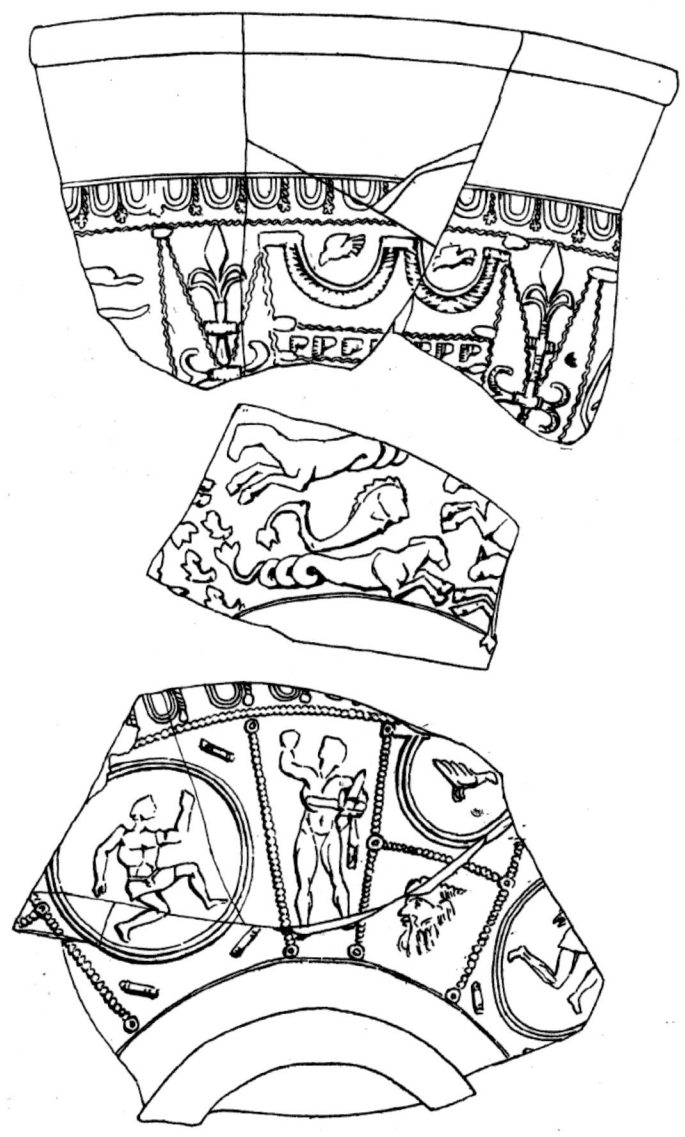

Figure 34 Figured Samian Ware Ambleside
by R.G.C.

(TCWAAS) a major task, working to deadlines. In the same year he completed for publication 'The Likeness of King Elfwald': A study of Northumbria and Iona at the beginning of the Viking Age. The story attempts to reconstruct the history of the years 792 to 808, set partly in Carlisle and elsewhere in Cumberland, also partly in the Hebrides and York. He also completed a paper in collaboration with Dr Charles Parker presenting a reconsideration of the Gosforth Cross. Robin too continued his university work as far as it was possible during the war.

The large gallery rooms at Hertford House were ideal for the study and drawing of maps. Some rooms were occupied by translators abstracting information thought to be critical; the map rooms had large tables, each devoted to a particular area where cartographers were busy preparing maps. Maps had fascinated Gershom since a young boy and he did a good deal of his learning by reading or making maps.

Douglas H. Johnson writing in Collingwood (R.G.) Studies in 1994 stated 'More importantly, he [Gershom] often conceived problems in terms of maps and attempted their answers in the style of maps. The origin of some of his most important historical scholarship, and his most successful historical fiction, lay in his attempt to resolve and explain many of the puzzles in the map of his adopted home in the Lake District: to put features to names and to trace the pattern of relationship between them. He had a painter's care for the detail of outward form, and a geologist's interest in deep structure.'

Robin and his sisters had become well used to father encouraging them to think through maps either by drawing or studying them. No doubt Robin had this experience in mind, knowing of his father's fine draughtsmanship, when he recommended him for a place at Hertford House. This appointment of Gershom was similar to that of other people in the organisation who were recruited mainly from universities. Somebody knew somebody, who knew somebody, who was thought suitable, unless the Director Reginald Hall was involved; he preferred to recruit people with large earlobes as an indicator of good character (we can only assume that all the people he knew of 'good character' had large earlobes and that he knew people of 'bad character' who had small earlobes). Possibly the most important connection Gershom had at the Naval Intelligence was Professor Henry Newton Dickson, author of a book 'Maps and Map Reading' (1912) who proposed the setting-up of the geographical section. Newton Dickson was Professor of geography at University College Reading until 1920 (when he left to take up an appointment as Assistant Editor of Encyclopaedia Britannica) and he was there during the period when Gershom lectured and became Professor of the Fine Art Department; he would know how appropriate Gershom's skills would be to the section. The most important task the Geographical Section performed was the production of maps and Dickson would know of Gershom's strong interest and skills in interpreting maps and map making. One female assistant liked to think of fictitious places, making them up from imagination, which caused some concern among more senior staff, taking the mapping of one imaginary 'place' seriously. Both Robin and Barbara as children, encouraged by mother and father, had similar flights of imagination and became close friends with the assistant, sharing what they felt to be a harmless pastime.

Academics worked voluntarily in intelligence, paid only expenses, yet by 1918 the staff at Hertford House numbered 120. Gershom's daughter Barbara who had been studying in London and had done work in munitions also chose to do war work with Naval Intelligence. Each of the three Collingwoods, Gershom, Robin George and Barbara had skills and knowledge to offer the department and in addition all three contributed languages: German, French, Spanish and Italian. Gershom too had contacts in Denmark and experience of that country, which was useful when producing a manual associated with the area of Schleswig-Holstein until then the standard approach, was to use only German sources. Both Gershom and his son had experience of sifting evidence, drawing maps and writing reports as part of archaeological work, experience of added value to the Geographical Department.

While at the Royal Geographical Society building Barbara shared a flat with her brother Robin, above a shop at 69 Church Street, Kensington. When the section moved to Hertford House, brother and sister shared another flat, 30 Bedford Gardens. When Gershom joined them later in the department, he lived separately at 82 High Street Hampstead, home of the Altounyan family, eldest daughter Dora and husband Ernest Altounyan and where their first child Barbara Harriet (changed to Taqui) was born there in 1917, while Ernest was in France.

**Maps and Manuals**

The first task Gershom had at Naval Intelligence was the production of a reference manual of geographical details with a focus upon military needs. Topographical intelligence becomes vitally important to military personnel. The manual was to be about European Russia, a massive undertaking made more difficult in 1917 when it became almost impossible to collect data during the year of revolution. By January 1918 it was decided to abandon the Russia project and Gershom was asked to do similar work but with the Middle East in mind. The area then known as Persia was strategically placed in relation to India, then part of the British Empire, the area also held large reserves of oil. There is no record of a manual being produced but it is believed that the work Gershom did was used in writing various memoranda at the Foreign Office to aid decision making with respect to that area.[112] Much of

---

[112] Johnson, P. 2012. A Philosopher at the Admiralty, Vol. 1. p. 92.Exeter: Imprint Academic.

the work done by Gershom during 1917 and 1918 at Hertford House was to be used at a planned peace conference, the intention was to use the information when deliberations took place between politicians of various countries. On hearing of Wilfrid Owen's death in battle in November 1918, Gershom must surely have thought about the evening spent with him six years earlier discussing Ruskin. He would have further thoughts, how for more than a year he had been working at Naval Intelligence preparing for the 'peace' conference in 1919; why did Owen and some of his colleagues have to die when preparations for the peace were already being made? After taking part in two battles of 1916 and 1917 Owen was at Craiglockhart House, Edinburgh recovering from shell shock; he wrote a poem 'Anthem for Doomed Youth' and shortly, after returning to the front, he became a doomed youth.

**After the War**

For various reasons Professor Dickson became distrusted by senior figures at the Foreign Office, the outcome was that none of the work done at Hertford House was used during the peace conference in 1919. The so-called peace conference simply provoked further conflict. There appeared to be a certain amount of stereotyping from the Foreign Office about 'Professors' not being sufficiently practical when called upon to make decisions. The manuals that were produced ceased to have any military importance after peace was declared (Original copies from the 1914-18 period can still be bought for around £100.00).

None of the senior people at Hertford House were represented at the peace conference, but for the Collingwoods there were family connections in attendance. Gershom's son-in-law Ernest Altounyan and his father Aram Assadour Altounyan, both medical doctors, were there to speak on behalf of the Armenians of Western Asia but their concerns were largely ignored, their country not being seen as of sufficient strategic importance. Representatives of various Arab States felt betrayed too; their calls for independence were set aside. Betrayal of Arabs by the British government continued to the present day, especially in Palestine. The outcomes from the conference can only be seen, in hindsight, as a disaster, but this must be left to generations of historians to explain. Gershom must have felt disappointment that so much work, injurious to his healt had been in vain, but by that time (April 1919) would be only too pleased to be back in Lakeland and away from London; wartime and a heavy work schedule did cause problems with his health, which had not been strong when he joined the Intelligence Service.

Robin George returned to Oxford, where he had continued to do some work during the war, to resume his successful career as historian and philosopher, almost as though nothing had happened over the past four years. His interest and involvement in archaeology was somewhat different. Francis Haverfield the famous archaeologist, and mentor to Robin, died in 1919 and a number of his students did not survive the war.

Francis Haverfield could be thought of as a victim of the 1914-18 European war; he had no children and loss of his students probably felt like family loss; especially the death in action (1915) of George Leonard Cheesman who was expected to become a colleague of Haverfield.[113] Robin George Collingwood, in his own words[114] was left as 'the only man resident in Oxford whom he [Haverfield] had trained as a Romano-British specialist', beginning around 1909.

Haverfield specialized in Roman epigraphy and Roman Britain. In 1907 he became Camden Professor of Ancient History at Oxford University and Fellow of Brasenose College. In Haverfield's own words when he first approached the study of Roman Britain (c. 1890) it was 'the playground of the amateur'. He maintained a strong interest in the antiquity and archaeology of the north. He joined CWAAS in 1890, and became President of the society in 1915. He was possibly the greatest influence in the direction taken by Robin George when studying Roman Britain and largely responsible for R.G. Collingwood becoming a well-respected authority on Roman Britain after the initial apprenticeship spent with his father. R.G. Collingwood had enormous respect for Haverfield 'whose interest embraced every branch and twig of Roman archaeology'. He felt that his skill and knowledge was comparable only with Mommsen himself. (Theodor Mommsen, 1817-1903. German Historian and Archaeologist who influenced the young Haverfield).

Shortley before he died, Haverfield asked Robin Collingwoodto act as draughtsman for his new collection of Roman inscriptions of Britain (RIB); each to be illustrated with a facsimile drawing. After Haverfield died (1919) Collingwood continued this work for the next 15 years.

---

[113] Freeman, P.W.M. 2007. The Best Training-Ground for Archaeologists: Francis Haverfield and the invention of Romano-British Archaeology. Oxford: Oxbow Books.
[114] Collingwood, R.G. 1939. An Autobiography. Oxford: Oxford University Press.

# Chapter XIII
# Later Research
# (1920-1930)

**Roman Sites**

Extensive archaeological research was done at Hardknot Castle between 1889 and 1893 and a large amount of pottery fragments discovered, much of it housed at Muncaster Castle to the west. Gershom concluded, firmly, that Hardknot is exclusively a Flavian-Trajanic site. (Flavian and Trajanic were Roman Imperial Dynasties covering the period AD 69 to 117) Two Roman sites, Ambleside and Hardknot, were most likely founded by Agricola around AD 79. This conclusion was supported by the research of Robin George Collingwood (R.G.C.) in the early 1920s (that the fort was Agricolan is no longer accepted, now thought to be Hadrian).[115] A more detailed description of R.G.C's work is necessary at this stage to help demonstrate how years of helping his father had born fruit by him becoming a well-established authority on Roman Britain, adding to his considerable reputation as an historian and philosopher. Robin had been taken to Hardknot Roman Castle with his father in 1891 when only three weeks old, carried in a carpenter's bag.

**Ambleside Roman Camp**

In a paper of 1921[116] R.G.C. brought together results from digging at the Ambleside Roman Fort, he had been closely involved with his father and Francis Haverfield on exploratory digs in 1913, 1914 and 1915, but war brought the work to an end until 1920. In one of his few references to his father in his autobiography[117] Robin George acknowledged how much he learned from his father when on archaeological digs; mainly the idea of constantly questioning rather than relying only upon 'authority', which he carried through to his work on history and philosophy. It is also worth mentioning that the idea of visualizing earlier events for re-enactment or reconstruction could be influential too, as when his father painted a scene at

---
[115]Collingwood, W.G. 1988. The Lake Counties, Revised, p. 59. London: J.M. Dent &Sons Ltd.
[116]Collingwood, R.G. 1921. Explorations in the Roman Fort at Ambleside (fourth year, 1920) and at other sites on the Tenth Iter. Transactions of the Cumberland and Westmorland Antiquarian and Archaeological Society, vol. 21, pp.1-42.
[117]Collingwood, R.G. 1939. An Autobiography. Oxford: Oxford University Press.

Hardknot, he visualised it during the time of the Romans. In addition, how Gershom visualised life in Lakeland 1000 years earlier when writing some of his fiction.

When exploration of the Ambleside Roman fort began in 1913, Haverfield opened the great meeting on the site with a short address and left Robin Collingwood to give a more detailed description. Haverfield visited the site until 1915 when war brought work to an end, until 1920.

The camp at Ambleside is the nearest to Hardknot and is of great interest to scholars of the Roman period, but in terms of early findings it was a disappointment to Gershom and his son. The original fort appeared to be of a temporary nature, the structures inside the walls had been of wood and even the post-holes had been obliterated by the building of a second fort. The first fort was established around AD 79 but on a site that flooded too easily and around 40 years later the area was raised and a second fort built which remained in use for 300 years until soldiers left the area. The fort became less and less important when the Romans felt that the North West had been pacified; they needed to concentrate upon Scottish rebels further north. The excavation work done at Ambleside provided an overall plan of the fort, drawn by son Robin George. A granary was positively identified, measuring 50 feet by 12 feet (15 m x 3.7 m) and estimated to hold 350 tons of grain; given a cohort of 500 men at any one time, they stored a two-year supply. This granary was similar to those found on other Roman sites. There had been a pottery finds at both Ambleside and Hardknot with the greatest amount at Hardknot, W.G.C. was able to add to this collection: a large part of a Samian bowl, a necked cooking pot and a jug made of red clay.

Fragments of pottery showing decoration and some figures were also found. The fragments from both sites were stored at Muncaster Castle (rather than thrown away) and proved valuable to researchers many years later when it had become possible to date periods of occupation by careful examination of pottery. These fragments were drawn in detail by Robin George (See Figure 34) following on from his father's example, and, in addition, he provided a description of the pottery found in 1915 by his father on that site and discussed the dates of occupation for Hardknot Castle based upon fragments of pottery found between 1889 and 1893, still held at Muncaster Castle. Possibly the most interesting part of the report, to the modern reader, is a survey of the Roman road from Ambleside by Little Langdale to Wrynose and to the coast, a route that can still intrigue some visitors to the area.

### The Tenth Iter

Both Gershom and his son were convinced that a road from Kendal (named 'Alone') to Ravenglass was the Tenth Iter. Identifying the course of the road and distances was a crucial part of their evidence. There had been much talk among antiquaries of a Roman road from Kendal, (at nearby camp of Watercrook) to Ravenglass passing by camps at Ambleside and Hardknot. There was an obvious link between the fort at Ambleside and another fort (castle) at the top of Hardknot Pass, both built by the Romans. The route from Ambleside to Ravenglass of 20 miles (32 km) was over very rough country; the actual course of the route has remained unclear but in 1900 W.G.C. spent time in a laborious attempt to trace a possible road from the fort, up Little Langdale to Fell Foot and over passes of Wrynose and Hardknot. The country would be too difficult to cover in one day for heavily laden or heavily dressed Roman soldiers so a camp at the top of Hardknot Pass was built around 9 miles (14 km) from Ambleside, roughly half-way between the fort and the port they had established at Ravenglass.

Two main questions were raised during the Collingwoods' earlier excavations of Roman sites in mid-Lakeland, which were to be followed up during the 1920s: dating the sites of Ambleside and Harknot camps and establishing the line of a Roman road connecting the camps that fortunately could all be studied together.

R.G.C. accepted as fact that the road from Kendal by Ambleside (Galava) and Hardknot to Ravenglass (Clanoventa) on the coast is the Tenth Iter. The Tenth Iter was part of the 'Itinerary of Emperor Antoninus' which registered roads and distances between centres of the Roman Empire. The British section of the itinerary (Iter Britanniarum) registers 15 Iter from place to place throughout England and parts of Wales, not Scotland. Of all 15 Iter the one to cause the most controversy among antiquaries is the Tenth Iter. Throughout the nineteenth century many theories were put forward to describe the course of the Tenth Iter. Possibly the first scholar, a friend of Gershom and Robin, to identify the sea-end (all other Iter had either a beginning or end at the sea) was Professor Haverfield when he identified Ravenglass as Clanoventa the coastal end of a Roman road. Haverfield, who taught Robin Collingwood at Oxford, remains to this day one of the most outstanding Roman scholars and continues to be one of the most influential figures in Romano-British research. Professor Haverfield, in 1915, suggested the identification of the Ravenglass Kendal road with the Tenth Iter, making Ravenglass and Ambleside the first two stations Clanoventa and Galava respectively. In 1919, C.R.B. McGilchrist wrote (CW2 vol. 19) that Haverfield's work was cursory because no digging had been done. In a note to the same article, Haverfield replied that:

> 'Mr Gilchrist thinks my examination to be cursory. No doubt it was.....I believe that I should be justified in calling Mr Gilchrist's own examination also 'cursory'. It does not seem that he used a spade, and any exploration of a Roman road must be called cursory which omits the spade'. Writing in 1899 about exploration on Hadrian's wall (CW1 vol.15) Haverfield said

the spade was rarely used to prove theories which were suggested by the appearance of the ground.'

One question at once suggesting itself to the mind of any interested reader was 'why Hardknot should be omitted?' Hardknot stands actually on the proposed Roman road, and its strong position makes it an unlikely place to be overlooked by any compiler of road-books. It was doubtless never a large station and the rough remote situation saved it from destruction by the plough or by stone-robbing for other buildings, making it of great interest to later Antiquarians but possibly a less important place to the Romans than either of its neighbours, Ravenglass and Ambleside: *its omission, though by no means unparalleled, suggests the possibility that when the Itineraries were drawn up it was already abandoned. If so, its omission is explained and the one objection to Haverfield's interpretation of the Tenth Iter is removed.*

The attempt by W.G.C. to trace this road was not an easy task because the land is swamp-like in places around Ambleside and positive trace of an ancient road was not found until a short distance beyond Skelwith where the road would have crossed the river Brathay; one of the few possible crossing points available. He felt that the Roman road would have followed the north bank of the Brathay to Skelwith. The road went past Fell Foot to the start of a climb over Wrynose pass. This was a packhorse track and not a metalled road when W.G.C. traced the route and not too different from the route used by Romans. The track is steepest on the east side, in places with a gradient of 1:4. On the far side of the pass there is a level section, now known as Wrynose Bottom, which leads to Hardknot Pass. A short distance north from the summit of this pass Romans built Hardknot Castle (or fort) situated in a magnificent position surrounded by mountains and looking down Eskdale to the west and beyond to Ravenglass on the coast; the Romans chose the site well, and W.G.C. who loved rough hill country would be overjoyed to spend time there excavating the site. In his paper of 1921 R.G.C. gives clear description and reasoning when plotting the course of the most controversial part of the Fifteen Iter, that is 15 recorded Roman roads in Britain; the road between Ambleside and Ravenglass going over the passes of Wrynose and Hardknot was claimed to be the Tenth Iter, the last Iter to be positively identified. The most difficult section to trace was from Ambleside to the summit of Wrynose Pass.

(The reader not familiar with this beautiful area may be helped by having a Lake District Ordnance Survey Map to hand).

R.G.C. described this problematic part of the route. Note: in the paper R.G.C. refers to right and left banks of a river or stream, sometimes referring to 'true' right or left bank without explaining that true in this sense means in the direction of water flow, not in the direction of walking and all his references to right or left refer to being 'true' (as further explanation: the true right or left bank of a glacier is taken to be when looking in the direction of ice flow, down the valley). Robin George describes the mountainous part of the Tenth Iter as:

> 'The distance between the fort at Ambleside and the summit of the pass [Wrynose] is exactly six miles in a straight line, but the distance by road is necessarily a good deal longer. The straightness normally shown by Roman roads in a flat country is here not to be expected: the country is mountainous and contains streams which cannot everywhere be crossed without substantial bridging; for a third of a mile due west from the Ambleside fort, the ground is entirely marsh which must have been even less penetrable in the Roman period than it is now. Further, it was intersected by two powerful streams, separate or united, much too deep to ford. If the Romans wished to take their road across here in the direct line for Wrynose they must have built a heavy causeway nearly half a mile long, and one or two bridges. The ground shows no trace of such works, vestiges of which would certainly survive if they had ever existed. We may therefore infer that the Roman road went up the left bank of the Rothay,[River] through flat and swampy meadows for about 300 yards, to Rothay Bridge, the first point where the river Rothay offers an easy crossing. A corduroy road of Roman date was discovered on this line in 1900 [TCWAAS, CW 2, pp. 30-37] evidently leading from the neighbourhood of the east gate to that of Rothay Bridge. After crossing the Rothay (presumably by a ford) the road must have taken the line of the modern road to Clappersgate. Here we may question whether it crossed to the right bank of the Brathay or kept to the left or Westmorland bank. The following points bear on this question: (1) The south (right) bank gives the more direct route. Consequently this is the more likely bank. (2) West of Skelwith, the road certainly was on the south bank. But on the other hand (3) no trace of any road along the south bank has been seen, though the opportunities for observation are extremely good. For quite half a mile east of Skelwith there are open sloping meadows in which the road, if it were there, could hardly escape notice. There is no footpath, no line of farmhouses such as we find in Little Langdale, in short no trace of any kind. The Brathay had to be crossed somewhere, and Skelwith is a much easier crossing than Clappersgate. In fact, Skelwith is the first easy ford which one reaches while ascending the Brathay from its mouth. I conclude that the Roman road followed the left (north) bank of the Brathay to Skelwith, taking the line of the modern road, which though an important coachroad is not a new line, but is undoubtedly a very old line from Waterhead to Skelwith. At Skelwith the Brathay is easily fordable, just above the modern bridge, and here I presume the Roman road crossed the river. A quarter of a

mile south-west of this point I find the first actual traces of the old road. The coach-road from Skelwith to Coniston climbs steeply up the hill to a much greater height than is necessary either to approach the houses (which are all below it) or to cross the hill, which would be more easily crossed, and in a shorter line further north. This anomaly is explained by the fact that the summit-stretch of the road is Roman. From the very top of Skelwith hill to the brow above Colwith the modern road is on the Roman line ; on the summit the two diverge, the Roman road still mounting slightly before it begins to descend to Skelwith, the other descending at once. The Roman road plunges into a dense coppice, where it is just visible as a terrace striking across the hill and dipping upon the modern road where the road from Bull Close enters it. From this point to Skelwith the two, I think, coincide. At the brow above Colwith the modern road swings round to the south for Coniston; the Roman road has to go straight on. But a deep lateral valley lies in its way. Into this it descends by turning boldly to the north and skirting down the hill at a gradient of 1 in 4. It is here very conspicuous as a steeply sloping terrace cut out of the hillside. Just before reaching the brow known as Scar Coppice, which falls abruptly into the Brathay below Colwith, the road makes a hairpin turn to the left and continues its descent. It now crosses the modern Colwith road close to the foot of its steep hill, and continues S.S.W. as a grassy lane between stone walls, descending into the lateral valley above- mentioned, which enters the Brathay at Colwith. Arrived at the bottom of this valley it fords the two streams, which drain it, and turning N.W. climbs once more. Its course is here marked by a stonewall dividing rough moorland to S.W. from coppice to N.E.: the road is sometimes on one side of the wall and sometimes on the other, but soon swings round to the west in a curve enclosed by a right angle between two walls. Here a gradient of 1 in 3 has been at some period modified by the addition of a loop reducing it to 1 in 5. At the top of this loop a stone wall is crossed, on the N. side of which runs the footpath from Colwith Bridge to High Park farm. The Roman road ca easily be made out sometimes to north of this footpath, sometimes coinciding with it. For some 300 yards [274 metres] west of High Park the Roman road coincides with the modern road to Stang End. After this they part, the Roman road being very conspicuous as a metalled causeway in the fields north of the modern road, and about 8 feet wide [2.4 metres]. It passes close under the walls of Stang End farm, which lies to the south of it (the front door, in fact, still opening towards the Roman road, though the modern road is on the other side of the house), and then appears to curve first to the right and then to the left, descending the slope from Stang End to the river. On reaching the river it disappears, but is seen again

200 yards to the west, where it appears as a flat bed of very hard gravel lying in the river itself, and emerging a few inches from its waters near the right bank. This section of road lying in the Brathay is only 20-30 yards [18-27.4 metres] east of the footbridge and ford by which the road from Tilberthwaite crosses the river ; it is therefore, though grass-grown, very conspicuous and was the first portion of the road to be discovered. Its position in the river is due to the fact that the Brathay here makes a strong left-handed bend, and has obviously eroded its right bank a good deal in what, for geology, is a very short space of time. The Romans found a flat space between the river and Pierce How, the conical hill that stands above the stream, and along this they built their road. The river has now destroyed most of the road, but a section 60 feet long by about 10 feet wide [18 x 3 metres] of good rammed gravel, is still to be seen, though this too is gradually being eaten away. At the east end, where all the metal has gone, the large stones with which the road was bottomed are visible in the water, terminated on the south by a neatly laid row of kerbstones. Above the modern ford the road appears still to lie on the very edge of the river; but it soon begins to ascend the slopes to the left hand. All traces of this ascent for about a quarter of a mile have been obliterated by the spoil banks of a large quarry, but further on, due south of Slater Bridge (which has sometimes been erroneously described as Roman), the road can be seen as a terrace of stones, mounting at a gentle gradient. Immediately afterwards another quarry has completely destroyed it. West of this second quarry a modern field-road appears to claim a Roman origin: but its line and its construction make this impossible. The true line is somewhat higher up the slope, and strikes a modern road once more at High Hall Garth, the third of the old farms which mark the line of the Roman road in Little Langdale. West of this the road is easily traced; it soon joins the path from Tilberthwaite to Fell Foot, and follows it to Bridge End. The direct line from this point would be across Greenburn Beck and up the true right of Wrynose Bottom. But no trace of a road can be found here, and it seems more reasonable to suppose that the Romans crossed the Brathay, now a small stream, at Fell Foot and took the easier line, like all subsequent road- builders, up the true left [true left of a stream is when looking in direction of flow] or north side. Indeed, there are places here where an old road is visible which may be Roman in origin, though no doubt reconstructed. The present road, though not now fit for wheeled traffic except of the roughest kind, is of modern origin and departs here and there from the line which is probably Roman. On the summit of Wrynose it is possible to distinguish four roads: the modern, though now dilapidated, carriage road; an earlier cart track; a third which is probably a mediaeval pony-track, and

fourth, which is perhaps the Roman road. All these appear to have run in the same direction, and none shows any sign of taking the direct line by the south bank of the Brathay to join the Roman road at or near Bridge End. [The way from the summit of Wrynose Pass down to Wrynose Bottom and along to Hardknot Pass is obvious.]

## Hardknot Castle

While Ambleside was soon abandoned, Hardknot was maintained as a garrison until thirty or forty years after Agricola's retirement, around AD 84 After this, the fort was never again occupied. There seemed to be no attempt to include the site as part of Hadrianic reconstruction of the frontier system, and therefore does not figure in the Antonine Itineraries.

The site of the Hardknot camp has the finest views of any Roman building in England, surrounded by some of the most rugged mountain scenery in Lakeland: Scafell, Scafell Pikes, Great End and Bowfell to one side and on another side stands the wonderfully craggy Harter Fell.

Not surprisingly, Gershom was drawn to Hardknot as one of his first ventures into excavation, and over the years Robin often accompanied his father to the site. Gershom was instrumental in organising a group of members of the CWAAS, their first aim being to explore the site rather than carry out formal excavation. The initial finds were so promising that they were encouraged to carry out some controlled digging which continued at intervals over the next five years (1889 to 1893). The camp is square in outline covering a little over three acres. A tower stood at each corner, each at a cardinal point of the compass. The north tower stood at the highest point, on a rocky knoll, and was most likely a signaling point because it was possible to see part of the port at Ravenglass. When doing his research at the Ambleside Roman Camp in 1912,[118] Gershom noted that the camp was in full view of Wrynose Pass 6 miles (9.6km) away, which in turn was visible to Hardknot Camp, making it possible to pass messages between Ambleside and the coast.

Both Gershom and his son felt that the critical part played by Hardknot Castle as mid-point along the Tenth Iter needed to be established, and it seemed that this could be settled at a very small expenditure of time and trouble by thoroughly examining the Hardknot pottery. At the time when the fort was excavated by Gershom and his colleagues (early1890s) it was impossible to date sites by pottery evidence. A few samples of Samian pottery were stored at Muncaster Castle, but the dating of Samian was little understood even in the later nineties, and the dating of the so-called 'coarse pottery' was only begun between1905-1908. By 1920,

---

[118] Collingwood, W.G. 1912. The Roman Camp at Ambleside. Ambleside: The St. Oswald's Press.

it was possible to date coarse pottery with reasonable accuracy, especially from the second century and the latter part of the first.

Fortunately, the antiquaries headed by William Slater Calverley had parcelled up fragments of pottery and deposited them at Muncaster Castle to be looked after by Lord Munster (Gershom and his son continued to owe a great deal to Calverley and his workers). Following on from his father, Robin George Collingwood made around 100 drawings from the collection of coarse pottery. After careful analysis of this collection R.G.C. had evidence, but not proof, that Hardknot was built no later than the Hadrianic period. The small amount of coin finds also supported this hypothesis. These data could not be used to begin writing a history of the fort. After R.G.C. scrutinised particular pieces of pottery he came to realise that the collection represented an unusually interesting series. This led R.G.C. to declare that:

> 'it may be said at once that the rarer types do nothing to weaken the inference to which these lead, that Hardknot was built in the late first century and abandoned probably not later than the middle of the second: after which it was never used again by the Romans. Thus the problem of the Antonine Itinerary is solved by the most cursory glance at the pottery: whatever view one takes of the exact dating of that document, there can be no doubt that it was drawn up after Hardknot had ceased to be an occupied site. It is noteworthy that it ceased not only to be a regular fort, but also to be used at all: not even a wayside meal has left its mark in the shape of a later potsherd or coin dropped under the shelter of the walls.'

Robin Collingwood discussed each category of the Hardknot pottery collection in relation to collections at other Roman sites, particularly along Hadrian's Wall at Corbridge and Haltwhistle Burn. In doing this, he displayed an extensive knowledge of Roman Britain that would rival that of Haverfield himself. Through this research, Hardknot entered into an extremely interesting series of sites whose history covers the dark period that lies between Agricola and Hadrian. Until the nineteenth century the existence of these sites was unknown; it was thought that Agricola's forts were evacuated when he left the country, or at least very soon after and the districts, so held, abandoned by the Romans till Hadrian re-occupied them. But later it became known that this was not the case. R.G.C. pointed out that several Agricolan forts, like Newstead on the Tweed and Inchtuthil in Strathmore were occupied for a considerable time after AD 85, and other forts like Throp and Haltwhistle Burn in Northumberland were actually added after the turn of the century. The conclusion, at the time, must be that the Roman sites of Ambleside, Hardknot and most likely Ravenglass are pre- Hadrian.

## Wild Northumberland

After tracing the Roman road from Ambleside to Ravenglass, the next spell of road tracing took place in 1923 on the wild moorland north of Hadrian's Wall in Northumbria. A route known as the Maiden's Way, referred to by Sir Walter Scott in 'Guy Mannering', ran with Roman-straightness north from Birdoswald on the wall to Bewcastle (Shopford), passing on the way a site of what became Spadeadam farm and further north a Roman signalling station. The station was well-placed to detect any tribe movement on moors north of the wall and signal back to guards on the wall and forward to the fort at Bewcastle. Previously, the last section of this road could not be found and a problem existed because the course of the road would pass Bewcastle fort some distance to the east. There seemed to be an assumption that the Maiden (Roman) way would continue northwards beyond Bewcastle into what was, for Romans, enemy country but an alternative assumption of ending at Bewcastle appeared to be the more reasonable.

Gershom was joined by Lady Dorothy Henley and Hon. Francis Robert Henley Sixth Baron Henley of Chadstock to form a digging party (an aristocratic digging party). A road thought to be built beyond Bewcastle from a place called 'Bush' and then over Borderrigg was thought by Gershom to be mediaeval. There was no history for the area in the twelfth century but Priories at Wetheral and Carlisle existed and they needed access to ecclesiastical sites over the border. Gershom gave examples of Monks in Abbeys developing paved roads to help their communication, based upon techniques used in Roman times and this seems to be a sound explanation for any paved road going beyond Bewcastle.

Returning to the question of where the Maiden's Way led: with help from a resident of High House they began tracing a road in the direction of the fort at Bewcastle; the digging party used spades to search below the moor and found a paved way. The road they discovered was 12 feet (3.7metres) wide and formed of two courses of stone laid upon peat. In following the road, Gershom could see how a Roman engineer planned the way. To continue in a straight line would take him into a difficult crossing of White Beck so he moved eastward to an easier crossing point. The engineer also adopted a zigzag course up a steep hill. He still had to build the road westward until near the fort. The last section, Gershom said, could only be uncovered with more digging work but there was no doubt that the road led to the eastern gate of the fort at Bewcastle and so to the end of the Maiden Way.

## Towards a Corpus

By 1926, Gershom had been researching stone crosses and other carved stonework throughout the North of England and south-west Scotland for around 30 years. During this period he had published in various journals 41 papers on the subject, and edited a book of 'Early Sculptured Crosses' based upon work of the late William Slater Calverley and wrote one chapter for a book Victoria County History Cumberland (1901), entitled 'Remains of the Pre-Norman Period'.These papers and books built a body of knowledge, which was utilised, along with additional techniques, to produce a most influential book 'Northumbrian Crosses of the Pre-Norman Age' (19270 an impressive work with numerous drawings by the author. Gershom's son Robin George pointed out that the book was not a corpus, but a treatise.[119] (But went on to criticise quality of the paper used in production of the book); certainly, the paper did not do justice to the fine illustrations. The subject material covered by the book is only a selection from the output of W.G.C.'s work. If we add to this publication the many papers on the subject written by Gershom and his edited book of Rev. Calverley's research there is a major contribution to a corpus of pre-Norman stonework in Northern England. If he had been granted more years, the task could have been progressed towards completion of his work (at the time of writing a project for a corpus of Anglo-Saxon Sculpture is being conducted at Durham University under the guidance of Dame Rosemary Cramp, Emeritus Professor in the Department of Archaeology).

**Gosforth Cross Reconsidered**

In early 1917, before Gershom joined his son at the Admiralty he sat down with Dr Charles Parker to reconsider research work done on the Gosforth Cross over the past 35 years. At the time of the first project (1882), the comparative study of stone crosses was at a primitive stage. During the intervening years, various papers were written at different times but each one was done independently, any attempt to provide a comprehensive explanation of what was found on each side of the cross proved fruitless. Parker and Collingwood decided to restate a few points in the light of what had been discovered, based upon their own experience of analysing many stone crosses.

Thirty-five years after the first scholarly interest in the cross both antiquaries (Parker and Collingwood) returned to reconsider the evidence;[120] both writers agreed that a lack of collaboration between researchers had hindered our understanding of the monolith. They began by re- visiting the figures on all four sides of the

---

[119]Collingwood, R.G. 1935. The Bewcastle Cross. Transactions of the Cumberland and Westmorland Antiquarian and Archaeological Society, vol. 35, pp.1- 29.
[120]Parker, C.A. and W.G. Collingwood, 1917. A reconsideration of the Gosforth Cross. Transactions of the Cumberland and Westmorland Antiquarian and Archaeological Society, vol. 17, pp. 99-113.

cross to reveal previously unknown features, they also made comparative study with other carved stonework: Dearham cross, Leeds cross, various hogbacks and Northumbrian stonework. The age of the cross they determined could not be later than twelfth century because nearby related hogbacks had been built into the foundations of the twelfth century church. The literary subjects on the shaft of the cross are taken from the Edda poem of the Völuspá. Images on all four sides of the shaft can be linked to stages in that poem; W.G.C. and Dr Parker at the end of their paper on the reconsideration of the cross, list the features on each side of the shaft and these match the Völuspá poem to a remarkable degree; the poem was known in Cumberland since around AD 1000.

Beginning at the base of the south side working upwards, then from the top of the west side working downwards, up from base of north side and finally down from the top of the east side to finish with the crucifixion of Christ. They concluded that the cross cannot be earlier than the tenth century; somewhat later than seventh century as thought by Professor Stephens of Copenhagen (date now given is around early tenth century). A problem was recognised when 'reading' sides of the shaft, whether to move from east to west and whether to work from top to bottom or bottom to top while changing from one side to the next. W.G.C and Dr Parker concluded that although the literary subject is Norse, the artistic character of the cross is English (Anglian). They also noted that a feature of figures carved on the shaft have irregular positioning, this has been noted with other carved stonework in the form of monoliths.

Writers of the 1917 paper point to careless carving with lack of forethought; a mason busy working on the stone lying flat may not consider the images when seen in an erect position. An interesting feature of the carvings is that on one side is found evidence of Norse mythology and on another of Christ crucified; heathen one side, Christian on another. Gershom pointed out that many Vikings of that time could be half Christian and half heathen, baptised and church going at home and praying to Thor in battle at sea. The story told on the shaft of the cross seems to support this idea.

**Dykes**

Towards the end of his life Gershom turned his attention to dykes or linear earthworks without losing any of his early enthusiasm or thoroughness when doing fieldwork.

In the second series (CW2) of TCWAAS vol. 30, was a paper he delivered in Penrith, April 1929 (published 1930). He researched the use of earthworks as

Figure 35 Thirlmere before the Dam
Thomas Allom c. 1832

boundary markers at Rydal in the Lake District[121] going back around 600 years. Gershom concluded that at least 70 dykes existed in the district and recommended that they be 'measured and plotted on Ordnance Survey maps of 6 inches to the mile'.

His interest in dykes extended to Galloway in Scotland where a much-disputed length of earthwork existed. Early Antiquarian Joseph Train (1779-1852) convinced himself that a lengthy earthwork known as Deil's Dyke was one continuous boundary or fortress of some kind. Later scholars noted changes in construction methods and concluded that it was a series of dykes. The whole length was walked during 3 days in June 1926 by R.C. Reid and Dr Semple, who wrote two papers giving descriptions, but no attempt was made to identify the date or purpose of Deil's Dyke until Gershom presented a paper on the subject in 1930.[122] It was the

---

[121]Collingwood, W.G. 1930. The Mediaeval Fence of Rydal. Transactions of the Cumberland and Westmorland Antiquarian and Archaeological Society, vol. 30, pp. 1-11.

[122]Collingwood, W.G. 1932. The Deil's Dyke. Transactions of the Dumfriesshire and Galloway Natural History Society, Series 3, vol. 17, pp. 72-79.

unexplained nature of Deil's Dyke that attracted Gershom, he began by quoting writer Herbert Maxwell, Conservative Member of Parliament in saying 'There is a certain attraction in unexplained phenomenon' and Gershom added that there are few things more unexplained than Deil's Dyke. There was general agreement that the dyke was never defensive; like the wall of Hadrian, it simply set a limit or boundary to an area of country. Gershom seemed to think that the dyke had been intended to enclose the good lands of Galloway. There was no sign of it being a complete ring-fence but was clearly more than a field or community boundary. In places, Gershom likened it to a miniature and rude copy of Hadrian's Wall. With regard to earlier scholars thinking it a series of earthworks, Gershom's reply was that differences in building along its length was not surprising, given that it would be built by different groups of men not efficiently coordinated, he referred again to Hadrian's Wall and how similar differences can be observed along its length. Gershom, in his typical style of working posed many questions in his paper as a means of reasoning about possible date and purpose of the dyke, including a contribution from Mr R.G. Collingwood when questioning possible Romano-British links.

Gershom questioned and reasoned by working backwards chronologically from the twelfth century, drawing upon his extensive knowledge of northern history. he ventured south only to use as an example Offa's Dyke on the border with Wales. He speculated that building of the dyke could be done during the Norse occupation of Galloway or, when that area was Kingdom of Strathclyde, Cumbria, which was noted in the Anglo-Saxon Chronicles. From the evidence gathered, Gershom favoured the builders as being from a Christian settlement of Romano-British people in Galloway shortly before the Romans left Britain, around early fifth century.

With the completion of this work, no more learned papers were written. Appendix A can claim to be a definitive record of published work by Gershom, though it is just possible that one or two items have slipped through the net.

# Chapter XIV
# Future of Lakeland
# (1932-)

**Difference of Opinion**

Among the many interests of Gershom was the future of the area he chose to make his home but not in the normal way at the time, as a preservationist. People described as preservationists were inclined to be dogmatic, insisting upon the total preservation of an area that they had come to love. In contrast, Gershom was ready to accept change on condition that a sensible balance was achieved between satisfying the needs of local people while not going so far as to destroy areas of beauty and tranquility, in practice a balance difficult to achieve but one he felt worth working towards.

William Gershom Collingwood was a very private man, sociable with family and close friends, amusing and kind, but happiest when alone with his work. Now, the term laid-back would be applied to him, rarely finding quarrel with anyone. At Lanehead, a quiet corner of the Lake District, he had found an ideal home surrounded by loved- ones in a peaceful and beautiful setting. Future of The Lake District, however, provided the subject for what has been called quarrels with Canon Rawnsley, discussed by Karen Welberry in 'Collingwood (RG) and British Idealism Studies' vol.10 in 2004.[123] On reflection this was little more than a difference of opinion concerning the future 'management' of the Lake District when faced with proposed industrialisation and increasing tourism bringing railways, motor-roads and an increase in the building of houses and hotels. Hardwick Drummond Rawnsley, three years older than Gershom, was a student at Oxford University when Gershom arrived. After Oxford, Rawnsley settled in the Lake District to take a position with the church, and best known as Canon Rawnsley after his association with Carlisle Cathedral. His first post in the District was as Vicar of Wray near Windermere before a move to become Vicar of Crosthwaite near Keswick, a position held until his retirement. He campaigned most of his life for the preservation of the Lake District, which for him meant keeping the area as a sanctuary where higher thoughts and feelings could flourish, he would not have tolerated ice cream-eaters beside Windermere; almost inevitably a view seen by

---

[123] Welberry, K. 2004. H.D. Rawnsley, W.G. Collingwood and the German Miners of Keswick, 1565-1645 in 'Collingwood and British Idealist Studies', vol. 10. Cardiff: R.G. Collingwood Society.

some people as elitist. This preservationist-view was how Rawnsley interpreted the writing of Ruskin on developments in the Lake District. Ruskin was not a preservationist it would be more accurate to describe him as open-minded. He supported the aims of science and advancement of knowledge; even in art he supported Turner when most prominent figures in the art world would reject his painting as being unconventional.

Although Rawnsley knew Ruskin at Oxford and helped on the road-building project at Ferry Hinksey (after volunteering rather than being invited by Ruskin) he did not enjoy the close working relationship Gershom had with the Professor. Rawnsley also followed closely the views held by Wordsworth gathered mainly from his poetry but also from Wordsworth's campaigning against railways and building work within the district. In contrast Gershom, like Ruskin, seldom referred to the great Lakeland poet apart from in his book 'The Lake Counties'. In a book to the memory of John Ruskin, Dr. W.R. Inge Dean of St. Pauls made a relevant point that, '*Wordsworth averted his eyes from the ugliness of industrialisation because it meant nothing to him. Ruskin could not avert his eyes because it meant a great deal to him, and all that it meant was distasteful*'.

Gershom interpreted Ruskin's views rather differently from Rawnsley, recognising him as a modernist who saw a need to develop the area for the benefit of people escaping from sordid industrialised towns and cities who looked upon the area mainly as a place of recreation, rather than for any form of spiritual inspiration. This approach led inevitably to popular, sometimes rowdy, pastimes, which have to be accepted if local people are to benefit from wealth brought into the area. Ruskin did object to the introduction of railways into the Lake District and made this known to Rawnsley, possibly leading him to think that this was a typical stance held by Ruskin. Gershom wrote that especially in the English Lake District, the scenery is in miniature and easily spoiled by embankments and viaducts, and by rows of ugly buildings which usually grow up around railway stations, a sentiment also shared with Ruskin. Gershom stated that criticism of Ruskin as inconsistent in his views about railways was wrong; he never objected to mainline trains, which he used from time to time, but like many people he objected to their introduction into districts where chief interest is in the scenery. Generally the Professor was rather ambivalent about changes in the district during his lifetime, his concerns being primarily for social reform within the whole country and not only the North West. When thinking of Cumberland and Westmorland, Ruskin did appreciate the need for local people to have means of employment so judged each proposed change on its merit, whether a balance was being achieved between protection of the 'natural' environment and needs of the local population. Both Gershom and Rawnsley supported the Lake District Defense Society formed around 1883 at the time Gershom settled in Lakeland. Rawnsley already established in the area was a founder member of the society.

In a paper written towards the end of his life for the Journal of the Fell and Rock Climbing Club of the English Lake District (1930)[124] Gershom stated his position clearly with respect to development of the district. *'We begin by fancying that all is wild and primeval, untouched by man and his sophistications. When we were very young we rejoiced in the notion that God made the country by himself, whoever built the nasty towns we had come from. We can't escape from the works of man; and, after a while, we learn that much of the romance of the fells means that man has been there before; that this is no undiscovered country, and that we are not the first whoever burst into this silence.'*

Gershom fully appreciated that the Lake District, an area that so many people came to love, had been modified by man over centuries; he wrote that *'untouched nature is not picturesque landscape, though it may have its moments'*. People who see wild country as waste land will not be concerned about any harm being done by mans' building work, in contrast people who see beauty in wild country will actively oppose any development. Rawnsley supported the second category, preferring that Lakeland remained untouched, or rather without any further development. Gershom also leaned towards the second category while being prepared to accept well-justified change.

To say that a quarrel raged on between Gershom and Canon Rawnsley is an exaggeration; they were friends holding different views about how, or whether, their adopted home-district should be developed. They also disagreed about how some of Ruskin's writing on the subject should be interpreted. Gershom was simply more open-minded towards any proposed change and it was this attitude that upset Rawnsley.

Over the years whenever preservation, or conservation, of the Lake District was discussed Canon Rawnsley has become the dominant figure of the two (Gershom and himself). However, it can be argued that Gershom has had a bigger part to play in helping outsiders appreciate the 'Lakes' through his writing of learned papers, writing very readable non- fiction guide-type books about the district, and works of fiction set within the area that can stir peoples' imagination about times long ago. Gershom's natural reticence in contrast to Rawlinson's gift for self-publicity leads automatically to our current view of the two men. Their respective contribution to Lakeland can be too easily distorted by relying upon the current and shallow practice of 'image making'. Rawnsley is now best known for being a founder of the National Trust but he would be horrified by the Trust's activities

---

[124]Collingwood, W.G. 1930. Leavings of the German Miners. Fell and Rock Climbing Club of the English Lake District, vol. 8, p. 283.

in the Lake District and Gershom too, even with his more open attitude to some of the changes.

## Reflections

What Rawnsley and Gershom 'argued' about more than 100 years ago is still debatable. People join or resign from the organisation 'Friends of the Lake District' depending upon whether they agree or disagree with declared views about which developments should or should not be allowed in the area. Debate goes on about whether the National Trust is a fit body to look after any wild area and whether they ought to confine their attention to historic houses. More debate takes place about whether masts should be built to provide residents and visitors with telephone access, or amenities be constructed in wild places to provide amusement. No doubt, Canon Rawnsley would be apoplectic about almost every change that has been introduced or proposed since his death in 1920. Wordsworth too would be horrified by what has been done to the area. Gershom after careful consideration would be likely to support some actions and oppose others.

During the 50 years Gershom spent in Lakeland, he witnessed major changes and unlike some people close to him who feared for the area's future he remained optimistic; he never wanted Lakeland to be a museum dedicated to fine scenery. The main changes he supported included various mining schemes, also railways, which encouraged tourism, and the building of more homes for working people local to the district. However, changes have taken place since his death in 1932 that most surely would not have pleased him, overall he felt there had been too much meddling in wild country and Gershom, like Wordsworth, would be horrified by some of the changes. Construction of artificial paths, regimented plantations of trees, building of an ugly and potentially dangerous nuclear re-processing plant, dual-lane highways, needless reservoirs, and masts, pylons or wind turbines around the periphery of the area but well within sight of anyone on hills and mountains. The meeting of wild country with cultivated areas need only be a few steps for the walker and this has been a strong feature throughout the Lake District. The planting of alien trees in regimented rows destroys any sense of wildness. H.H. Symonds writing in 1933[125] about the valley of Ennerdale said '*Now a few years later trees have won a more cruel victory than sheep, and moss and grasses and all the seedlings which wind and birds set among them have gone back to paleness and oblivion, under the shadow of a wood*'. Later, the intrusion of artificial paths has blurred the sharp distinction between wildness and non-wildness.

---

[125] Symonds, H.H. 1933. Walking in the Lake District. London: A. Maclehose & Co.

Gershom recalled Ruskin talking about his favourite seat at Beck Leven and saying; if a single chimney of the Barrow ironworks appeared in the outlook from his rural retreat, he should never take joy in it more. Gershom wrote that *'Gray the poet and Turner the painter saw the dales at their best, and if Wordsworth had been born a century later he could not have been Wordsworth.'*

Gershom lived through a time when for walkers and climbers Lakeland was at its best despite the changes, mainly the introduction of mining and railways. He did live to see the damage done to Thirlmere; writing in his book 'The Lake Counties':

> 'Thirlmere has no expanse, but it was once the richest in story and scenery of all the lakes. The old charm of its shores has quite vanished, and the sites of its legends are hopelessly altered, so that a walk along either side is a mere sorrow to anyone who cared for it before; the sham castles are an outrage and the formality of the roads, beloved of car drivers and cyclists, deforms the hill-sides like a scar on a face'.[126]

To help show what has been lost by the thoughtless building of a dam see Figure 35 drawn by Thomas Allom around 1832[127] the view of Thirlmere is from low ground at the foot of Raven Crag looking north.

Only a rough track led along the west shore suitable for horse or on foot. A narrow peninsular almost divided the mere in two but bridged by three 'arches' made of oak with handrails. A rough causeway of stones led to the bridge. The bulk of Helvellyn can be seen on the east side of the mere; a beautiful scene captured by artist Thomas Allom, which is in sharp contrast to the drab artificial view today. Earlier comments about Thirlmere before the dam came from Samuel Taylor Coleridge in October 1803, when writing in his notebook; Coleridge was ecstatic about the view of that mere.

Gershom was upset by the pointless spoiling of a mere, just so that water-wasteful people of a city (Manchester) could have water from the mountain Helvellyn and from hills around the mere. One influential protester against the Thirlmere water scheme was Robert Somervell (1851-1933) an original Companion of St. George and follower of Ruskin. After Cambridge University, he became a schoolmaster at Liverpool College, then Harrow School where he taught a young Winston Churchill the rudiments of English grammar. He produced a pamphlet in 1877 distributed with Ruskin's Fors Clavigera, but protest of this kind fell upon

---

[126] Collingwood, W.G. 1902. The Lake Counties. London: J.M. Dent.
[127] Rose, T. 1832. Westmorland, Cumberland, Durham and Northumberland Illustrated. London: Fisher Son & Co.

stony ground as so many continued to do over the years; we have seen how a once beautiful mere has been condemned to be a reservoir.

A debate throughout Gershom's life, at times fierce, took place between conservationists and preservationists. As already pointed out, Gershom could be open-minded about new developments in Lakeland and in this respect was a conservationist, but with regard to the building of a dam on Thirlmere he spoke like a preservationist, he preferred to see the mere and its valley remain as natural as possible, in a pristine state. Had he lived to see a period of rapid change and development, it is possible that he could follow the preservationists in their thinking about how to manage Lakeland.

During Gershom's life, the people of Mardale in the east of the district lived without any thought of their beautiful village being drowned under a reservoir. He did not live to see yet another example of this mindless destruction among the hills. During Gershom's final months, a dam was being built at the foot of Haweswater to fill the valley and swamp the village of Mardale. The seventeenth century church would be under water. Gershom wrote a short time before, *'What will be the end of this once beloved corner of Lake District nobody can tell. It is certain that the damage is done and cannot be undone'*. Also during his lifetime, the sea to the west was free from contamination; walkers on the mountain Blencathra could enjoy their day free from traffic noise; singing waters of the Liza River could be followed up Ennerdale without sight of surrounding mountains being obliterated by alien conifers. Summit views could be enjoyed without the sight of hideous constructions. He was spared the horrendous sight of an artificial path made up Sail Fell, and on other mountains and fells of Lakeland. He was fortunate not to have lived during the fifty years beyond 1960 when the area is close to being ruined beyond repair; much the work of the National Trust. Gershom realised and wrote about how the slightest alteration to the landscape has an impact because, unlike the Alps, the area is so small; a strong walker like himself could stride through it in one day whether from north to south or east to west. As for many lovers of Lakeland today, Gershom felt that the only hope for any return to wildness would be for humans to leave the scene altogether, in his words:

> 'And someday, Nature will have got the better of all the builders and engineers, and Lakeland will be left to itself again. But meanwhile?'[128]

---

[128] Collingwood, W.G. 1930. Leavings of the German Miners. Fell and Rock Climbing Club Journal of the English Lake District, vol. 8 page 287.

# Chapter XV
# Father and Son
# (1889-1932)

## Father's Influence

Today it is not fashionable to speak only of father-son relationships but it was common for people brought up in the nineteenth century to focus only upon males in the family when thinking of higher education and careers. Robin George Collingwood more than fulfilled any expectations his father may have held for his son, though this idea does not come from Robin's own assessment.

Peter Johnson writing about the Collingwoods at the Admiralty[129] suggested that Robin George Collingwood had not found a way to live that matched his aspirations and that he lived his life, at least partially, adrift from his ideals. Robin's sisters Dora, Barbara and Ursula, all became gifted artists, as well as devoted wives and mothers and Ursula worked as a Midwife, but R.G.C. did not appear to recognise his aspirations as being fulfilled, this has been left for other people to acknowledge.

There is a Jesuit saying: *'Give me a child until he is seven and I will give you the man'*; Vladimir Lenin claimed to need a child only to the age of five and it would be his for life. There have been many changes in the study of child development over the past hundred years, but there is still some truth to be found in claims from Jesuits, or Lenin.

Influences upon any child up to the age of seven are crucial in determining future approaches to life. Robin Collingwood was educated at home until the age of thirteen, along with his three sisters. Robin was an accomplished amateur musician; encouraged by his mother. Historical research, especially the use of methodologies, was encouraged by his father, particularly in archaeology. However, the full extent of personal influence, in any situation, is almost impossible to determine.

Robin's accomplishments in philosophy are more difficult to trace back to either parent, for this we must look more to his later life and to his study of philosophers Hegel and Groce. Groce was a contemporary of R.G. Collingwood, Hegel, the more famous, died in 1831 and Robin has been compared less favourably with the German philosopher. A possible reason is put forward by William M. Johnston[130] that Robin laboured in a less favourable atmosphere in Oxford of the

---
[129] Johnson, P. 2012. Philosopher at the Admiralty. Exeter: Imprint Academic.
[130] Johnston, W.M. 1967. The Formative Years of R.G. Collingwood. The Hague: Martinus Nijhoff.

1920s and 1930s, suggesting, unlike Hegel 100 years earlier in Heidelberg or Berlin. Johnston adds three further important points: first, that R.G.C's affinity with the ideas of Hegel comes not from the great philosopher but from his father who had received it from John Ruskin. Second, 'the study of R.G.C. properly begins with the study of his father'. And third, 'R.G.C. did not dream up the ideal of a many-sided intellectual life; he inherited it'.

Robin became a noted philosopher, influential today around seventy years after his death; he recalled, as a child of no more than eight years old, taking down a book of philosophy from his father's bookshelves. There were many books at home in Lanehead, some from the time his father was a student at Oxford and Robin made full use of the library. The book he took down from the shelves was about Kant's Ethics, translated by Rev. Thomas Kingsmill Abbott. In his autobiography, Robin recalled, *'disgraceful to confess, here was a book whose words were in English and whose sentences were grammatical, but whose meaning baffled me'*. Robin grew up at Lanehead surrounded by idealist literature and much talk of alternative ideas; also, while a student at Oxford his father had contact with Thomas Hill Green, probably the most influential idealist at that time.

Educated at home until the age of thirteen meant with mother a musician and artist; father an artist and polymath both would have a strong influence upon young Robin and much of this showed in his professional writing. While other philosophers studied and wrote about the subject for its own sake, Robin George wrote 'The Principles of Art', 'Outlines of a philosophy of Art', 'The Idea of Nature' and 'The Idea of History'. The idea of History, a rapprochement between history and philosophy was respected by most philosophers and historians. He would explore philosophy historically and history philosophically; an aim being to bridge between the two subjects of philosophy and history; including their respective theories and practices. However in these discussions, archaeology was largely ignored. (W.J. Van der Dussen, 'History as Science')

Robin was something of a polymath, much like his father and like him an idealist too, though early in his career Robin would reject this last claim.

Methods of working learned during his home-based education largely determined his approach to working life. Students and followers of Robin's philosophy, debate today about early influences upon his thoughts and writing. As noted by Ray Monk,[131] Robin Collingwood as philosopher was a lonely figure, *'swimming against every identifiable tide'*, and reasons for his rather novel approach to history and philosophy are open to many interpretations; his father is one person who cannot be overlooked, whatever interpretation is adopted.

---

[131] Monk, R. 1998. Preface in R.G. Collingwood by Johnson, P. Bristol: Thoemmes Press.

Parents, Gershom and Dorrie taught Robin at home, or rather helped him to learn how to learn, that during the most impressionable period of his life it would be surprising if the education received at this time did not influence him, to some extent, during his later life. Questions about influences upon Robin's development have to be, not whether his parents influenced Robin but in how many ways was he influenced, and to what degree and for how long?

There can be little doubt that mother and father had a strong influence upon Robin up to the age of thirteen when he left home to become a school pupil for the first time, but whether further influences from them continued well into adult life is open to question. To say, as one commentator did, that Robin George Collingwood was a more brilliant version of his father may appeal to the general observer or student reading R.G.C's books and papers, but behind the comment is the question whether in stature Robin stood independently apart from his father or gained brilliance by standing upon his father's shoulders. There is a strong case for saying that the greatest influence upon Robin during his early years came from the habit of both parents working each day at creative activity whether art, literature or craftwork.

Robin's formal education at home for nine years from the age of four consisted mainly of classics and modern languages from father, music from mother and art from both. Early home-education consisted of three to four hours study in the morning, followed by education of the more practical kind in the afternoon.

Both mother and father were well qualified to cover Robin's art education. Robin's appreciation of music, and associated knowledge, came from his mother and became a vital part of his life, to the extent that during early days as a student at Oxford he seriously considered making it the subject of his studies. Despite discovering Kant at a young age in his father's library, it seems that Robin George did not come naturally to philosophy. Encouraged by his mother, music became his main interest he played the piano and violin tolerably well but never mastered either. Later as recreation, he composed tunes. Had he become a prominent musician, we would now be debating the influence of his mother alone. Robin became well known not for his music but for his scholarly writing on philosophy, history and archaeology.

Being a slave to my time, I was reluctant to discuss Gershom's influence with his son Robin unless the same approach could be taken with respect to his three daughters with mother included too. The only justification for devoting a major part of this chapter to son Robin is that of the four children he was the only one to achieve greatness or at least has demanded the attention of serious scholars worldwide for the past 70 years. Any claim that Gershom had a direct part to play in his son's career, or that he did not, can only be supported with clear evidence from scholars of history or philosophy.

## Summary

Previous writers have claimed that Gershom's wider influence is *generally* recognised in particular W. Jan van der Dussen in 'History as a Science'.[132] Dussen discussed R.G. Collingwood as an archaeologist and historian and argued that his role as an archaeologist has been underestimated, especially with regard to his question and answer approach said to be based upon Sir Francis Bacon's approach to inductive reasoning. Both his father and Haverfield used similar methods of asking relevant questions before planning an excavation. Gershom's influence was recognised in the Editor's introduction to the second edition of R.G. Collingwood's book 'The Idea of History'.[133] The idea of history was discussed by Douglas Johnson in Collingwood Studies as 'Beginnings of the Idea of History' in 1994[134] emphasising the part played by Gershom. Robin himself finally recognised his father's contribution when writing his obituary for the Times newspaper and in his paper for the Transactions (TCWAAS) titled 'Bewcastle Cross', two years after his father's death. Robin delivered a paper at Bewcastle in June 1934. He addressed members of the Cumberland and Westmorland Antiquarian and Archaeological Society with the words, *'your committee was, I know, thinking of me not as an authority on the difficult problem of pre-Norman history and art, but as representative of the great scholar who for many years directed our Society's study of those problems. His loss has removed from among us the only man who could describe the Bewcastle Cross as it deserves to be described, with full justice done to its art, its archaeology, and its setting in the history of our age. The only reason that could induce me to accept so difficult a task is the fact that, having watched him at work so closely and so long, I have learned to see in these things a little of what he saw. But it would show scant respect for the memory of a great scholar, if one merely repeated views resting on his authority, instead of reconsidering the problems for oneself.* Robin was thinking here only of his late father; a fine tribute and ended by following his father in questioning rather than falling back on authority.

Douglas Johnson described Gershom as *'one of RG's philosophical ancestors: as the scholar, more than any other, who provided him with the example of an historian's work, the practical demonstration of re- enactment, and an insight into the idea of history.'* There is a suggestion that R.G.C's question and answer approach to the study of logic could be gathered, at least initially, from a similar approach of his father to archaeology.

---

[132] Dussen, van der, J.W. 1981. History as a Science: The Philosophy of R.G. Collingwood. The Hague: Martinus Nijhoff.
[133] Collingwood, R.G. 1994. The Idea of History, second edition. Oxford: Oxford University Press.
[134] Johnson D.H. 1994. W.G. Collingwood and the Beginnings of the Idea of History in Collingwood Studies vol.1, David Boucher (ed.) Swansea: R.G. Collingwood Society.

There is ample, though rather superficial, evidence of strong connections between son and father during Robin's adult life: As can be read in the chapter on Naval Intelligence, Robin after serving a year with the Geographical Section recommended his father for work in the section so by 1917 father, son and daughter Barbara were all working for Naval Intelligence. In addition to collaboration on war work Robin and father worked together on archaeological digs and Robin followed his father in becoming editor of Transactions (TCWAAS) and President of the (CWAAS).

No consideration of influences upon Robin Collingwood can ignore the art critic and social reformer John Ruskin. As a boy of impressionable age, Robin met Ruskin a number of times as he lived less than a mile from the Collingwood home and during visits would often enjoy cakes made by Joan Severn. Ruskin, near the end of his life and suffering ill health from the time that Robin was born was still an impressive figure, and who enjoyed the company of children. Later in his writing, Robin overlooked any influence that Ruskin may have had, treating the Professor much in the same way as he did his father. In 1919, this was corrected in impressive style when he delivered a paper on 'Ruskin's Philosophy' at the Ruskin Centenary Conference at Coniston under the auspices of Ruskin Museum. Eventually his paper was published in 1922 by Titus Wilson, Kendal, and reprinted in 1971. Robin George Collingwood took care to point out that he was not writing about Ruskin the philosopher, making clear that he was not a philosopher. Ruskin's reading of philosophy was limited, apart from Plato, which he read and re-read to the end of his life; he looked upon philosophy as a futile and dangerous pursuit, which it was his duty to avoid. Robin showed in this paper that Ruskin did have an impact upon his thinking by declaring that Ruskin nevertheless had a philosophy, a very different thing from reading philosophy or being a philosopher. R.G.C. ventured to suggest that philosophers are the least likely to have a philosophy of their own; likening them to a man who is always taking his watch to bits to see how it works, is not the best man to tell you the time.

Tracking any influence from Ruskin can be done in two ways, directly and indirectly. Directly, Robin as a boy read books by Ruskin held in his father's library and Ruskin's various writings and influence would be ever-present during his student days at Oxford. It is possible that despite reading a number of Ruskin's published works Robin failed to be influenced by the Professor, but anyone reading Robin's paper on Ruskin's Philosophy would find this idea hard to accept. He shows a great depth of understanding by discussing characteristics of Ruskin's thoughts: his belief in unity and solidarity of the human spirit, his focus on causes of historical events and his tolerance. In theory, unity of experience comes from philosopher Hegel but in practice, at the time, it is more likely that the idea came from Ruskin to Collingwoood R.G. through his father Collingwood

W.G. (See Johnston W.M. earlier in chapter). It is difficult to describe Ruskin as a follower of Hegel because, as already stated, he had little time for philosophers in general; Plato being an exception. Ruskin's strong power of synthesis enabled him to see unity in experiences, independently of what any philosopher may have said earlier. Another insight provided by R.G.C. was in Ruskin's approach to art, that he could not consider any work of art without thinking about religion, morality and politics.

What is virtually certain is that any influence coming from his father [Gershom] would have elements of Ruskin's ideas. Robin was only 11 years old when Ruskin died. Difficult to have any direct influence upon Robin from Ruskin, it had to come, if at all, through his father or from reading books by Ruskin, or both. Robin's form of education, with stress put upon a combination of theoretical and practical learning, came from his father following the teaching and guidance of Ruskin. Gershom had a natural inclination towards a broad multi-subject approach to learning, seeing connections and overlaps between subjects that could be seen as a forerunner of systems thinking practised today. This approach was further reinforced by Ruskin; Robin's strong attempts to merge history and philosophy in his writing may have their origins from seeing his father at work, which was not without influence from the work of Ruskin.

When thinking about the life of Gershom, the work of his son could be seen as a form of legacy along with other legacies of Gershom: his artwork that brings to life the early Icelandic sagas; exploring and elucidating what it means to be a Northerner in England. He provided essential groundwork for the completion of a countrywide corpus of Pre-Norman stonework. In addition, writing vivid saga-type stories about early life in Lakeland; providing, through the pages of numerous journals, a history of the north; a clear readable biography of John Ruskin in two volumes; writing works of non-fiction, a guidebook about Lakeland to rival Wordsworth's guide; an accolade for any writer of guidebooks.

Peter Johnson described R.G. Collingwood[135] as a philosopher who was also a distinguished historian, that as a historian R.G.C. wrote mainly on the archaeology of Roman Britain. The title of a book he wrote which became influential among archaeologists, and which can be described as his most successful book. In this respect he can rightly be thought of as an archaeologist of importance rather than a historian interested in Roman Britain. W.J. Van der Dussen said that: 'he had met archaeologists who were surprised to learn that R.G. Collingwood was also a philosopher, and philosophers who either did not know he had been a practising

---

[135] Johnson, P. 1998. R.G. Collingwood: an introduction. Bristol: Theommes.

archaeologist and historian, or thought it no more than a private hobby.' R.G.C. wrote a great amount of influential books and papers about his specialization Roman Britain between 1913 and 1939 with only a break during the war years 1917-18.

Looking from the outside in, I feel that R.G.C. was more successful as an archaeologist, especially the Romano-British period, than as a historian or philosopher and in this respect his father had unquestionable influence, in addition to that of Professor Haverfield at Oxford who tutored R.G.C.

# Chapter XVI
# Last Years
# (1928-1932)

**Coming to a Close**

The four years following the death of Dorrie had been difficult for Gershom he lost himself in work by writing for journals: Yorkshire Archaeology, D&G Transactions, Fell and Rock, TCWAAS and Antiquity. Despite fruitful work completed during these years it did appear that with Dorrie gone it was time for him to go too. Intellectually he was still active but physically he could no longer walk the hills and strokes beginning in 1927 made writing extremely difficult. Three years earlier, Arthur Ransome wrote in a letter: 'the old Collingwoods are,I fear, getting very old indeed'. He went for a short walk with Gershom and found that he tired very quickly. Gershom, wrote in 1930: *'That I am still alive is the wonder after all'*. In July of that year another stroke left him paralyzed on his right side.

Gershom, sat at his writing table on October 1 1932, took his pen and wrote a one-page letter to his son Robin,[136] a few hours later he would be dead. In the letter, he told Robin that Barbara (Robin's sister) had gone to Windermere to meet a friend travelling on her way south. When Barbara returned she took her father for a drive and when near Little Langdale, in sight of his beloved Pikes, he died. We cannot chose when and where to die naturally and unexpectedly, but we can be almost certain that given a choice Gershom would think of only one better place and that would be sitting at home at Lanehead, looking across to Coniston Old man.

Regular correspondence passed between Robin and his father during the final months. On May 13 1932,[137] Robin wrote from Oxford mainly about teaching and the writing he had to complete, with difficulty, beginning letters My Dearest Daddy and closing with Yours R.G.C. People who relish Robin's flowing style would be surprised to read in one letter how he paced up and down his room at Oxford trying to think of first words, a feeling he likened to having constipation, until suddenly the words come to him and then 'writing goes moderately well'.

---

[136]Letter 1932, W.G. Collingwood to R.G.Collingwood. Collingwood Archive. Abbot Hall, Kendal.
[137]Letter, R.G. Collingwood. to W.G. Collingwood. April, 1932. Collingwood Archive, Cardiff University .

Figure 36
Acca Cross Upper

Figure 37
Acca Cross Lower

**Final Works**

One of Gershom's last tasks was a major revision of his classic guide 'The Lake Counties'[138] which was carried out 30 years after its first publication, and published during the last year of his life. There was much to alter for things had moved over these years *'and that under my very eyes'*. At Whitsuntide 1932 he wrote, *'it is like looking at a kaleidoscope. But in such a toy other changes are never for the worse: always into something rich and strange. Can we hope for the same for our country? I should like to be one who, as the Romans put it, does not despair of the republic'*

The time had to come when Gershom sent a paper to an appropriate journal that would prove to be his last. This was 'A Pedigree of Anglian Crosses' and the journal was 'Antiquity'.[139] Gershom returned to the question of when stone crosses

---

[138] Collingwood, W.G. 1932. Lake Counties, revised edition. London: Frederick Warne.
[139] Collingwood, W.G. 1932. A pedigree of Anglian crosses. Antiquity, vol. 6, pp. 35-54.

were first introduced and provided, in his view, the development and Chronology of Christian monuments from AD 740 to the time that this form of Anglian art merged with Scandinavian interest and methods of working in stone (around 900).

Only 50 pieces of sculptured stonework survived from the period of pure Anglian art in stone (740 to 900) to be available to scholars like Gershom. There were crosses in Britain before the time of Venerable Bede (672-735) but they were of wood or un-ornamental stone columns, as at Iona in Scotland and St. Oswald's Church, Heavenfield in Northumberland. There was little evidence of ornamental stonework before AD 740; at least during Gershom's time.

The Acca Cross (Acca, Bishop of Hexham, died in 740) from Hexham Abbey in Northumberland was described by Gershom in his last paper as one of the earliest examples (740-745) and though found at Hexham he felt that the design and carving came from someone foreign to the country. In Gershom's words, *'No Englishman at any time in the Anglo-Saxon age conceived such a set of artistic delicate lines* (which can be seen in Figures 36 and 37).

*'There is nothing in our ancestral art to match it for variety and beauty'*. It was a unique design done before there could be anything worked beforehand that could be followed. The cross was found near his grave but not bearing his name, so Gershom expressed doubts about it being directly associated with the Bishop, despite being called the Acca Cross. Gershom, in his last paper, described also schools of stone-cross design and development: Hexham, Hoddam, Lancaster, Durham and Yorkshire. He felt that such an important centre as York during this period ought to be included but evidence, if any, could have been lost during attacks by the Danes.

Figure 38 Gravestone for Gershom and Dorrie

# Appendix

Published writing of William Gershom Collingwood, books and periodicals including edited (ed.) work; based upon a list by Mathew Townend, 2009, Cumberland and Westmorland Antiquarian and Archaeological Society Extra Series 34, with additions from the present author.

1876
The Economist of Xenophon with Alexander, D. Wedderburn (translation for John Ruskin ed.).

1882
Lady Diana's prayer book, The Art Journal, pp. 337-339.

1883
The Philosophy of Ornament, 8 lectures (University College, Liverpool) Orpington: George Allen.

1884
The Limestone Alps of Savoy: Deucalion Supplement, 1. Orpington: George Allen.

1885
A Book of Verses. Orpington: George Allen.
On Lake Basins of the Neighbourhood of Windermere, Transactions of the Cumberland Association for the advancement of Literature and Science, vol. 9, pp. 1-10.

1886
'Astrology in the Apocalypse': An Essay on Biblical Allusions to Chaldean Science. Orpington: George Allen

1889
'John Ruskin': A Biographical Outline. London: Virtue and Co.
The Missal of Kaiser Max. The Ruskin Reading Guild Journal (Igdrasil) pp. 65-69.
A New School II. The Ruskin Reading Guild Journal (Igdrasil) pp. 182-184.
Recent Paintings and Ruskin's Principles. The Ruskin Reading Guild Journal (Igdrasil) pp. 273-275.
Two Sonnets. The Ruskin Reading Guild Journal (Igdrasil) p. 317

1890
The Genesis of 'Modern Painters' The Ruskin Reading Guild Journal (Igdrasil) pp.3-9.
The Philosophy of 'Modern Painters'. Igdrasil pp. 42-50.
The Influence of Reynolds on Ruskin. Igdrasil pp. 126-131.
Ruskin and Reynolds: Their Theories of Art. Igdrasil pp. 219-225.
The Purport of 'Modern Painters'. Igdrasil pp. 314- 319.
The Fable of Convolvulus. Igdrasil p. 376.

1891
(ed.) 'The poems of John Ruskin', 2 vols London: George Allen.
'The Art Teaching of John Ruskin'. London: Methuen.
Cassandra's Prophecy, Ruskin Reading Guild Journal (Igdrasil) pp. 1-10.
1892
The Vikings in Lakeland: their place names, remains, history. Saga Book of the Viking Society, vol.1 part1 pp. 182-196.
1893
'The Life and Work of John Ruskin' 2 vols London: Methuen.
(ed.) 'John Ruskin': the poetry of architecture. Orpington: George Allen.
(ed.) 'Selections from the Writing of John Ruskin', 2 vols Orpington: George Allen
Practical Fly-Fishing by John Beever (Memoir by W.G.C.) London: Simpkin and Marshall.
1894
(ed.) 'John Ruskin, Verona and Other Lectures'. Orpington: George Allen.
1895
'Thorstein of the Mere': a saga of the Northmen in Lakeland. London: Edward Arnold.
Some Manx Names in Cumbria, Transaction of the Cumberland and Westmorland Antiquarian and Archaeological Society. vol. 13 pp. 403-414.
(ed.) 'The Ruskin Reader'. Orpington: George Allen.
(ed.) 'John Ruskin, Studies in Both Arts'. Orpington: George Allen.
1896
Furness a thousand years ago, Barrow Naturalists' Field Club.
'The Bondwoman': a story of the Northmen in Lakeland. London: Edward Arnold.
(ed.) 'John Ruskin': Fors Clavigera 4 volumes. Orpington: George Allen.
Seventeenth Century MS. Epistles of Early Friends, Transaction of the Cumberland and Westmorland Antiquarian and Archaeological Society. vol. 14 pp. 155-59.
1897
'The Book of Coniston'. Kendal: Titus Wilson.
(ed.) John Ruskin: Lectures on Landscape (delivered at Oxford in 1871). Orpington: George Allen.
Reports from Cumberland and Westmorland. Saga Book of the Viking Club. vol. 2 part 1, pp. 33-146.
King Eirík of York. Saga Book of the Viking Club. vol. 2 part 1, pp. 313-327.
1898
Reports on excavations at Springs Bloomery, Coniston. Transaction of the Cumberland and Westmorland Antiquarian and Archaeological Society. vol. 15 pp. 223-228.

Lost Churches in the Carlisle Diocese, with John Rogers. Transaction of the Cumberland and Westmorland Antiquarian and Archaeological Society. vol. 15 pp. 288-302.

Ulpha Old Hall, Transaction of the Cumberland and Westmorland Antiquarian and Archaeological Society. vol. 15 pp 315-320.

The Ormside Cup, Transaction of the Cumberland and Westmorland Antiquarian and Archaeological Society. vol. 15 pp. 381-387.

'An Old Master', C.K.G. British Quarterly Magazine, July pp. 29-33.

1899

'A Pilgrimage to the Saga-steads of Iceland' with Jón Stefánsson. Ulverston: Wm. Holmes.

'Coniston Tales'. Ulverston: Wm. Holmes.

(ed.) W.S. Calverley: Notes on the Early Sculptured Crosses, Shrines and Monuments in the Present Diocese of Carlisle. Cumberland and Westmorland Antiquarian and Archaeological Society. Extra Series 11. Kendal: Titus Wilson.

1900

Forward to John Ruskin Exhibition. July 21 to September 8. Pp. 1-2.

So-called 'Cockpit' at Monk Foss, in the Parish of Whitbeck, Cumberland. Transaction of the Cumberland and Westmorland Antiquarian and Archaeological Society. vol. 16, pp. 117-119.

The 'Wissonsett Cross'. Transactions of the Norfolk and Norwich Archaeological Society. vol. 15. pp. 316-323.

'Traces of the Norse in Cumberland'. The Norwegian Club Yearbook. pp. 8-21.

The Story of the Bewcastle Cross. Northern Counties Magazine. October. pp. 32-42.

1901

'The Ruskin Cross at Coniston'. Ulverston: William Holmes.

Remains of the Pre-Norman Period in the Victoria History of the County of Cumberland. pp. 253-293. James Wilson (ed.).

Pre-Norman Cross-fragments from Glassonby. Transaction of the Cumberland and Westmorland Antiquarian and Archaeological Society. pp. 289-291

Fragments of an early cross at the Abbey, Carlisle. Transaction of the Cumberland and Westmorland Antiquarian and Archaeological Society. pp. 292-294.

Tumulus at Grayson-lands, Glassonby, Cumberland. Transaction of the Cumberland and Westmorland Antiquarian and Archaeological Society. pp. 295-99.

The 'Gosforth Cross'. Northern Counties Magazine. vol. 2 pp. 312-321

1902

'The Lake Counties'. London: Dent.

The Northmen in the Lake Counties, II. The Norwegian Year Book. pp. 21-35.

The Life and Death of Cormac the Skald with Jón Stefánsson. Viking Club Translation Series. Ulverston: William Holmes.

Ruskin's Ilaria. American Periodicals: The Critic. vol. 40 number 4.

Ruskin's Jump. American Periodicals: The Critic. vol. 40 number 6.

Report on excavations at the Holy Well, Gosforth. Transaction of the Cumberland and Westmorland Antiquarian and Archaeological Society. pp. 77-83.

The Battle of Stainmoor in Legend and History. Transaction of the Cumberland and Westmorland Antiquarian and Archaeological Society. pp. 231-241.

Pre-Norman cross fragments at Lancaster. The Reliquary and Illustrated archaeologist, vol. 8. pp. 272- 274.

The Ancient Ironworks of Coniston Lake. Transactions of the History Society of Lancashire and Cheshire. New Series 17, pp. 1-22.

Traces of the Norse in Cumberland, The Norwegian Club Year Book, pp.8-21.

1903

Ruskin's Bibles. The Living Age, February. vol. 14. pp. 441.

'Ruskin Relics'. London: Isbister.

On some ancient sculptures of the Devil Bound, Transaction of the Cumberland and Westmorland Antiquarian and Archaeological Society. vol. 3, pp. 380-89.

An Anglian cross-fragment at Kendal, The Reliquary and Illustrated Archaeologist, vol. 9. pp. 204- 205.

Some Pre-Norman finds at Lancaster The Reliquary and Illustrated Archaeologist, vol. 9. pp. 257-266.

1904

King William the Wanderer, an Old British Saga from Old French Versions. Saga Book of the Viking Club, vol.4 part 1, pp. 171-181.

Notes in advance on the Tour to the Hebrides, privately printed, Kendal.

The County Palatine of Lancaster, Gazetteer and Royal Blue Book, pp.15-56.

Two Bronze Armlets from Thirlmere. Transaction of the Cumberland and Westmorland Antiquarian and Archaeological Society. vol. 4 pp. 80-84.

An Anglian cross-fragment at Kendal. Transaction of the Cumberland and Westmorland Antiquarian and Archaeological Society. vol. 4 pp. 330-333.

The Dove in the Osprey's nest, Good Words, pp. 196-199.

Some crosses at Hornby and Melling in Lonsdale. The Reliquary and Illustrated Archaeologist, vol. 10. pp. 35-42.

A Hebridean Pilgrimage. The Reliquary and Illustrated Archaeologist, vol. 10. pp. 248-259.

1905

On a sculptured trough in Tullie House Museum, Transaction of the Cumberland and Westmorland Antiquarian and Archaeological Society. vol. 5 pp. 202-212.

Brampton Mote. Transaction of the Cumberland and Westmorland Antiquarian and Archaeological Society. vol. 5 pp. 290-291.

Bewcastle Cross. Transaction of the Cumberland and Westmorland Antiquarian and Archaeological Society. vol. 5 pp. 296-300; and in Proceedings of the Society of Antiquaries of Newcastle-upon-Tyne, pp. 219-226.

1906

The Fésole Club Papers: Lessons in Sketching for Home-Learners. Ulverston: William Holmes.

Kunst, Arbejde, Opdragalse: The Foredrag om Ruskin, translated by Andreas Mollerup. Copenhagen.

'Ruskin', in H.B. Baildon et al. Homes and Haunts of Famous Authors. London: Wells, Gardner, Darton. pp. 91-104.

Coniston, in Guide to the Church Congress and Ecclesiastical Art Exhibition held in Barrow-in- Furness, September 29 to October 5, pp. 97-106.

Late and Magic Runes in Cumberland, Transaction of the Cumberland and Westmorland Antiquarian and Archaeological Society. vol. 6 pp. 305-312.

Some antiquaries of Canna. The antiquary, vol. 42. pp. 372-377.

John Ruskin, Temple Bar new series. vol. 6 pp. 481-494.

Some illustrations of the Viking Age in England. Saga Book of the Viking Club. vol. 5 pp. 111-141.

A Legend of Shetland from Fljótsdaela Saga, Saga Book of the Viking Club. vol. 5 pp. 272-287.

1907

Illustrations of the Archaeology of the Viking Age in England. Saga Book of the Viking Club, vol. 5  pp. 111-141.

The Lowther Hogbacks. Transaction of the Cumberland and Westmorland Antiquarian and Archaeological Society. vol. 7 pp. 302-304.

Bampton Crosses. Transaction of the Cumberland and Westmorland Antiquarian and Archaeological Society. vol. 7 pp. 302-304.

Anglian and Anglo-Danish Sculpture in the North Riding of Yorkshire. Yorkshire Archaeological Journal. vol.19 pp. 267-413.

Some Antiquities of Tiree. The Antiquary. vol. 43 pp. 174- 180.

The Ballad of Hildina: old-lore miscellany of Orkney, Shetland, Caithness and Sutherland. (1) pp. 211-216.

1908

Three More Ancient Castles of Kendal, Transaction of the Cumberland and Westmorland Antiquarian and Archaeological Society. vol. 8 pp. 97-112.

A Shetland Legend from Flötsdaela Saga. Saga Book of the Viking Club, vol. 5 part 2. pp. 272-287.

An award concerning sheep-gates, Seathwaite-in-Dunnerdale, 1681. Transaction of the Cumberland and Westmorland Antiquarian and Archaeological Society. vol. 8 pp. 352-354.

'Scandinavian Britain.' London: Society for Promoting Christian Knowledge.
Anglian and Anglo-Danish sculpture in York. Yorkshire Archaeological Journal. vol. 20 pp. 149-213.

1909
High Furness in Fishwick, H. and P.H. Ditchfield (eds) Memorials of Old Lancashire, 2 vol part II pp. 159-190.
Report on the Exploration of the Romano-British Settlement at Ewe Close, Crosby Ravensworth. Transaction of the Cumberland and Westmorland Antiquarian and Archaeological Society. vol. 9 pp. 355-368.
New Finds of Pre-Norman Stones at Bedale Church, Yorkshire Archaeological Journal. vol. 20 pp. 259-260.
Aldingham Mote. The Antiquary. vol. 45 pp. 252-258.
Anglian and Anglo-Danish Sculpture at York. Yorkshire Archaeological Society. vol. 20 pp. 149-213.

1910
'Dutch Agnes Her Valentine': Being the Journal of the Curate of Coniston, 1616-1623. Kendal: Titus Wilson.
A Pre-Norman cross-shaft from Urswick Church. Transaction of the Cumberland and Westmorland Antiquarian and Archaeological Society. vol. 10 pp. 307-311.
An Exploration of the Circle on Banniside Moor, Coniston, Transaction of the Cumberland and Westmorland Antiquarian and Archaeological Society. vol. 10 pp. 342-351.
Coniston Hall. Transaction of the Cumberland and Westmorland Antiquarian and Archaeological Society. vol. 10, pp. 354-368.
Germans at Coniston in the Seventeenth Century. Transaction of the Cumberland and Westmorland Antiquarian and Archaeological Society. vol. 10 pp. 369-394.

1911
'Foreword' in John Ruskin by Andreas Mollerup (ed.) pp. 3-6
A Rune-inscribed Anglian cross shaft at Urswick Church. Transaction of the Cumberland and Westmorland Antiquarian and Archaeological Society. vol. 11 pp. 462-468.
Anglian and Anglo-Danish Sculpture in the East Riding. Yorkshire Archaeological Society. vol. 21 pp. 254-302.

1912
'Elizabethan Keswick': extracts from the original Account Books, 1564-1577.
Anglo-Saxon Sculptured Stones, in William Page (ed.) 'The Victorian History of the County of York, vol. 2 pp. 109-131.
A cross-shaft of the Viking Age at Kirkby Stephen. Transaction of the Cumberland and Westmorland Antiquarian and Archaeological Society. vol. 12 pp. 29-32.

Anglian cross-shafts at Dacre and Kirkby Stephen. Transaction of the Cumberland and Westmorland Antiquarian and Archaeological Society. vol. 12 pp. 157-163.

'Roman Camp at Ambleside'. Ambleside: The St. Oswald Press.

1913

Recent Opinion on the Bewcastle Cross, CW2 13, pp. 409-411.

On a Group of Northumbrian Crosses. The Antiquary new series 9, pp. 167-173.

1914

The early crosses of Leeds. Miscellanea of the Thoresby Society. vol. 22 pp. 269-338.

The Antiquities of the Doe Crag Track, Journal of the Fell and Rock Climbing Club of the English Lake District. vol. 3 pp. 11-16.

1915

Notes on Early Crosses at Carlisle, Bewcastle and Beckermet. Transaction of the Cumberland and Westmorland Antiquarian and Archaeological Society. vol. 15 pp. 125-131.

Anglian and Anglo-Danish Sculpture in the West Riding. Yorkshire Archaeological Society. vol. 23 pp. 129-299.

Untitled Paper on the Bewcastle Cross, Proceedings of the Antiquities of Newcastle-upon-Tyne. Series 3, vol. 6 pp. 214-218.

1916

The Castle Rock of St. John's Vale. Transaction of the Cumberland and Westmorland Antiquarian and Archaeological Society. vol. 16 pp. 224-228.

An Anglian Cross at Tullie House. Transaction of the Cumberland and Westmorland Antiquarian and Archaeological Society. vol. 16 pp. 279-281.

The Ruthwell Cross in its Relation to other Monuments of the Early Christian Age. Transactions of the Dumfries and Galloway Natural History and Antiquarian Society. Series 3. vol. 4 pp. 34-84.

1917

'The likeness of King Elfwald': A Study of Northumbria and Iona at the Beginning of the Viking Age. Kendal: Titus Wilson.

With C.A. Parker, A reconsideration of Gosforth Cross. Transaction of the Cumberland and Westmorland Antiquarian and Archaeological Society. vol.17 pp. 99-113.

Fragment of Early Grave-Monument at Kirkheaton. Yorkshire Archaeological Society. vol. 24 pp. 213-215.

1918

Mountain names. Transaction of the Cumberland and Westmorland Antiquarian and Archaeological Society. vol. 18 pp. 93-104.

The name of Birdoswald. Transaction of the Cumberland and Westmorland Antiquarian and Archaeological Society. vol. 18 pp. 238-240.

1920

The Giant's Thumb. Transaction of the Cumberland and Westmorland Antiquarian and Archaeological Society. vol. 20 pp. 53-65.

A few more mountain names. Transaction of the Cumberland and Westmorland Antiquarian and Archaeological Society. vol. 20 pp. 243- 245.

1921

Angles, Danes and Norse in the District of Huddersfield, Tolson Memorial Museum Publications 2.

Thirteenth-century Keswick. Transaction of the Cumberland and Westmorland Antiquarian and Archaeological Society. vol. 21 pp. 159-173.

Norse influence in Dumfriesshire and Galloway. Dumfries and Galloway Transactions. Series 3. vol. 7 pp. 97-118.

The cattle of the saga times. The Vasculum, vol. 8 no. 1. pp. 48-49.

1922

A Calendar of Grinsdale and Kirkandrews documents, 1635-1817. Transaction of the Cumberland and Westmorland Antiquarian and Archaeological Society. vol. 22 pp. 252-280.

A cross base at Winchester, Papers and Proceedings of the Hampshire Field Club and Archaeological Society. vol. 9 pp. 219- 20.

The country of Ruskin and Wordsworth. The Landmark, pp. 421-424.

1923

The Giant's Grave, Penrith. Transaction of the Cumberland and Westmorland Antiquarian and Archaeological Society. vol. 23 pp. 115-128.

Tillesburc, with R.G. Collingwood. Transaction of the Cumberland and Westmorland Antiquarian and Archaeological Society. vol. 23 pp. 138-141.

An inventory of the ancient monuments of Cumberland. Transaction of the Cumberland and Westmorland Antiquarian and Archaeological Society. vol. 23 pp. 206-276.

The Brailsford cross. Journal of the Derbyshire Archaeological and Natural History Society. vol. 45 pp. 1-13.

The first English in Northumberland. The Vasculum vol. 9 pp. 34-39.

1924

The end of the Maiden Way. Transaction of the Cumberland and Westmorland Antiquarian and Archaeological Society. vol. 24 pp. 110-116.

Who was King Eveling of Ravenglass? Transaction of the Cumberland and Westmorland Antiquarian and Archaeological Society. vol. 24 pp. 256-259.

The Angles in Furness and Cartmel. Transaction of the Cumberland and Westmorland Antiquarian and Archaeological Society. vol. 24 pp. 288-294.

A relic from the dark age of Hexham. The Vasculum vol. 10 pp. 38-41.

Review of English Place-names in 'ing' by Eilert Ekwal. Oxford: Oxford University Press, 1923. In The Vasculum, vol. 10 pp. 90-91.
1925
'Lake District History'. Kendal: Titus Wilson.
Patron Saints of the Diocese of Carlisle with T.H.B. Graham. Transaction of the Cumberland and Westmorland Antiquarian and Archaeological Society. vol. 25 pp. 1-27.
The Waberthwaite Crosses. Transaction of the Cumberland and Westmorland Antiquarian and Archaeological Society. vol. 25, pp. 81-85.
The Early Crosses of Galloway, Dumfries and Galloway Transactions Series 3. vol. 10 pp. 205-231.
Early carved stones at Hexham. Archaeologia Aeliana Series 4. vol. 1 pp. 65-92.
The First English in Northumberland. The Vasculum. vol. 11, pp. 34-39.
1926
(ed.) The Gosforth District, C.A. Parker, Revised Edition. Cumberland and Westmorland Antiquarian and Archaeological Society. Extra Series 15.
An Inventory of the Ancient Monuments of Westmorland and Lancashire North-of-the-Sands. Transaction of the Cumberland and Westmorland Antiquarian and Archaeological Society. vol. 26 pp. 1-62.
Dr William Stratford the Benefactor, with Caesar Caine. Transaction of the Cumberland and Westmorland Antiquarian and Archaeological Society. vol. 26 pp. 63-76.
Rockcliff Cross and the Knowes of Arthuret. Transaction of the Cumberland and Westmorland Antiquarian and Archaeological Society. vol. 26 pp. 378-389.
Candida Casa. Transaction of the Cumberland and Westmorland Antiquarian and Archaeological Society. vol. 26 pp. 523-528.
The dispersion of the wheel cross. Yorkshire Archaeological Journal. vol. 28 pp 322-331.
The Early Church in Dumfriesshire and its Monuments, Dumfries and Galloway Transactions. Series 3. vol. 12 pp. 46-72.
1927
'Northumbrian Crosses of the Pre-Norman Age'. London: Faber and Gwyer.
Rey Cross. Transaction of the Cumberland and Westmorland Antiquarian and Archaeological Society. vol. 27 pp. 1-10.
Fragments of Early Grave-Monuments at Kirkheaton. Yorkshire Archaeological Journal. vol. 24 pp. 213-215.
Ardwall Island and its Ancient Cross with R.C. Reid, Dumfries and Galloway Transactions Series 3, vol. 13 pp. 125-129.
Christian Vikings. Antiquity vol. 1 pp. 172-180.

Arthur and Athelstan, Saga-Book of the Viking Club, vol.10 (1919-1927) part 1 pp. 132-144.

1928

(ed.) The Memoirs of Sir Daniel Fleming, transcribed by R.E. Porter. Cumberland and Westmorland Antiquarian and Archaeological Society. Tract Series 11.

Whithorn Priory: Wigtown Official Guide, with R.C. Reid. London: H.M.S.O.

The Early Monuments of West Kirby in West Kirby and Hilbre by John Brownbill. Liverpool. pp. 14-26.

The Keswick and Coniston Mines in 1600 and later. Transaction of the Cumberland and Westmorland Antiquarian and Archaeological Society. vol. 28 pp. 1-32.

The Inventory of Mistress Fleming of Skirwith, 1639. Transaction of the Cumberland and Westmorland Antiquarian and Archaeological Society. vol. 28 pp. 33-40.

Wigton Old Church. Transaction of the Cumberland and Westmorland Antiquarian and Archaeological Society. vol. 28 pp. 96-102.

Packhorse-bridges. Transaction of the Cumberland and Westmorland Antiquarian and Archaeological Society. vol. 28 pp. 120-128.

Hut-Circles at Greendale. Transaction of the Cumberland and Westmorland Antiquarian and Archaeological Society. vol. 28 pp. 371- 376.

1929

The Register and Record Books of Holm Cultram with Francis Granger. Cumberland and Westmorland Antiquarian and Archaeological Society. Record Series 7.

A Book of Old Quaker Wills. Transaction of the Cumberland and Westmorland Antiquarian and Archaeological Society. vol. 29 pp. 1- 38.

Ravenglass, Coniston and Penrith in ancient deeds. Transaction of the Cumberland and Westmorland Antiquarian and Archaeological Society. vol. 29 pp. 39-48.

Anthorn Cross. Transaction of the Cumberland and Westmorland Antiquarian and Archaeological Society. vol. 29 pp. 211-213.

Explorations on Thwaites Fell, South Cumberland with Marjorie Cross. Transaction of the Cumberland and Westmorland Antiquarian and Archaeological Society. vol. 29 pp. 250-258.

Hoddam and its Monuments. Transaction of the Cumberland and Westmorland Antiquarian and Archaeological Society. vol. 29, pp. 318- 322.

Leavings of the German Miners. Journal of the Fell and Rock Club of the English Lake District. vol. 8 pp. 283-287.

Arthur's Battles, Antiquity 3, pp. 292-298.

Crosses Lately Found at Hovingham and Hawnby. Yorkshire Archaeological Journal. vol. 28 pp 111-112.

A Cross Fragment at Sutton-on-Derwent. Yorkshire Archaeological Journal. vol. 28 pp. 238-240.

1930
The medieval fence of Rydal and other linear earth works. Transaction of the Cumberland and Westmorland Antiquarian and Archaeological Society. vol. 30, pp. 1-11.
Crewgarth. Transaction of the Cumberland and Westmorland Antiquarian and Archaeological Society. vol. 30 pp. 132-136.
1931
Gleanings from Rydal Muniments. Transaction of the Cumberland and Westmorland Antiquarian and Archaeological Society. vol. 31 pp. 1-7.
1932
The Deil's Dyke, Dumfries and Galloway Transactions. Series 3, vol. 17 pp. 72-79.
A pedigree of Anglian Crosses. Antiquity vol. 6 pp. 35-54.

# Acknowledgements

Thank you to: Professor David Boucher of Cardiff University for all his help in facilitating use of the Collingwood (RG) Archives, and for his kind hospitality during my first visit.

Alison Harvey at the Special Collections and Archives, Arts and Social Studies Library, Cardiff University for collating archive material and making the search so much easier, and for her work in keeping me supplied with many boxes of material.

Peter Keelan, Head of Special Collections and Archives for making the research work possible.

Suzannah Brown for all her help in guiding me through the Collingwood Archive at Abbot Hall Art Gallery, Kendal.

Glyn Hughes of the Alpine Club for locating details of Gershom's membership.

Vicky Slowe, Director and Curator Ruskin Museum for permission to use image of John Ruskin in Brantwood study, and for making his museum a continued success.

Staff at the University Library Cambridge, particularly in the Rare Books Room.

My daughter Alison for her computer expertise when the machine kept saying 'no'.

My wife Margaret Craig for constant interest in the work, checking and making valuable comments.

# Books by the Author

1994. Analysing Learning Needs. Aldershot: Gower.
2000. Thinking Visually. London: Continuum.
2011. Gable: biography of a mountain and its upper valleys. Wilmslow: Sigma Press.
2013. Shackles of Convention: women mountaineers before 1914. Wilmslow: Sigma Press.
2014. Communicating with Diagrams. Printed by Create Space for Amazon.
2014. Alpine Mountain Guides of the Nineteenth Century. Printed by Create Space for Amazon.

# Index

Abbot Hall, x, 248
Acca Cross, 234
Admiralty, 107, 216
Aleppo, 7, 95, 98
Alpine Club, vi, 3, 185–186, 248
Alps, v, 4, 71, 147
Al-Thing, 173
Altounyan Ernest, 95, 98, 101, 111, 203, 204
Altounyan family, 96, 111
Ambleside, 22, 201, 206, 208–209, 213–215
Anglo-Saxons, 125
Antiquaries, vii, x, 119, 191, 197, 208
Antiquities, 95, 100, 120, 146, 153, 241, 243
Archaeology, 133, 216, 229, 233
Barmouth, 89, 153
Bede, 144
Beever, Susie, 81
Bewcastle, 197, 215, 229
Bondwoman, vi, 171
Bosanquet, v, 34–35
Brantwood, v–vi, 49–50, 70, 73, 75, 77–79, 82–83, 85, 91–93, 197, 248
Cardiff University, x, 64, 193, 248
Calverley, vi, 71, 139, 141, 145, 147, 191, 216
Collingwood, viii, x–xi, 1, 8, 15, 17–23, 25, 31, 55, 57, 61, 63–64, 68, 82–83, 90–91, 97, 104, 106–108, 124, 152, 171, 181, 186, 190, 193, 197, 206, 214, 216, 226, 229, 248
  Barbara, vi, viii, 106–107, 113, 190
  David, v, 27–28, 31, 248
  Dorothy (Dora), vi, ix, 1, 3, 38, 65, 67, 68, 70, 98, 104, 105–107, 109, 111, 182, 183, 190–192, 203, 226
  Family, vi, 14–15, 17–19, 21–23, 25, 27, 46, 56, 60, 63, 69–70, 75, 84–85, 94, 104–106, 113, 133, 165, 190, 226
  Frances, 22, 63
  Francis, 206, 229
  Robin George, x, 8, 107, 206, 216, 226
  Ruth, v, 27, 31, 105
  Society, vi–vii, x–xi, 8, 15, 31, 35, 53, 87, 93, 113, 116–117, 145, 148, 181, 187, 197, 229
  Ursula, vi, 73, 75, 105–106, 190, 196
  William, v, vii, xi, 14–15, 18, 20–22, 25, 27–28, 31, 65, 68, 71, 77, 79, 108, 141, 174, 180, 216
Coniston, vi–vii, 4, 15, 51, 77, 79, 82, 86, 94, 104, 108, 133, 158
Cowper, H.S., 133, 156, 187, 188
Crosses, viii, 4–6, 12, 59, 119–123, 135, 137, 139–141, 143, 144, 153, 154, 174, 198, 211, 212, 215, 234
Cumberland and Westmorland, vi, x, 5, 116, 159, 187, 229
Danes, 146, 155
Darwin Charles, 180
Denmark, vii, 85, 155, 173, 191, 194
Dorrie, vi, x, 47, 50, 61, 63–67, 69–70, 73, 75, 94, 97, 104–106, 108, 165, 167, 190–191, 196–197, 233, 236
Dressler Conrad, ix, 36, 77
Dutch Agnes, vii
Dykes, 217
Economist of Xenophon, 40
Edda, 141, 142, 169, 171, 179, 217
Ellwood Thomas, 133, 147, 156, 158, 161, 162
English Lake District, vii, 3, 73, 147
Ennerdale, 147
Ewe Close, 118, 119, 242
Fell and Rock Climbing Club, vii, 3, 73
Fellfoot, 187
Ferguson Chancellor, 139, 152
Ferguson Robert, 154, 156, 163, 189
Furness, 124
German Miners, 195
Giant's Thumb, 138, 143
Gillhead, vi, 31, 49, 63, 67, 69–71, 73, 75, 94
Gnosspelius, 113, 119
  Barbara, vi, viii, 106–107, 113, 190
  Janet, 119

Gosforth Cross, 136, 141, 216
Guild of St. George, ii, 50, 81, 86–90, 153, 237
Great Gable, viii, 107
Green Thomas, 34
Groce, 226
Hardknot, 206–209, 213–214
Hardknot Pass, 208
Hegel, 46
Hertford House, 200, 204
Hilliard Lawrence, ii, vi, 41, 50, 81, 86, 87
Hinksey Ferry, v, ix, 38, 39, 81, 221
Hogbacks, 120, 144–146
Holland Henry, 31, 63, 176
Holmes William, 32, 186, 239
Holt Emma, 10, 44, 110, 111
Hunt Holman, 80, 92
Hunt William, 9
Iceland, vi–vii, 31, 82, 147, 168, 173–174, 177, 180–181, 185–186
Igdrasil, vi, x
Ilaria Correto, 54, 56, 183
Imhoff Marie, 22, 65
Isaac Georgina, 62
Isaac Sara, 60
Isaac Thomas, 60
Isle of Man, 134, 146, 159, 165
Italy, v, 53
Johnson Douglas H, 229
Johnson Peter, 3, 226, 231
Johnson, W.M., 226, 231
Jumping Jenny, 41
Jungfrau, 4, 15
Jutes, 125, 126
Kaber Rigg Plot, 151
Kendal, x, 207–208, 248
Kensington, vi, 63, 68, 141
Keswick, vii, 132, 197
Kist Panel, ix, 154, 157, 163
Lake Artists Society, 113
Lake Counties, vii–viii, 234
Lakeland, 4, 31, 69, 73, 79, 82, 94–95, 97, 99, 101, 103, 105, 107, 109, 111, 113, 115–116, 124, 148, 151, 155, 158, 161, 165, 170–171, 176, 180, 187, 190–191, 194, 207, 221, 223, 225
Lanehead, vi, 74–75, 83, 94, 100, 104, 106, 108, 143, 165, 167, 190–191, 193, 195, 197, 199–200
Langdale Pikes, 4
Legros Alphonse, I, v, 44
Lenin Vladimir, 111, 226
Lindop Grevel, 2
Liverpool, v, 15, 19, 21, 27–28, 30–31, 34, 45, 78, 176
London, vi, 14–15, 22, 43, 45, 49–50, 60, 63, 65, 79, 85, 94, 107–108, 113, 141, 143, 158, 174, 176, 181, 185, 190, 198, 200
Luard Selby R.B. Rev., 102, 107
Lucca, 54–56, 58
Magnusson Eirkr, 169, 171, 173–177, 179, 186
Maiden Way, 119, 153, 215
Manchester, 15, 30, 87
Maps, 82, 105, 165, 203
Maw Family, 18
Matterhorn, 15, 25
Mediaeval, 186
Mont Blanc, 4, 34
Morris William, iii, 8, 37, 49, 77, 95, 170, 171, 174–176, 180, 183, 192
Muncaster Castle, 206
Naval Intelligence, 143, 200–201, 203–205
Nettleship, R.L., 34, 35
Newcastle-upon-Tyne, vii, x, 197
Normans, 5, 127, 149–150
Norse, 31, 82, 124, 134, 146–147, 149–151, 155–156, 158–160, 165–166, 170, 173, 186, 194
Northern England, 5, 31, 72, 115, 117, 120, 127, 151, 159, 174, 216
North West (England), 5, 6, 12, 30, 104, 115, 117, 124, 135, 144, 146, 147, 150, 153, 159, 163, 171, 189, 207, 221
Northernness, 115
Northumbria, 215
Northumbrian Crosses, viii, 6, 216
Nothing Much, 101, 104–105
Norwegian, 5
Ormside Cup, 129

230, 231
Ruskin Museum, 15, 51, 248
Ruskin Relics, vii, 51
Russia, 108, 203
Saga Book, 122, 128, 129, 148, 156, 169, 173, 188
Sagas, 165, 168, 170–171, 174, 180–181, 186
Scafell, 75
Scandinavian, vii, 31, 146, 150, 155, 157–159, 161, 163, 165, 167, 169, 171, 173–175, 177, 179, 181, 183, 185, 187, 189
Schlegwig Holstein, 126, 203
Scott Walter, 32, 41, 84, 171, 207, 215
Scott William Bell, 112
Seascale, vi
Severn Arthur, 84, 85, 93, 117
Sheepscombe Gloucester, 90
Shelley Percy, 34
Silver Wedding, 193
Slade School, v, 43–44, 174
Smith Teresa, 8, 105
Social Reform, 78
Southey Robert, 168
Stephens George Prof., 142, 149, 151, 191
Swallows and Amazons, 111
Switzerland, v, 21–22, 53, 65
Tpahouse H.J., ix, 74
Tenth Iter, 207, 209
Thingbrekka, 173, 177
Thingvellir, 178
Thirlmere, 218, 224
Thorstein of the Mere, vi–vii, 158, 171
Thurston Water, 165, 167
Thwaite, 83, 164, 188
Times Newspaper, 229
Townend Mathew, 7, 155, 156, 168, 169, 237
Translation Work, v, 40, 180
Trevelyan family, 112
Trotsky Leon, 111
Troutbeck, 32, 108
Troyes, 55
Tulley House Museum, 130
Turner J.M.W., 18, 44, 48–51, 84, 88, 89, 91, 92, 221, 224

Owen Robert, 88
Owen Wilfred, 197, 204
Pagan, 146
Parker, C.A., viii, 7, 141, 142, 156, 168, 172, 202, 216, 217
Parliament (Icelandic), ix, 28, 178, 184, 185, 188
Pavey Ark, 147–148
Peace Conference, 204
Peel Island, vi
Philosophy, v, x, 8, 34–35, 78, 206
Place Names, 134, 147–148, 158–159, 165–166
Plymouth Brethren, 14, 21
Powell E.V., 60
Praeterita, 41, 85, 89
Pre-Norman, viii, 5, 31, 71, 115–116, 144, 151–152, 216, 229
Pre-Raphaelite, 8, 48, 88
Prout Samuel, 15, 17–19, 48, 49, 51, 92
Puff and Fluff, ix, 100, 101
Quaker, 93
Quakerism, 102
Randall Frank, ix, 57, 58
Ransome Arthur, ii, 4, 7, 9, 95, 96, 100, 108–112, 153, 192, 233
Ravenglass, 147, 187, 207–209, 214–215
Rawnsley Hardwick Cannon, 38, 82, 220–223
Reading University College, 190
Religion, 100, 173, 197
Rey Cross, 121, 245
Reykjavik, 31
Rollinson William, 12, 47
Roman, 30, 116, 124–125, 151, 206, 208–209, 214–215
Romano-British, 165
Rossetti Gabriel, 46, 91, 92, 112
Royal Academy, v, 44, 71, 94, 107
Rugby School, 190
Runic, 64
Ruskin John, i, ii, v, vii, ix, x, 1-13, 15, 17, 25, 34–43, 45, 48–59, 65, 68, 80–93, 95–97, 99–104, 106, 107, 112, 135, 165, 171, 182, 184, 191, 193, 197, 204, 221, 224, 227,

Tympanum, 122, 137
Tynwald, 187, 188
Unicorn Press, 108
University Fellowships, v
Urswick Cross, 122
Vasculum, 4, 125, 126, 244
Victoria Queen, 10, 70, 176
Viking, vi–vii, 5–6, 31, 71, 146, 155–156, 158, 173, 181, 185–187, 194
Viking Club, vi–vii, 31, 156, 158, 173, 194
Wainwright Alfred, 124, 125
Wainwright David, 28
Wales, 125, 152
Wasdale Head, 86
Water Colour Society, x
Wawn Andrew, 142, 175, 176
Wedderburn Alexander, v, 38, 40, 41, 84, 89, 237
Wetherlam, 94
Whitehouse John Howard, 87, 93
Wilde Oscar, 8, 9, 37, 38, 89
Windermere, vi, 31, 68, 71, 73, 75, 86, 124
Wirral, 115, 147
Woolf Leonard and Virginia, 98
Wordsworth William, 19, 37, 168, 221, 223, 224, 231
Worsaae Jens, 155, 156, 158, 160, 189
Wrynose Pass, 209, 213
York, 121, 122, 128, 134, 149, 160, 189, 202, 235
Yorkshire, xi, 115, 145–146, 233